A-Level
Physics
Exam Board: AQA

A-Level Physics is a heavyweight challenge, that's for sure — and the exams can knock you flat if you don't know what to expect. What you need is some intensive training, which is exactly what's on offer in this fantastic CGP book.

It's packed with exam-style questions covering both years of the AQA course, with full answers and mark schemes included at the back. Along the way, we've thrown in plenty of expert exam tips to help you pick up every mark you can.

All in all, it's the best way to make sure you can square up to any question the examiners throw at you. So put on your most scientific sweatband and get ready for a workout...

A-Level revision? It has to be CGP!

Contents

☑ Use the tick boxes to check off the topics you've completed.

Published by CGP

Editors:
Sarah Armstrong, Duncan Lindsay, Ethan Starmer-Jones, Hannah Taylor, Stephen Walters, Charlotte Whiteley, Sarah Williams.

Contributors:
Stuart Burditt, Sam Pilgrim, Oliver Rigg, Frances Rooney.

ISBN: 978 1 78294 916 9

With thanks to Emily Garrett, Glenn Rogers and Mark Edwards for the proofreading.
With thanks to Ana Pungartnik for the copyright research.

Printed by Elanders Ltd, Newcastle upon Tyne

Based on the classic CGP style created by Richard Parsons.

Exam Advice

To pick up every mark you can, you'll need tip-top exam technique as well as your knowledge of physics.

Get Familiar with the **Exam Structure**

If you're sitting AS-level Physics rather than A-level you'll be sitting different exams to the ones described here.

For **A-level Physics**, you'll be sitting **three papers**.

Paper 1 — this will test you on **Sections 1-7** of this book. **2 hours** **85** marks **34%** of your A-level	**Section A: 60 marks** of **short** and **long** answer questions. **Section B: 25 marks** of **multiple choice questions**.
Paper 2 — this will test you on **Sections 8-12** of this book **2 hours** **85** marks **34%** of your A-level	**Section A: 60 marks** of **short** and **long** answer questions. **Section B: 25 marks** of **multiple choice questions**.
Paper 3 — this will test you on **Sections 1-12** of this book and your **optional topic** from **Section 13**. **2 hours** **80** marks **32%** of your A-level	**Section A: 45 marks** of questions on **practical skills** and **data analysis**. **Section B: 35 marks** of questions on your chosen **optional topic**.

1) **Papers 1 & 2** will test you on the **facts** that you need to know and on whether you can **apply your knowledge** to unfamiliar contexts. You can also have your **practical skills** tested in these papers.

2) You could get asked an **extended response question**, which could require a **written English** answer or an **extended calculation**, or a combination of the two. These questions are marked based on the **quality** of your responses as well as their physics **content**. Your answers will need to be **coherent** and **fully explained**, and have a **logical structure**.

3) **Paper 3, Section A** can test you on anything from **Sections 1-12**. The majority of the marks up for grabs will be for demonstrating your **practical skills** knowledge and ability to **analyse experimental data**.

4) **Paper 3, Section B** will test you on the **optional topic** you've studied. The following optional topics are covered in **Section 13** of this book: Astrophysics, Medical physics, Engineering physics and Turning points in physics.

Manage Your Time Sensibly

1) Use the **number of marks** available to help you decide **how long** to spend on a question.

2) Some questions will require **lots of work** for only a **few** marks but others may be much quicker. **Don't** spend ages struggling with questions that are only worth a couple of marks — move on. You can always **come back** to them later when you've bagged loads of marks elsewhere.

3) **Multiple choice** questions can sometimes be quite **time-consuming**, but they're still only worth **one mark** each. So if you're pressed for time, you might want to focus on the **written answer** questions, where there are **more marks** available.

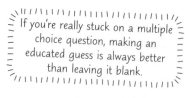
If you're really stuck on a multiple choice question, making an educated guess is always better than leaving it blank.

Be **Careful** with **Calculations**

1) At least **40%** of the marks will be for **maths skills**, so you'll be doing a lot of calculations in the exams.

2) Make sure the values you're using are in the **correct units**, and always **show your working** — you may get some marks for your method even if you get the final answer wrong.

3) Don't **round** the values you use in a calculation, only round your answer at the very end. Remember to always give your **final answer** to the **same** number of **significant figures** as the data that you use from the question with the **least number** of significant figures.

Remember to Use the **Exam Data Booklet**

1) In your exams, you'll be given a **data booklet** — it'll contain lots of useful data values and equations.

2) The information you'll be given in this data booklet is given on **pages 196-198** of this book.

3) Unless you're told otherwise in the question, you should **always** use the values given in the data booklet.

Particles — 1

Are you confident you know your leptons from your hadrons? Do you know the ins and outs of quarks? Are you whispering conservation rules in your sleep? Then you're ready — give these questions a go.

For each of questions 1-4, give your answer by ticking the appropriate box.

1 Which row in the table correctly describes a $^{215}_{87}$Fr nucleus?

	Hadrons	Leptons	Baryons	
A	87	87	87	☐
B	215	0	215	☐
C	215	87	87	☐
D	87	0	87	☐

(1 mark)

2 The neutral lambda baryon (Λ^0) has the quark composition uds. Which of the following is the only interaction that could occur?

A $\Lambda^0 \rightarrow p + \pi^-$ ☐

B $\Lambda^0 \rightarrow p + \bar{p}$ ☐

C $\Lambda^0 \rightarrow p + e^- + \nu_e$ ☐

D $\Lambda^0 \rightarrow p + \pi^- + e^- + \bar{\nu}_e$ ☐

(1 mark)

3 The diagram shows the fundamental particles involved in a beta-plus decay.

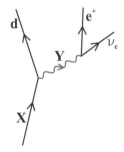

Which of the following rows correctly identifies particles X and Y?

	X	Y	
A	p	W⁻	☐
B	n	W⁺	☐
C	d	W⁻	☐
D	u	W⁺	☐

(1 mark)

4 What is the quark composition of an antineutron?

A uud ☐

B udd ☐

C $\overline{uud}$ ☐

D $\overline{udd}$ ☐

(1 mark)

5   The element oganesson has the highest atomic number of all known elements.

Oganesson can be made by colliding californium-249 and calcium-48 nuclei.
An incomplete equation of this process is shown below.

$$^{249}_{98}\text{Cf} + ^{48}_{20}\text{Ca} \rightarrow ^{294}_{118}\text{Og} + 3\text{X}$$

5.1   State which particle is represented by X.

....
(1 mark)

5.2   Nuclear binding energy is the energy that would be needed to separate all the nucleons of an atom's
nucleus. It is equal to the difference between the rest energy of the nucleus and the sum of the rest
energies of its constituent nucleons.

Oganesson-294 has a rest energy of 274 059 MeV.
Calculate the nuclear binding energy of oganesson-294.

Nuclear binding energy = ... MeV
(3 marks)

5.3   Oganesson-294 decays rapidly by alpha emission into livermorium (Lv).
Write the decay equation for this process.

....
(2 marks)

5.4   The alpha decay of oganesson-294 into livermorium releases 11.65 MeV of energy.
Calculate how many decays would be necessary to provide one kilojoule of energy.

Decays = ...
(2 marks)

6   Particle interactions obey a number of conservation laws.

Table 1 shows three particle interactions that have never been observed.

Table 1

Interaction 1	$n \rightarrow p + e^+ + \nu_e$
Interaction 2	$p + p + n \rightarrow p + p + p + \bar{p}$
Interaction 3	$\mu^- \rightarrow e^- + \bar{\nu}_e$

6.1   State which law of conservation is violated in interaction 1.

....
(1 mark)

6.2   State and explain which particle in interaction 2 could be removed to give an interaction
that obeys all conservation laws.

....

....
(2 marks)

6.3   State **one** particle that should be added to the products in interaction 3 to give an
interaction that obeys all conservation laws. Explain your answer.

....

....
(2 marks)

6.4   Energy must be conserved when a particle decays.
Explain why it is not possible for a free proton to decay into a neutron without the input of energy.

....
(1 mark)

6.5   Explain why strange particles must always be created in pairs when produced via the strong interaction.

....

....

....
(2 marks)

6.6   Scientists believe that there is more matter in the observable universe than antimatter. Explain why
this is surprising and suggest what this may imply about particle interactions in the early universe.

....

....

....

....
(2 marks)

7   **Table 2** shows a list of particles and the years in which they were discovered.

Table 2

Year of discovery	Particle
1897	Electron
1919	Proton
1932	Neutron
1937	Muon
1947	Pion
1947	Kaon
1956	Neutrino

7.1 State the name of the only stable baryon and give its quark composition.

Particle: ....

Quark composition: ....
(2 marks)

7.2 State the **three** particles in the table which do not experience the strong nuclear force.

1. ....

2. ....

3. ....
(1 mark)

7.3 Pions are an exchange particle. Explain what an exchange particle is.

....

....
(1 mark)

7.4 Compare the properties of an electron and a positron.

....

....
(2 marks)

7.5 The existence of the neutrino was hypothesised more than 30 years before it was detected.
Explain why the existence of the neutrino was hypothesised.

....

....
(1 mark)

EXAM TIP
Decay equations come up all the time in exams, so you need to know them. The key is figuring out what happens to the nucleons. For example, with beta decay you need to make sure you know what happens to the individual nucleon, then you can look at the bigger picture and see how this affects the proton number and nucleon number in the atom.

Score

29

Particles — 2

1 The PET (Positron Emission Tomography) scanner is a device that can be used to detect a variety of diseases. A patient is injected with a radioactive tracer, which produces positrons. The positrons then annihilate with electrons in the body, producing photons which are detected by a scanner.

1.1 State the type of radioactive decay that produces positrons.

....
(1 mark)

1.2 Write an equation showing the annihilation of a positron and an electron.

....
(1 mark)

1.3 The photons produced in the annihilation have a frequency of $f_{min} = 1.24 \times 10^8$ THz.
Show that the rest energy of an electron is 8.2×10^{-14} J.

(2 marks)

1.4 Explain why it is not possible for one of these photons to produce an electron and positron.

....

....
(1 mark)

1.5 Rubidium-82 ($^{82}_{37}$Rb) is often used as a radioactive tracer. Generators of this tracer contain strontium-82 ($^{82}_{38}$Sr), which decays to produce rubidium-82 without emitting any charged particles.
Describe what happens in the nucleus when strontium-82 decays to rubidium-82.

....

....

....
(2 marks)

1.6 Positrons are also produced in pair production.
Explain why both positrons and electrons must be produced in pair production to conserve charge.

....

....

....

....
(2 marks)

2   Kaons and pions are both types of meson.

2.1 State what is meant by a meson.

....
(1 mark)

Kaons are produced in the interaction shown in the equation below. The interaction is mediated by the strong force. All particles in the interaction are made up of a combination of up, down and strange quarks and antiquarks.

$$\pi^+ + p \rightarrow K^+ + \Sigma^+$$

2.2 Determine the quark composition of the positive sigma baryon (Σ^+). Explain your answer.

....

....

....

....

....
(3 marks)

The equations below show two possible paths for the decay of a kaon.

Equation 1 $K^+ \rightarrow Y + \mu^+ + \nu_\mu$

Equation 2 $K^+ \rightarrow \pi^+ + \pi^0$

2.3 State which particle is represented by Y.

....
(1 mark)

2.4 Write an equation to show the change in quark character that happens during the decay shown in equation 1.

....
(1 mark)

2.5 Show that baryon number is conserved in equation 2.

....

....
(1 mark)

2.6 State and explain which interaction is responsible for the decay shown in equation 2.

....

....

....
(2 marks)

3 A scientist studies the light emitted from different lasers.
Each laser emits a beam of photons at a known frequency.

3.1 State the rest mass and the charge of a photon.

....

(1 mark)

3.2 One of the lasers produces a beam of photons with 200 mJ of energy each second. The photons
have a wavelength of 650 nm. Calculate the number of photons produced by the laser each second.
Give your answer to two significant figures.

Number of photons = ...

(3 marks)

3.3 The scientist determines the average energy of the photons produced by each laser.
She plots the average photon energy against the laser frequency in **Figure 1**.

Figure 1

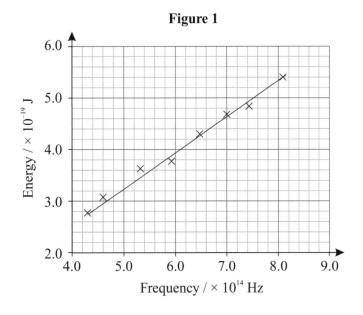

Use the graph to determine the scientist's value for the Planck constant and thus determine
whether the scientist is within 10% of the accepted value.

(3 marks)

4 **Figure 2** shows a diagram that a student has sketched of three nuclides. They have used black circles to represent protons and white circles to represent neutrons.

Figure 2

X   Y   Z

4.1 State which two nuclides are isotopes. Give a reason for your answer.

....

....

(1 mark)

4.2 Calculate the specific charge of nucleus X.

Specific charge = ...

Unit = ...

(3 marks)

4.3 Explain how the range of the strong force enables it to hold nucleons together in the nucleus and suggest why large and stable nuclei often have a high ratio of neutrons to protons.

....

....

....

....

....

....

....

....

....

....

....

....

(6 marks)

Remember, you're given a data booklet in the exam with lots of useful particle information in it. Particle symbols, particle rest energies and quark and lepton properties are given, in addition to all the constants you need. Make sure you get familiar with what is and isn't in the booklet so you don't get any nasty surprises in the exam.

Score

35

Particles — 3

1   The radioactive isotope $^{40}_{19}K$ can decay through beta-minus decay.

1.1   Complete **Table 1** to show the daughter nucleus and one of the particles emitted.

Table 1

Type of beta decay	Daughter nucleus	Particle emitted
Beta-minus	$^{......}_{......}Ca$	$^{......}_{-1}.........$

(2 marks)

1.2   If beta-minus decay only produced a daughter nucleus and a beta particle, it would violate the conservation of lepton number. State the particle which is also emitted in beta-minus decay.

....

(1 mark)

1.3   Describe what happens to the quarks in a proton when a beta-minus decay occurs.

....

....

(2 marks)

1.4   The exchange particle in beta-minus decay is the W^- boson. Compare the properties of this particle to those of the exchange particle used in electromagnetic interactions.

....

....

....

(3 marks)

$^{40}_{19}K$ can also decay through beta-plus decay.

1.5   State the daughter nucleus that is produced when $^{40}_{19}K$ undergoes beta-plus decay to form argon (Ar).

....

(1 mark)

1.6   Draw a diagram to show the particle interactions in a beta-plus decay.

(3 marks)

2   Most of the energy the Sun produces is released through a process called the proton-proton chain, in which hydrogen nuclei are converted to helium nuclei via a series of fusion events.

One mechanism by which helium nuclei are produced consists of the three equations shown in **Table 2**.

Table 2

Equation 1	$^1_1H + ^1_1H \rightarrow ^2_1H + e^+ + \nu_e$
Equation 2	$^1_1H + ^2_1H \rightarrow ^3_2He + \gamma$
Equation 3	$^3_2He + ^3_2He \rightarrow ^4_2He + ^1_1H + ^1_1H$

2.1   State what happens to the e^+ particle produced in equation 1 when it interacts with a nearby electron, including which particles are produced.

....

....

(2 marks)

2.2   Explain why a ν_μ particle would never be produced instead of a ν_e particle in equation 1.

....

....

....

....

(2 marks)

2.3   Determine the net amount of ^1_1H particles required to produce one ^4_2He particle in the mechanism above.

Net amount = ...

(1 mark)

2.4   In reality, the two hydrogen atoms in equation 1 briefly form a nucleus called a diproton, which is made up of two protons. One of the protons then rapidly decays into a neutron. Explain how this decay affects the stability of the nucleus.

....

....

....

....

....

(2 marks)

3   A nuclide undergoes two beta plus decays. The resulting nuclide is manganese-53, or $^{53}_{25}\text{Mn}$.

3.1   State the relative charge and nucleon number of the original nuclide before the decays.

Relative charge = ...

Nucleon number = ...

(3 marks)

A proton in the nucleus of the manganese-53 atom then captures an electron and turns into a neutron.

3.2   Explain how the quark composition of a neutron gives it a charge of zero.

....

....

(2 marks)

3.3   Draw a diagram of the electron capture.

(3 marks)

4   Different methods have been developed to detect different types of radiation.

Alpha radiation can be studied using cloud chambers. Charged particles collide with particles inside the chamber, forming vapour trails along their paths. **Figure 1** shows the tracks produced when a source that produces alpha particles is placed in a cloud chamber. A cosmic ray is also seen passing through the chamber.

Figure 1

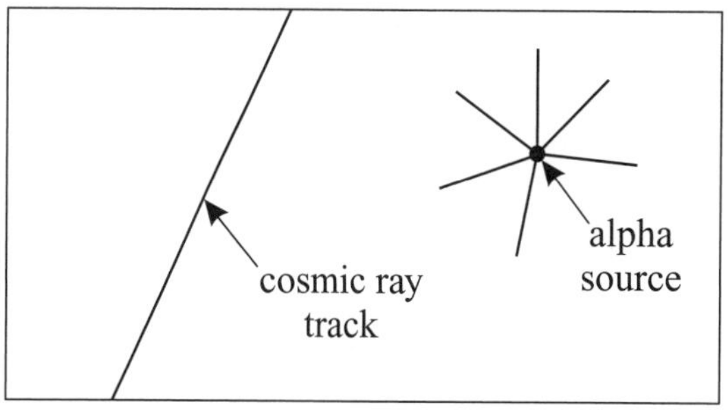

cosmic ray
track

alpha
source

4.1   Suggest what **Figure 1** implies about the range of alpha particles.

....

(1 mark)

14

A pair telescope can be used to detect gamma rays. A simplified diagram showing the interaction that takes place inside a pair telescope is shown in **Figure 2**. When a gamma ray hits the conversion foil, an electron and a positron are produced through pair production. The properties of the electron and positron are then measured to determine the momentum and energy of the gamma ray.

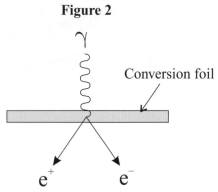

Figure 2

4.2 Explain how the momentum and energy of the gamma ray can be determined from the properties of the electron and the positron.

....

....

....

(2 marks)

4.3 The positron and the electron each have a kinetic energy of 0.64 MeV immediately after they are created. Calculate the wavelength of the gamma ray that hit the detector.

wavelength = ...m

(3 marks)

4.4 Pair telescopes are surrounded by a shield that detects charged particles.
Explain how this can be used to distinguish gamma rays from other particles.

....

....

....

....

(2 marks)

4.5 Suggest **one** limitation of this method for detecting gamma rays.

....

(1 mark)

EXAM TIP

You might be asked to draw a particle diagram in the exam, so you could get some easy marks if you learn the rules behind them. Here's a refresher if you've forgotten — incoming particles move upwards, baryons and leptons can't cross sides, charges on both sides should balance and W⁻ particles going to the left have the same effect as W⁺ particles going to the right.

Score

36

Electromagnetic Radiation and Quantum Phenomena — 1

Things you thought were waves behaving like particles. Things you thought were particles behaving like waves.
It's a crazy universe. Soothe your shattered nerves by trying out these questions...

For each of questions 1-4, give your answer by ticking the appropriate box.

1   Monochromatic light is shone on the surface of a metal and photoelectrons are emitted.
     Which of the following will increase the kinetic energy of the electrons emitted?

     A   Using a metal with a higher threshold frequency   ☐

     B   Increasing the frequency of the light   ☐

     C   Increasing the surface area of the metal   ☐

     D   Using a metal with a higher work function   ☐

                                                                     (1 mark)

2   A ground-level atomic electron is excited by an incident photon. It then emits a total of two photons,
     with frequencies 1.51×10^{14} Hz and 2.96×10^{15} Hz respectively, on its return to ground level.
     What was the energy of the incident photon?

     A 6.39×10^{-41} J   ☐

     B 3.11×10^{15} J   ☐

     C 2.06×10^{-18} J   ☐

     D 2.96×10^{-18} J   ☐

                                                                     (1 mark)

3   The work function of gallium is 4.32 eV.
     What is the threshold frequency for photoelectric emission in gallium?

     A 1.04×10^{15} Hz   ☐

     B 6.91×10^{-19} Hz   ☐

     C 6.55×10^{35} Hz   ☐

     D 2.70×10^{19} Hz   ☐

                                                                     (1 mark)

4   A subatomic particle with kinetic energy E has a de Broglie wavelength λ.
     What is the kinetic energy of an identical particle with de Broglie wavelength 2λ?

     A $2E$ ☐

     B $\dfrac{E}{\sqrt{2}}$ ☐

     C $4E$ ☐

     D $\dfrac{E}{4}$ ☐

                                                                     (1 mark)

5   Monochromatic light is shone on a metallic surface, resulting in the emission of photoelectrons.

The kinetic energy possessed by an individual photoelectron never exceeds $E_{k\,(max)}$.
Figure 1 shows how $E_{k\,(max)}$ varies as the frequency of the light, f, is increased.

Figure 1

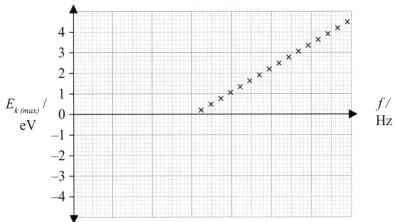

5.1   Explain why no photoelectrons are emitted unless f is greater than a threshold value.

....

....

(1 mark)

5.2   Explain why the kinetic energy of most photoelectrons is less than $E_{k\,(max)}$.

....

....

(1 mark)

5.3   Using **Figure 1**, determine the work function of the metal.

....

(1 mark)

5.4   Calculate the maximum speed of a photoelectron emitted when 9.3×10^{14} Hz light is incident on the metal.

speed = ... ms^{-1}

(2 marks)

5.5   Calculate the potential difference required to stop a photoelectron travelling at this speed.

stopping potential = ... V

(1 mark)

5.6   Predict how **Figure 1** would be affected if the intensity of light incident on the surface were increased.

....

(1 mark)

6   A detergent manufacturer develops a new "whiter-than-white" detergent for washing white clothes.

The detergent contains an optical brightener, a chemical which, when exposed to ultraviolet light, emits visible blue light. After washing, clothes retain small particles of the detergent. The visible blue light that is now emitted when the clothes are exposed to natural ultraviolet light from the sun disguises yellowing of the fabric.

6.1   Describe, with reference to energy levels, the process of photon absorption and re-emission in atoms. Explain how the optical brightener in the detergent emits visible light when exposed to ultraviolet light.

....

....

....

....

....

....

....

....

....

....

....

....

....

(6 marks)

6.2   Fluorescent tubes also rely on the conversion of ultraviolet light to visible light.

Explain how ultraviolet light is generated within a fluorescent tube.

....

....

....

....

....

....

(3 marks)

EXAM TIP

If you want to sound like a pro when you're writing about the photoelectric effect, use the proper vocabulary. Those electrons emitted from the metal's surface aren't just any electrons, they're photoelectrons. It's not simply light arriving at the metal's surface, it's photons of light. Using the right vocabulary could earn you easy marks in the exam.

Score

20

Electromagnetic Radiation and Quantum Phenomena — 2

1 Line spectra produced by gases can be used to investigate the configuration of electrons in the atom.

1.1 Explain how line spectra produced by gases support the idea that the electrons within an atom may only occupy fixed energy levels.

....

....

....

....

(2 marks)

Figure 1 shows a diagram of the electron energy levels of a hydrogen atom.

Figure 1

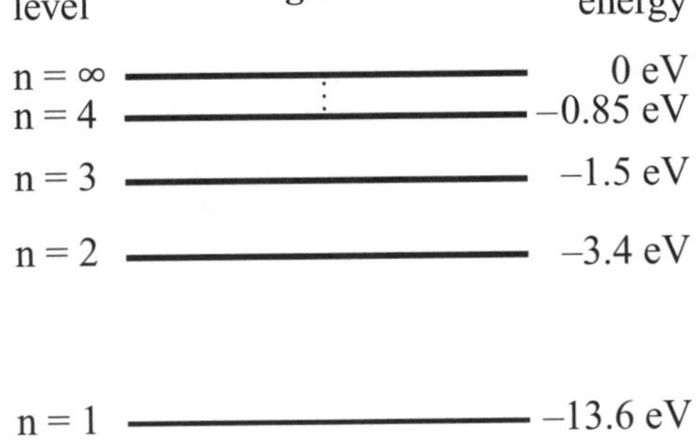

level		energy
n = ∞	———————— ⋮	0 eV
n = 4	————————	−0.85 eV
n = 3	————————	−1.5 eV
n = 2	————————	−3.4 eV
n = 1	————————	−13.6 eV

1.2 On **Figure 1**, draw an arrow identifying the electronic transition associated with the absorption of 4.6×10^{14} Hz electromagnetic radiation.

(2 marks)

1.3 When a very cold sample of hydrogen gas is exposed to 1.9 eV photons, very little absorption takes place.

However, when the same sample is simultaneously exposed to 1.9 eV and 10.2 eV photons, the rate of absorption of the 1.9 eV photons is increased.

Suggest why the presence of 10.2 eV photons leads to an increase in the rate at which 1.9 eV photons are absorbed by the cold hydrogen gas.

....

....

....

....

....

....

....

(3 marks)

2 The concept of wave-particle duality is supported by experimental evidence.

2.1 Explain how the photoelectric effect contradicts the idea that light always behaves like a wave.

....

....

....

....

....

....

....

(4 marks)

2.2 It is possible to observe subatomic matter behaving in a wave-like manner.
For example, neutrons may diffract as they pass through a silicon crystal.

Explain why it is not possible to observe much larger objects behaving in this way.

....

....

....

(2 marks)

2.3 A physicist is investigating the arrangement of carbon atoms within graphene, a form of pure carbon.

She uses a potential difference to accelerate free electrons, initially at rest, through a vacuum and towards a graphene sheet.

When the potential difference is equal to 75 V she is able to observe evidence of the electrons diffracting as they pass through the graphene sheet.

Calculate an estimate of the separation between adjacent carbon atoms in graphene.

separation = ... m

(4 marks)

> **EXAM TIP**
> Electron volts are much more useful than joules when it comes to thinking about the tiny amounts of energy emitted and absorbed by electrons. However, the all-important relationship $E = hf$ will only work if you input an energy that is in joules. But don't despair — all you need to do to convert from electron volts to joules is multiply by 1.60×10^{-19}.

Score

17

Waves — 1

Here comes phase one of a bumper section on waves. Dive straight into these multiple choice questions.

For each of questions 1-4, give your answer by ticking the appropriate box.

1   Light is shone through a single narrow slit, creating a diffraction pattern on a screen. How does the central maximum of the diffraction pattern change when the width of the slit is increased?

     A   The central maximum becomes wider and its intensity increases. ☐

     B   The central maximum becomes narrower and its intensity increases. ☐

     C   The central maximum becomes wider and its intensity decreases. ☐

     D   The central maximum becomes narrower and its intensity decreases. ☐

(1 mark)

2   Light with a wavelength of 750 nm is incident on a diffraction grating. The angle between the normal and the first order maxima is 30°. What is the spacing between slits on the diffraction grating?

     A 1.5×10^{-3} m   ☐

     B 1.5×10^{-6} m   ☐

     C 6.7×10^{-4} m   ☐

     D 8.2×10^{-6} m   ☐

(1 mark)

3   A wave is travelling at 20.0 ms^{-1}. Two points on the wave are separated by 14.0 cm. The two points have a phase difference between them of $\pi/6$ radians. What is the time period of the wave?

     A   0.021 s   ☐

     B   0.042 s   ☐

     C   0.084 s   ☐

     D   0.105 s   ☐

(1 mark)

4   A stationary wave is created on a string. The frequency of the first harmonic is 12.0 Hz. The tension on the string is increased by 40%. What is the new frequency of the first harmonic?

     A   1.2 Hz   ☐

     B   8.0 Hz   ☐

     C   14.2 Hz   ☐

     D   16.8 Hz   ☐

(1 mark)

5   A student wants to investigate the factors affecting the frequency of stationary waves on a string.

5.1   Explain how stationary waves are formed.

....

....

....

....

(2 marks)

Figure 1

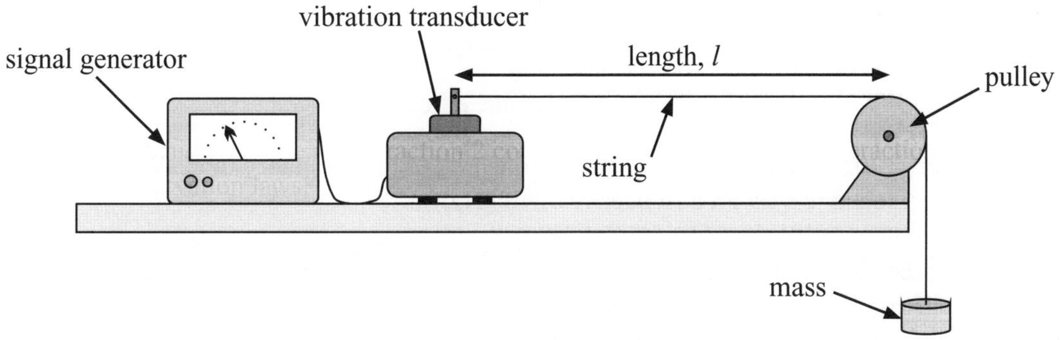

5.2   Describe how the student could use the apparatus shown in **Figure 1** to obtain measurements of the frequency of the string's first harmonic as the string's length, *l*, is varied.

....

....

....

....

(1 mark)

5.3   The string used in the investigation has a total length of 0.80 ± 0.020 m and a total mass of 2.0 ± 0.10 g. Calculate the string's mass per unit length in grams per metre and the absolute uncertainty in this value.

mass per unit length = ... $\pm$ .... gm^{-1}

(3 marks)

5.4   In this experiment the mass per unit length of the string is a control variable. Identify **one** other control variable in this experiment.

....

(1 mark)

6 The apparatus shown in **Figure 2** is used to form stationary sound waves in a column of air.

Figure 2

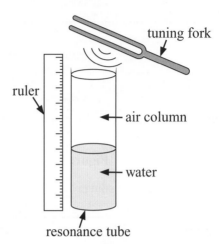

The tuning fork is struck and held just above the opening of the resonance tube. When struck, the tuning fork produces a sound wave with a frequency of 400 Hz.

The length of the air column in the resonance tube is adjusted by changing the volume of water in the tube. At certain lengths, the air column is a suitable length for a stationary wave to form.
Every stationary wave that forms has an antinode just above the open
end of the resonance tube and a node at the water's surface.

6.1 The total length of each stationary wave is assumed to equal the distance
between the water's surface and the rim of the resonance tube.

State what type of error is introduced by making this assumption and explain how the measurement of the length of each stationary wave will be affected.

....

....

(2 marks)

6.2 **Figure 3** shows a diagram of the first stationary sound wave that forms in the resonance tube.

Figure 3

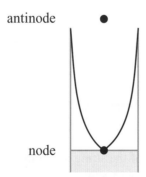

Draw arrows on **Figure 3** indicating the directions in which an air molecule located at the stationary wave's antinode would vibrate.

(1 mark)

6.3 On the **Figure 4**, sketch the second stationary wave that forms in the resonance tube as the length of the air column is increased. Include labels indicating the location of its nodes and antinodes.

Figure 4

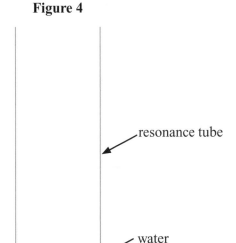

resonance tube

water

(2 marks)

After eliminating the error discussed in 6.1, the second stationary wave is found to be 63.75 cm in length.

6.4 Predict the length of the third stationary wave to form in the resonance tube.

length = ... m

(2 marks)

6.5 Calculate the speed of sound in air using the results of this experiment.

speed = ... ms^{-1}

(1 mark)

6.6 Unlike progressive waves, stationary waves do not transmit energy.
With reference to how stationary waves are formed, suggest why stationary waves do not transmit energy.

....

....

....

(1 mark)

Waves — 2

1 When two or more waves travelling through the same medium meet, their displacements will superpose.

1.1 Describe what is meant by the superposition of two waves.

....

....

....

(2 marks)

Figure 1 shows two wave forms travelling in opposite directions.

Figure 1

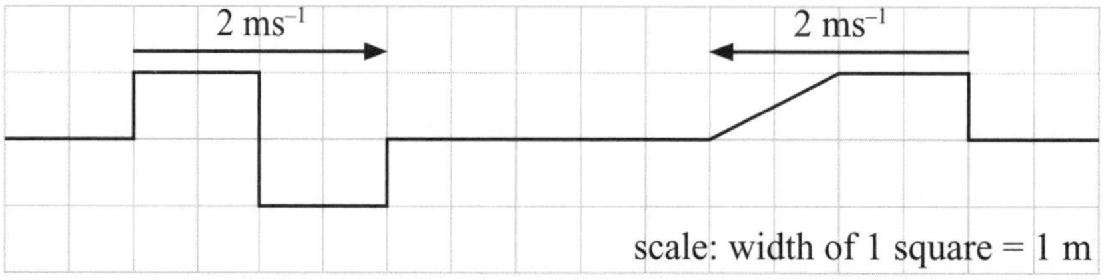
2 ms⁻¹
2 ms⁻¹
scale: width of 1 square = 1 m

1.2 Using **Figure 2**, draw the waveform that would be seen 2 seconds later.

Figure 2

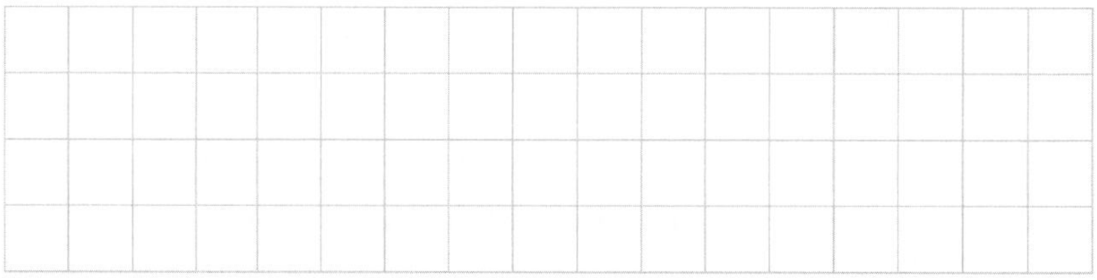

(2 marks)

1.3 On your drawing in **Figure 2**, place a cross on a point where destructive interference has occurred.

(1 mark)

1.4 When two sine waves of slightly differing frequency superpose, they will alternate between interfering constructively and destructively. The resulting waveform, shown in **Figure 3**, is called a beat pattern.

Figure 3

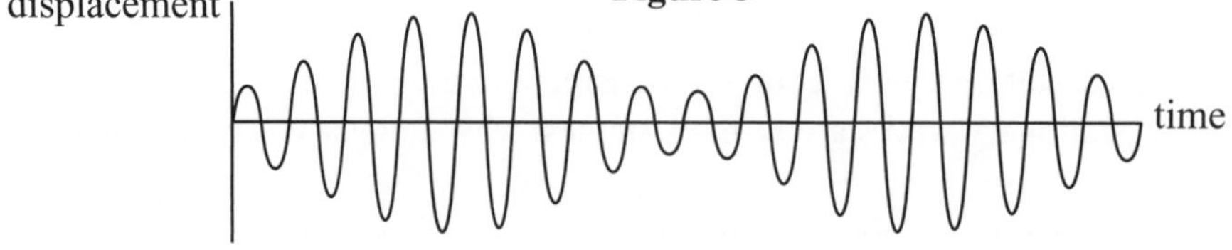
displacement
time

Traditionally, a piano string is tuned by comparing the sound it produces with the sound produced by a tuning fork which is known to be of the correct frequency. Both sounds are sine waves.

Suggest how the phenomenon of beat patterns could be used by a piano tuner to tune a piano string.

....

....

....

(1 mark)

2   A student passes monochromatic light through a diffraction grating, resulting in the formation of an interference pattern on a distant screen. **Figure 4** shows a diagram of the equipment he used.

Figure 4

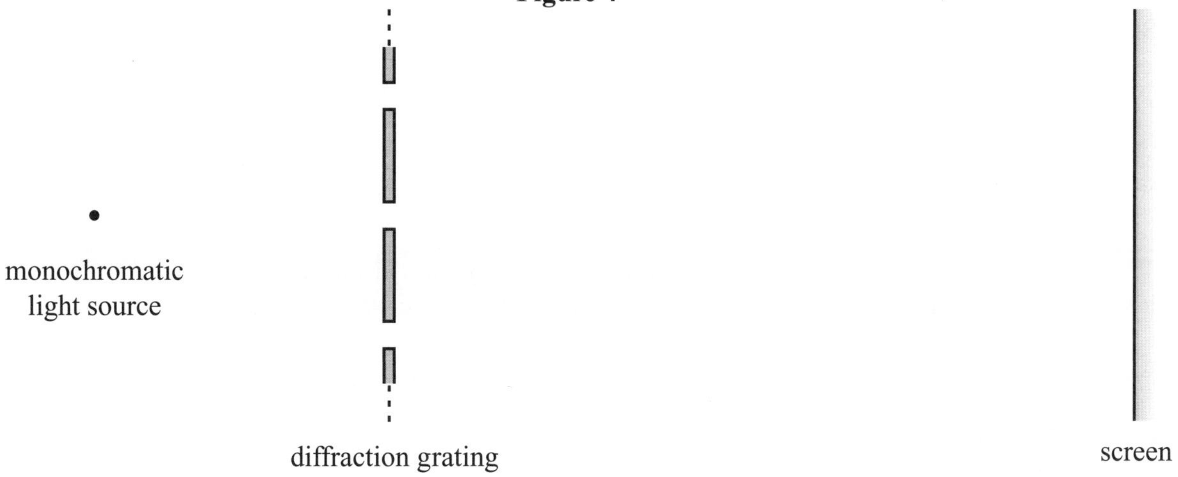

monochromatic
light source

diffraction grating   screen

The maxima of the interference pattern obey the following equation:

$$d \sin \theta = n\lambda$$

Where d is the separation between adjacent slits on the diffraction grating, θ is the angle through which light is diffracted in order to arrive at the maximum, n is the order of the maximum and λ is the wavelength of the light emitted by the light source.

2.1   Using **Figure 4**, derive this formula.

....

....

....

....

....

(3 marks)

2.2   The diffraction grating is stated to have 500 lines per mm, correct to 2 significant figures.
Light arriving at the interference pattern's second order maxima has been diffracted through 24.8°.
Calculate the wavelength of the light in nanometres.

wavelength = ... nm

(2 marks)

2.3   The monochromatic light source is now replaced by a source of white light.
Describe the interference pattern that can now be seen on the screen.

....

....

....

(2 marks)

3 3D movies use polarised light to create the illusion of depth.
Audience members wear glasses with lenses made of Polaroid material.
The transmission axes of these lenses are perpendicular to each other.

3.1 State what is meant by polarisation.

....

....

(1 mark)

3.2 The sound waves the audience hear during the movie are longitudinal waves.
Explain why longitudinal waves cannot be polarised, but transverse waves like light can.

....

....

....

....

(2 marks)

3.3 A child in the audience has removed the plastic lenses from the glasses and is playing with them.
She holds one lens in front of the other with their transmission axes perpendicular, as shown in **Figure 5**.
She then proceeds to rotate one of the lenses through 90°.

Figure 5

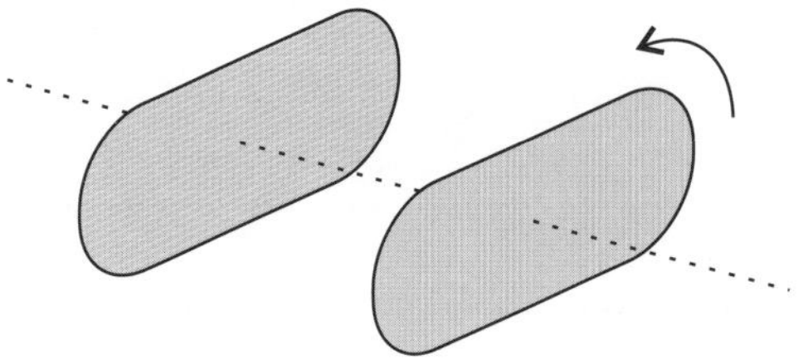

Describe what the child observes as the lens is rotated.

....

....

....

....

(2 marks)

3.4 Give **one** other use for polarised waves.

....

(1 mark)

EXAM TIP The examiners expect you to know the derivation of '$d \sin \theta = n\lambda$'. The derivation might look a bit daunting, but once you break it down you'll see it's just drawing some lines and some simple trigonometry. Knowing it off by heart might help you bag some easy marks in the exam.

Score

19

Waves — 3

1   A student shines monochromatic laser light on a card that has two thin slits cut out of it.
The two beams that are formed go on to produce an interference pattern on a distant wall.

1.1   Explain what is meant by monochromatic light.

....

....
(1 mark)

1.2   Explain why the student chose to pass light from a single source through two slits, rather than use two
separate light sources that produce light of the same wavelength.

....

....
(1 mark)

1.3   Working with lasers can be dangerous. Suggest **two** safety precautions the student should follow.

....

....

....
(2 marks)

An interference pattern of evenly spaced bright and dark fringes is produced.

1.4   The student measures the distance spanned by eleven bright fringes and divides this value by ten in order
to calculate the average spacing between two adjacent bright fringes.

Explain the advantage of using this method to obtain a value for fringe spacing, rather than directly
measuring the distance between two adjacent fringes.

....

....

....
(1 mark)

1.5   The student measures the fringe spacing to be 1.1 mm. The laser light has a wavelength of 510 nm and the
separation between the two slits is 1.0 mm.

Determine the distance from the slits to the wall.

distance = ... m
(1 mark)

2   Optical fibres, like the one shown in **Figure 1**, work by using total internal reflection.

A fibre-optic illuminator is used to transmit light rays into optical fibres.
You may assume that the refractive index of the illuminator is equal to that of air.

Figure 1

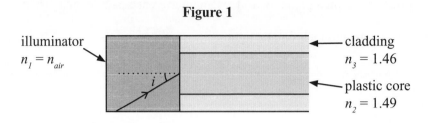

2.1   Light travelling in the fibre's plastic core is incident on the core's boundary with the cladding.
Calculate the critical angle for light at this boundary.

critical angle = ...°
(2 marks)

2.2   **Figure 1** shows a ray of light incident at an angle i on the illuminator-core boundary.
When this ray reaches the core-cladding boundary it undergoes total internal reflection.
Calculate the maximum possible value of i.

maximum angle of incidence = ...°
(3 marks)

2.3   Optical fibres are used to transmit digital signals. However, these signals can suffer from degradation.
Describe the types of signal degradation that can occur within optical fibres and explain their causes.

....

....

....

....

....

....

....

....

....

....

(6 marks)

3   A student uses the equipment shown in **Figure 2** to investigate interference between sound waves.

Figure 2

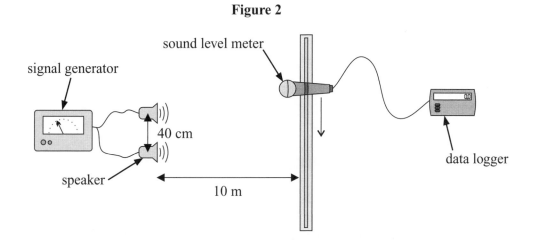

Two speakers are attached to a signal generator so that they produce coherent sound waves. The frequency of these sound waves is 13.5 kHz. The speakers are separated by a distance of 40 cm.

The sound pressure level (SPL) of the resulting interference pattern is measured by a sound level meter connected to a track which is positioned at a distance of 10 m from the speakers. The sound level meter moves at a speed of 0.25 ms⁻¹ along the track.

The measurements made by the sound level meter are recorded by a data logger.

3.1   Explain what is meant by coherent waves.

....

....

(1 mark)

Figure 3 shows a graph of the SPL measured by the sound level meter as it travels along the track.

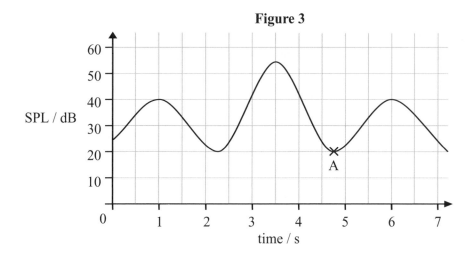

3.2   State the phase difference between the sound waves at point A on **Figure 3**.

....

(1 mark)

3.3 Calculate the speed at which the sound waves travel through the air.

speed = ... ms^{-1}
(3 marks)

The student slides the sound level meter along the track until it is positioned at a first order maximum of the 13.5 kHz interference pattern. She then clamps the sound level meter in place.

Using the signal generator, she steadily increases the frequency of the sound waves.

The student predicts that, as the frequency is increased above 13.5 kHz, the SPL will initially decrease to a minimum and then increase until it reaches a new maximum.

3.4 Explain why the student expects the sound level meter to record a secondary maximum in SPL as the frequency is increased.

....

....

....

....
(2 marks)

3.5 The sound level meter the student is using is only sensitive to frequencies below 22 kHz.
Determine whether the student will be able to measure the secondary maximum in SPL she predicted.

(3 marks)

EXAM TIP
When it comes to interference patterns, there are a truckload of variables involved. If you are asked how changing one of these variables will affect the pattern, always refer back to Young's double slit formula, $w = (\lambda D) \div s$: it'll tell you whether fringe spacing will shrink or grow.

Score

27

Waves — 4

1   A sucrose solution with a concentration of 10% has a refractive index of 1.35.

1.1   Calculate the speed of electromagnetic waves in this sucrose solution.

speed = ... ms^{-1}
(1 mark)

1.2   Laser light with a frequency of 5.0×10^{14} Hz passes from the 10% sucrose solution into air.
Calculate the change in the laser light's wavelength in nanometres.

change in wavelength = ... nm
(2 marks)

1.3   **Table 1** gives the refractive indexes of sucrose solutions of various concentrations.

Table 1

Sucrose Concentration (%)	Refractive Index
20	1.36
40	1.40
60	1.44
80	1.55

A researcher initially prepares a sucrose solution with a concentration of 20%.
She sets up a laser beam that passes from the sucrose solution into air.
The laser beam's angle of incidence on this boundary is 45.0°.
She increases the concentration of the sucrose solution in 20% intervals.

Determine the first concentration tested at which the researcher is no longer able to observe the laser beam leaving the sucrose solution.

concentration = ...%
(4 marks)

2   When light is reflected by a smooth surface, the reflected light is partially polarised.

2.1   State **one** other method for producing polarised light.

....

(1 mark)

When the angle of incidence is equal to Brewster's angle, θ_B, as shown in **Figure 1**, the reflected light is fully polarised.

The reflected light ray and the refracted light ray are perpendicular to each other.

Figure 1

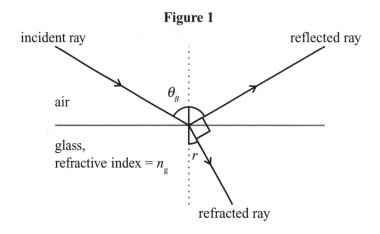

2.2   Suggest a method for measuring Brewster's angle for a pane of glass, using a polarising filter and a thin beam of unpolarised light.

....

....

....

....

....

....

(3 marks)

2.3   Brewster's angle for the pane of glass is found to be 56.6°.
Calculate the refractive index of the pane of glass.

refractive index = ...

(3 marks)

3 The frequency of the first harmonic on a string, f, depends on the string's length, l.

Figure 2 shows a graph of $1 \div f$ against l.

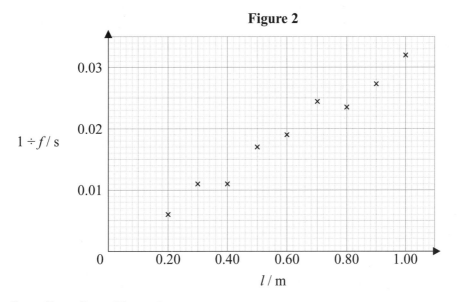

Figure 2

1 ÷ f / s

l / m

3.1 Draw a line of best fit on **Figure 2**.

(1 mark)

3.2 The string's mass per unit length is 1.5×10^{-3} kgm⁻¹.
Using **Figure 2**, calculate the tension in the string.

tension = ... N

(3 marks)

3.3 Using **Figure 2**, calculate the speed at which waves travel along the string.

wave speed = ... ms⁻¹

(3 marks)

The gradient of a straight-line graph can be a useful source of information. By finding
equations linking the variables on the x and y axes and putting them into the form $y = mx + c$
you can find out what the gradient of a particular straight-line graph represents.

Score

21

Section Three — Waves

Basics of Mechanics — 1

Mechanics is filled with vectors, forces and moments. Just like a tight-rope walk, mechanics can feel like a delicate balancing act — have a go at these questions to see if your revision is heading in the right direction.

For each of questions 1-4, give your answer by ticking the appropriate box.

1 Which of the following is **not** a vector quantity?

    A   Velocity ☐

    B   Speed ☐

    C   Displacement ☐

    D   Acceleration ☐

(1 mark)

2 Which of the following is a correct statement of the principle of moments?

    A   A moment about a point is defined as force × perpendicular distance from the point to the line of action of the force. ☐

    B   If the total clockwise moments around a point equal the total anticlockwise moments around the same point, the body is stationary. ☐

    C   A body is in equilibrium if the sum of the forces on one side of a point equals the sum of the forces on the other side of the same point. ☐

    D   For a body in equilibrium, the total clockwise moments around a point equal the total anticlockwise moments around the same point. ☐

(1 mark)

3 A 3 N force and a 4 N force act at right angles to one another. A third force is applied and the system is now in equilibrium. What is the magnitude of the third force?

    A   1 N ☐

    B   5 N ☐

    C   6 N ☐

    D   7 N ☐

(1 mark)

4 A 12 N weight and a 4 N weight are placed at either end of a 6 m long plank that has negligible mass. How far from the 4 N weight should the pivot be placed for the plank to be balanced?

    A   1.5 m ☐

    B   2.5 m ☐

    C   3.5 m ☐

    D   4.5 m ☐

(1 mark)

5 A valve in a water pipeline is opened by rotating a circular wheel of diameter 0.40 m.
An engineer uses one hand to apply a force of 120 N parallel to the edge of the wheel.

5.1 Calculate the moment of this force.

moment = ... Nm
(1 mark)

5.2 The engineer then uses both hands to apply equal and opposite forces at opposite sides of the wheel.
State the name given to such a pair of turning forces.

....

(1 mark)

5.3 The wheel requires a minimum turning force of 160 Nm to turn.
Calculate the minimum force the engineer would have to apply with each hand to turn the wheel.

force = ... N
(2 marks)

The engineer is not strong enough to apply the force required to turn the wheel.
He tries to turn the wheel by attaching a metal bar to the edge of the wheel, as shown in **Figure 1**.
The engineer pulls on the bar with a force F in the direction shown.

Figure 1

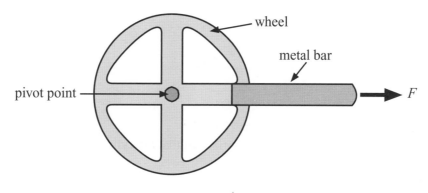

5.4 Explain why this method will not cause the wheel to turn.

....

....

(1 mark)

5.5 Explain how the engineer could use the bar to turn the wheel.

....

....

(1 mark)

6 A uniform cylinder is pushed so that it tilts at an angle of 5° from the horizontal, as shown in **Figure 2**.

Figure 2

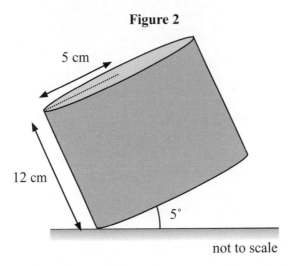

5 cm

12 cm

5°

not to scale

6.1 State what is meant by the centre of mass of an object.

....

(1 mark)

6.2 When the pushing force is removed, the cylinder drops back onto its base.
Using the ideas of moments and centre of mass, explain why the cylinder does not topple over.

....

....

....

....

....

(3 marks)

6.3 The cylinder has radius 5 cm and height 12 cm.
Calculate the maximum angle from the horizontal that the cylinder can be pushed before it topples over.

maximum angle = ... °

(2 marks)

Score

16

Basics of Mechanics — 2

1   **Figure 1** shows the location of a lighthouse, a ship and an island. The lighthouse is
1.5 km north of the island. The ship is anchored 3.2 km east of the lighthouse.

Figure 1

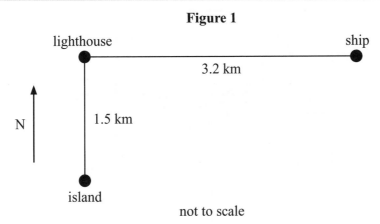

not to scale

1.1   Calculate the distance of the ship from the island.

distance = ... m

(2 marks)

1.2   A man is standing on the island, facing the lighthouse. He then turns clockwise to face the ship.
Calculate the size of the angle through which the man has turned.

angle = ...°

(2 marks)

1.3   The ship sails 2.1 km in a north-west direction.
Using a scale drawing, determine the new distance of the ship from the island in km.

distance = ... km

(2 marks)

2 A student is using a force board to investigate vectors and bodies in equilibrium.
She uses weights and smooth pulleys to exert forces on a metal ring.

2.1 The force board is set up so that three forces are exerted on the ring in the directions shown in **Figure 2**.

Figure 2

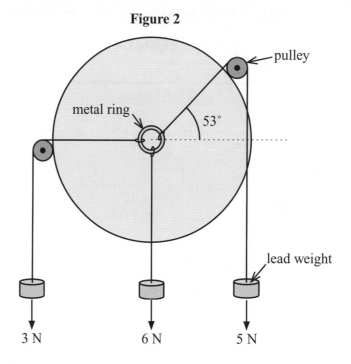

Explain why the ring begins moving vertically downward.
Include calculations of the horizontal and vertical components of the 5 N force in your answer.

....

....

....

....

(3 marks)

2.2 The student rearranges the force board. The 5 N force now acts at an angle of 60° above the horizontal.
She replaces the 3 N force with a new force F, but leaves the 6 N force unchanged.
The system is now in equilibrium.
Calculate the magnitude of F and the angle it makes with the horizontal.

magnitude = ... N

angle .... °

(4 marks)

3   Read the following passage and answer the questions that follow it.

Friction is a force that acts to resist relative motion between two objects that are in contact with one another. It is caused by the interaction of irregularities in the surface of each object. Even an object that appears smooth to the naked eye will look rough and irregular when magnified.

When a sliding force S is applied to a wooden crate resting on a stone floor, an equal and opposite frictional force F acts to oppose the sliding motion of the crate, as shown in **Figure 3**.

Figure 3

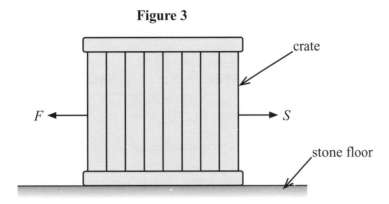

If the sliding force S is increased, F will increase to match it, until it reaches a maximum value, F_{max}.

Once S exceeds F_{max}, the sliding force is sufficient to overcome static friction, and the crate will begin to slide.

F_{max} is proportional to R, the reaction force exerted on the crate by the floor. If the crate is resting on a horizontal surface, R is equal and opposite to the weight of the crate, W. This is shown in **Figure 4**.

Figure 4

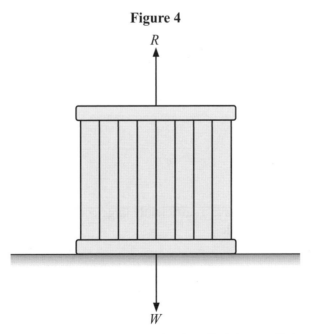

The constant of proportionality between F_{max} and R is called the coefficient of friction, μ. The value of μ depends on the properties of the two surfaces.

$$F_{max} = \mu \times R$$

3.1 The wooden crate is now resting on a slope, inclined at an angle θ. The crate doesn't slide down the slope.

Figure 5

Draw an arrow on **Figure 5** indicating the direction in which friction is acting.

(1 mark)

3.2 Write down the component of the block's weight acting parallel to the slope.

....

(1 mark)

3.3 The slope's incline is increased to a critical angle, such that the crate is on the verge of sliding. Show that:

$$\frac{\sin \theta}{\cos \theta} = \mu$$

....

....

....

....

....

....

(3 marks)

3.4 Explain why, if the crate and the slope have a sufficiently large coefficient of friction, the crate may move before the slope reaches this critical angle.

....

....

....

(2 marks)

EXAM TIP

If you're faced with a question which involves several forces acting on an object, make a start by drawing a diagram. Label the size and direction of each force clearly. If they are acting at awkward angles, try resolving each force into its horizontal and vertical components.

Score

20

Forces and Motion — 1

Here at CGP we regularly receive sacks full of fan mail from our adoring public. Mike, aged 17, wrote in to us recently, requesting a topic jam-packed with all kinds of thrilling graphs about motion. This one's for you Mike.

For each of questions 1-4, give your answer by ticking the appropriate box.

1   A 500 g football is moving at 7 ms⁻¹ towards a player. The player kicks the ball back in the opposite direction with an impulse of 5.5 Ns. What is the speed of the ball immediately after it is kicked?

    A   11 ms⁻¹ ☐

    B   3 ms⁻¹ ☐

    C   4 ms⁻¹ ☐

    D   18 ms⁻¹ ☐

                                                                   (1 mark)

2   Which of the following will give the instantaneous velocity of an object?

    A   The area under the object's acceleration-time graph. ☐

    B   The object's displacement divided by its total journey time. ☐

    C   The gradient of a tangent to the object's acceleration-time graph. ☐

    D   The gradient of a tangent to the object's displacement-time graph. ☐

                                                                   (1 mark)

3   A projectile is fired upwards with initial velocity u. At time t it has an upwards velocity of $\frac{u}{2}$. At what time will it have an upwards velocity of $\frac{u}{4}$? Ignore the effect of air resistance.

    A $\frac{3}{2}t$ ☐

    B $\frac{2}{3}t$ ☐

    C $2t$ ☐

    D $3t$ ☐

                                                                   (1 mark)

4   A constant braking force of magnitude F acts on an object of mass m that is initially moving with velocity u. How long does it take for the object to come to rest?

    A $\frac{uF}{m}$ ☐

    B $\frac{mu}{F}$ ☐

    C $\frac{F}{mu}$ ☐

    D $\frac{u}{mF}$ ☐

                                                                   (1 mark)

5 The velocity-time graph in **Figure 1** shows the motion of a car moving along a straight road.

Figure 1

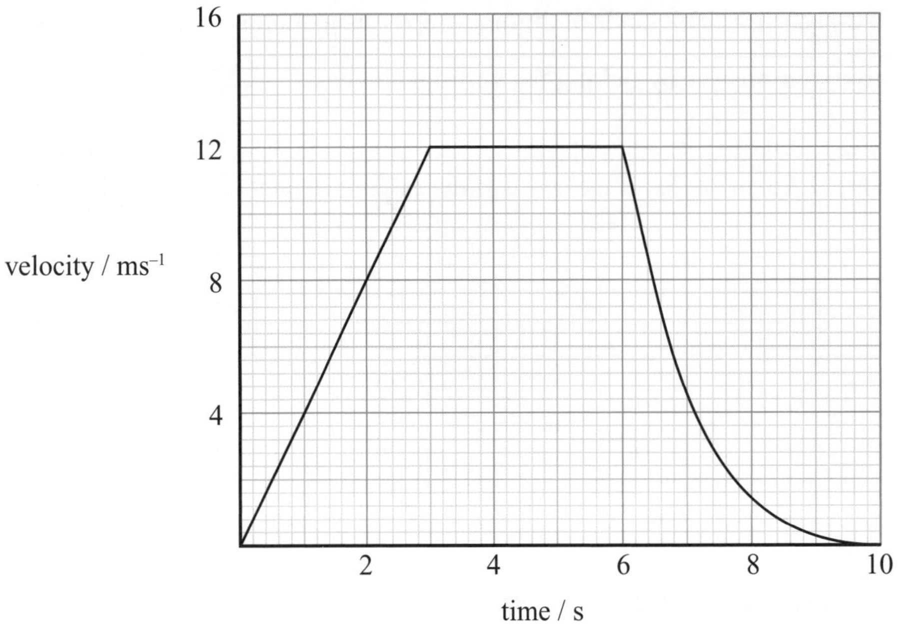

velocity / ms⁻¹

time / s

5.1 Describe the car's motion between 0 and 10 s.

....

....

....

....

(3 marks)

5.2 Estimate the distance travelled by the car in this time.

distance = ... m

(2 marks)

5.3 Draw a cross on **Figure 1** to indicate a point at which the magnitude of the car's acceleration is greatest.

(1 mark)

5.4 Calculate the average acceleration of the car during the final 4 seconds of its journey.

average acceleration = ... ms⁻²

(1 mark)

6 **Figure 2** shows a graph of the force acting on a 50 g tennis ball as it is hit.

Figure 2

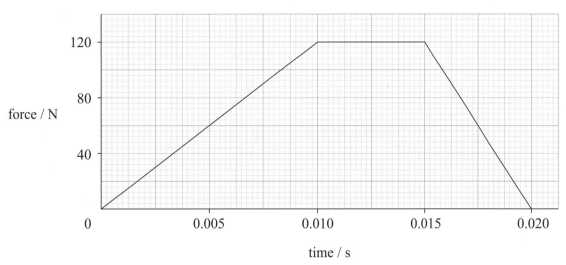

force / N

time / s

6.1 Calculate the increase in velocity of the ball as it is hit.

increase in velocity = ... ms⁻¹

(2 marks)

6.2 When a tennis player hits a ball they often continue to swing their racket
after the initial moment of contact. This is called 'following through'.
Explain how following through can allow a player to hit a faster shot than
if they were to stop their stroke immediately at the moment of contact.

....

....

....

(2 marks)

6.3 The tennis ball hits a wall. The speed of the ball immediately after the collision
with the wall is less than its speed immediately before the collision.
Give the name of this type of collision and explain why the ball's speed has decreased.

....

....

....

(2 marks)

 Sometimes you'll need to estimate the area under a graph that can't be easily split up into
nice simple shapes. In that situation, count up all the whole and half squares under the graph,
ticking them off as you go to make sure you don't count any more than once.

Score

17

Forces and Motion — 2

1   A prototype transportation system, shown in **Figure 1**, is designed to accelerate a vehicle to high speeds through a tunnel held at a low air pressure.

Figure 1

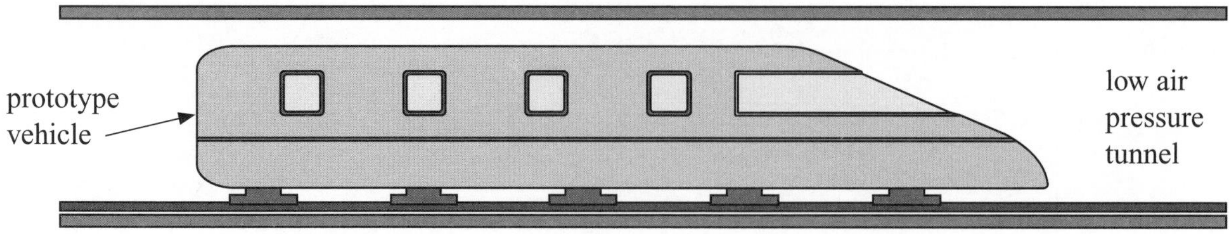

1.1   Explain why the low air pressure inside the tunnel allows the vehicle to reach very high speeds.

....

....

(1 mark)

1.2   A loop of track with a length of 1.10 km is built to test the system. During a test run, a detector records the vehicle travelling at 16.0 ms^{-1}. After completing two further circuits of the track, the detector records the vehicle's speed as 289 ms^{-1}. The vehicle's acceleration along the track is constant.
Calculate the amount of time between the two measurements taken.

time = ... s

(2 marks)

1.3   The prototype vehicle has a mass of 1250 kg.
Calculate the resultant force on the vehicle during the test run.

force = ... N

(2 marks)

1.4   The vehicle reaches a top speed of 320 ms^{-1} and maintains it along a straight part of the track.
Compare the driving forces and the resistive forces acting on the vehicle during this period.

....

....

(1 mark)

2   A student launches a model rocket.

The rocket accelerates upwards from rest at a constant rate until its engines cut out.
Figure 2 shows a velocity-time graph for part of the rocket's journey.

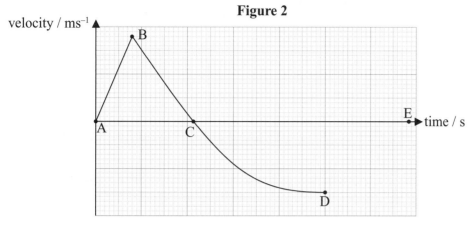
Figure 2

2.1 Identify the point at which the rocket's engines stopped.

....
(1 mark)

2.2 Describe and explain the motion of the rocket from point C to point D.

....

....

....

....

....
(3 marks)

2.3 At point D the rocket deploys a parachute, before eventually reaching the ground at point E.
On **Figure 2**, sketch the shape of the graph you would expect to see between points D and E.

(1 mark)

2.4 A second model rocket is launched. **Figure 3** shows how
the rocket's displacement above the ground varies over time.

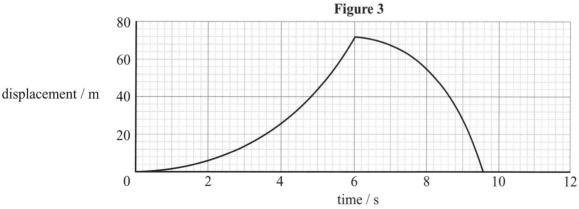
Figure 3

Determine the instantaneous velocity of the rocket the first time it is 40 m above the ground.

instantaneous velocity = ... ms⁻¹
(2 marks)

3   A snooker ball has a mass of 240 g and is initially at rest.

3.1   A player strikes the ball with a cue, delivering an impulse of 0.84 Ns to the ball.
Calculate the velocity of the ball after it is hit.

velocity = ... ms^{-1}
(1 mark)

3.2   The ball goes on to collide inelastically with a second ball of the same mass which is moving at a speed of
0.75 ms^{-1} in the opposite direction. State what is meant by an inelastic collision.

....
(1 mark)

3.3   After colliding, the two balls move off in the same direction. The speed of the leading ball is twice that of
the ball that follows. Calculate the velocity of the leading ball.

velocity = ... ms^{-1}
(2 marks)

3.4   After the collision, the leading ball falls into a pocket that is 84 cm from the point at which they collided.
Calculate the maximum size of the average frictional force acting on this ball.

force = ... N
(2 marks)

EXAM TIP   When you're answering a question about a collision, it can be really helpful to do a couple
of quick drawings of the objects before and after the collision, labelled with their masses and
velocities. It doesn't need to be the Mona Lisa though — blobs will work just fine.

Score

19

Forces and Motion — 3

1   The displacement-time graph for a high-speed lift over a 1 minute period is shown in **Figure 1**.

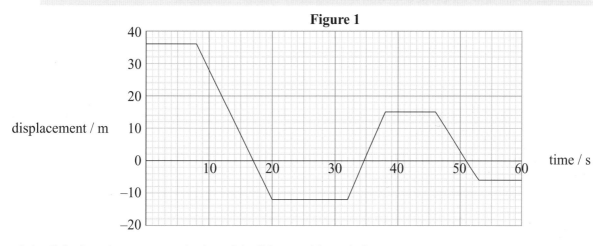

Figure 1

1.1   Calculate the average velocity of the lift over this period.

average velocity = ... ms⁻¹

(1 mark)

1.2   Calculate the average speed of the lift over this period.

average speed = ... ms⁻¹

(1 mark)

1.3   Using **Figure 2**, draw the velocity-time graph of the lift over this period.
You may use the space below **Figure 2** for any working.

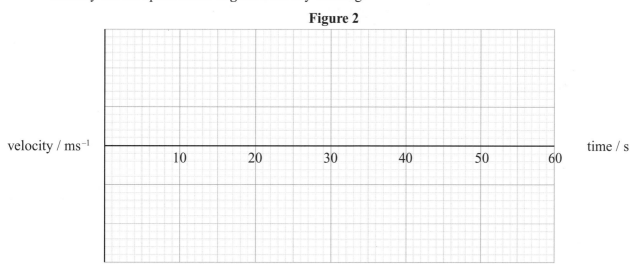

Figure 2

(2 marks)

2   A spacecraft consists of a probe of mass 60 kg attached to an engine.

2.1   Whilst travelling through space at a constant velocity, the probe and the engine separate.
The probe ejects the engine backwards.
Describe and explain how the probe's motion is affected by ejecting the engine.

....

....

....

(2 marks)

2.2   The probe approaches a rocky planet. It experiences a constant resultant force of 510 N due to the planet's
gravitational field. This force acts in the same direction as the probe's motion.
Calculate the acceleration experienced by the probe.

acceleration = ... ms^{-2}

(1 mark)

2.3   Calculate the increase in the probe's velocity due to this acceleration during an 18 second time period.

increase in velocity = ... ms^{-1}

(1 mark)

2.4   **Figure 3** shows a diagram of the probe as viewed from the side.

Figure 3

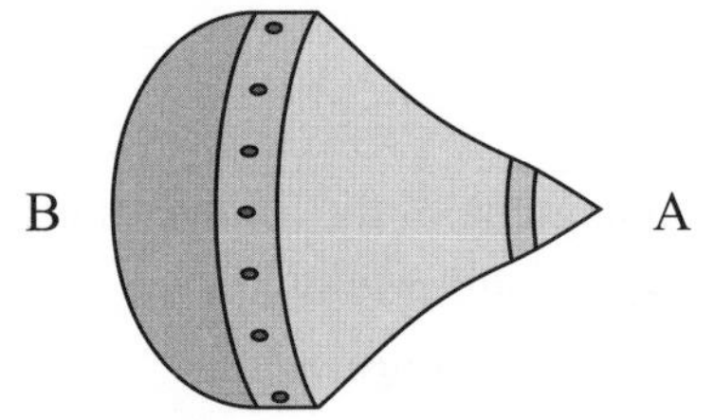

Before entering the planet's atmosphere, side A of the probe is facing its direction of travel.
Upon entry the probe rotates itself by 180° so that side B faces the direction of travel.
Suggest and explain how the probe's motion would be affected by this rotation.

....

....

....

(2 marks)

2.5   Before hitting the surface of the planet, the probe inflates airbags.
Explain how these airbags reduce the damage sustained by the probe as it strikes the planet's surface.

....

....

....

(2 marks)

3 A student is conducting an experiment to determine the value of the acceleration due to gravity on Earth.

Figure 4 shows the apparatus used by the student.

Figure 4

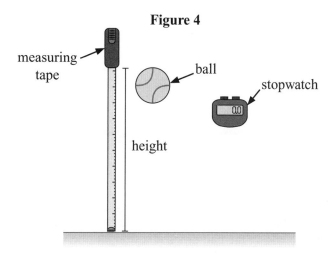

She releases a ball from rest from a known height, as shown in **Figure 4**. She uses a stopwatch to record the drop time between the ball's release and when the ball hits the ground.
For each height the ball is released from, the student carries out three measurements of drop time.
Her results are shown in **Table 1**.

Table 1

Release Height / m	Mean Drop Time / s	Mean Drop Time Squared / s^2
1.6	0.78	
1.8	0.82	
2.0	0.85	
2.2	0.88	
2.4	**0.91**	
2.6	0.94	

3.1 Using **Figure 5** and the data from **Table 1**, draw a graph of release height against mean drop time squared. The final column in **Table 1** is provided for any calculations you need to make. Include a line of best fit.

Figure 5

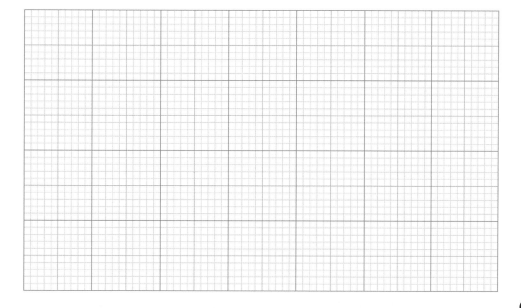

(3 marks)

3.2 Using the graph you plotted in 3.1, calculate a value for the acceleration due to gravity.

acceleration = ... ms^{-2}

(2 marks)

3.3 In order to improve the accuracy of her result, the student suggests dropping
the ball down a plastic tube to ensure the ball drops in a straight line.
Discuss whether this suggestion is likely to improve or reduce the result's accuracy.

....

....

....

(2 marks)

3.4 The actual value of the acceleration due to gravity is 9.81 ms^{-2}. Discuss the possible reasons that the
student's results differ from this value. Suggest ways in which she could improve her result.

....

....

....

....

....

....

....

....

....

....

....

(6 marks)

With questions like 3.4 that require an extended written response, it can be hard to know
where to start. How well your answer is structured can have an effect on your mark. A good
strategy is to brainstorm your ideas on scrap paper before committing to your final answer.

Score

25

Forces and Motion — 4

1   An air rifle fires pellets with a mass of 0.60 g at a target 100 m away.

1.1   The air rifle delivers an impulse of 0.15 Ns to a pellet.
Calculate the pellet's velocity immediately after it has been fired.

velocity = ... ms^{-1}
(1 mark)

1.2   The target is circular with a diameter of 1.2 m. Its centre is 1.4 m off the ground.
The pellet is fired horizontally, also from a height of 1.4 m off the ground.
Determine whether it is possible for this shot to hit the target. Ignore the effects air of resistance.

(3 marks)

1.3   A second pellet is fired from the same height with the same initial speed.
However, this pellet is fired at an angle θ above the horizontal and hits the centre of the target.
Ignoring the effects of air resistance, show that:

$$\sin\theta\cos\theta = 0.0008g$$

(4 marks)

2   A radio-controlled car of mass 750 g is driven up a ramp resting on the ground, as shown in **Figure 1**.

Figure 1

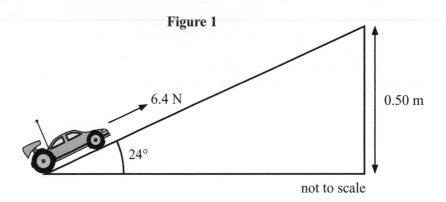

6.4 N

0.50 m

24°

not to scale

2.1   The car's motor provides a driving force of 6.4 N.
Calculate the acceleration of the car up the ramp.

acceleration = ... ms⁻²

(3 marks)

2.2   State **one** assumption that you made when calculating the car's acceleration up the ramp.

....

....

(1 mark)

2.3   The car starts from rest at the bottom of the ramp.
Calculate the car's speed when it reaches the top of the ramp.

speed = ... ms⁻¹

(2 marks)

A second radio-controlled car is driven up the same ramp.
Its speed as it reaches the top of the ramp is 4.4 ms⁻¹.

2.4 Calculate the maximum height above the ground that the second car reaches
after driving off the edge of the ramp. You may ignore the effect of air resistance.

height = ... m

(3 marks)

2.5 Calculate the horizontal distance the second car travels between leaving the ramp
and returning to the ground. You may ignore the effect of air resistance.

distance = ... m

(4 marks)

2.6 Other than by increasing the speed of the car or altering the ramp, suggest **one** way to increase the actual
horizontal distance the car travels between leaving the ramp and returning to the ground.

....

....

(1 mark)

There's no doubt about it — projectile motion questions can get hectic. The key is to keep
calculations about the vertical and horizontal components of motion separate. I'd go as far as
drawing a big line down the middle of the page and titling one side 'vertical motion' and the
other 'horizontal motion'. But, hey, that's just me.

EXAM
TIP

Score

22

Work and Energy

You're nearly there. Three pages of questions on work and energy is all that stand between you and the completion of this mammoth mechanics section. Then you can put your feet up for a bit and have a nice cup of something.

For each of questions 1-4, give your answer by ticking the appropriate box.

1 Which of the following would **not** be a correct unit of energy?

A Nms⁻¹ ☐ B kgm²s⁻² ☐

C J ☐ D Nm ☐

(1 mark)

2 A wind exerts a constant force of $0.5X$ N on a windsurfer, doing Y joules of work on him per second. What is the speed of the windsurfer?

A $2Y \div X$ ☐

B $2YX$ ☐

C $Y \div 2X$ ☐

D $0.5YX$ ☐

(1 mark)

3 **Figure 1** shows a horse-drawn carriage being pulled along flat ground with a force H at an angle of 15° to the horizontal. A constant frictional force F acts on the carriage. What is the total work done on the carriage to move it through a distance d?

Figure 1

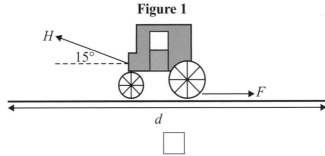

A $Hd\cos15°$ ☐

B $Hd\cos15° - Fd$ ☐

C $(H + F)d\cos15°$ ☐

D $Hd\cos15° + Fd$ ☐

(1 mark)

4 Two snowmobiles of equal mass are racing across a flat frozen lake. Snowmobile 1 does W joules of work to accelerate from rest to a top speed of v. Snowmobile 2 does $1.5W$ joules of work to accelerate from rest to a top speed of $1.2v$. The efficiency of snowmobile 1 is e. What is the efficiency of snowmobile 2?

A $0.8e$ ☐ B $1.04e$ ☐

C $1.25e$ ☐ D $0.96e$ ☐

(1 mark)

5 A student conducts an experiment to determine the efficiency of an electric motor. A 250 g mass is connected to the motor by a piece of string. The string is assumed to be light and inextensible, and rests on a smooth pulley. **Figure 2** shows the set-up of the equipment in the experiment.

Figure 2

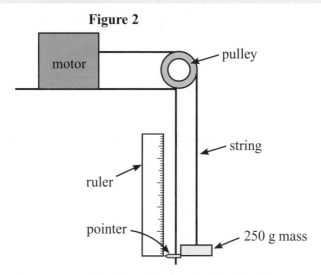

The student uses a stopwatch to measure how long it takes for the electric motor to raise the masses vertically upwards by 0.50 m. She repeats the experiment three times, and calculates the mean time taken to be 1.28 s.

5.1 State the principle of conservation of energy.

....

....
(1 mark)

5.2 Calculate the useful power output of the electric motor.
Give your answer to an appropriate number of significant figures.

useful power output = ... W
(2 marks)

5.3 The electrical power supplied to the motor from the power supply is 1.3 W.
Calculate the efficiency of the motor. State your answer as a percentage.

efficiency = ... %
(1 mark)

5.4 The student estimates the absolute uncertainty in his timing measurements to be approximately 150 ms.
Use this to determine the percentage uncertainty of the student's timing measurements.

percentage uncertainty = ... %
(1 mark)

5.5 Suggest **one** way in which the percentage uncertainty of the measurements could be reduced.

....

....
(1 mark)

6 A bungee jumper stands at the edge of a bridge. He uses an elastic bungee cord with an unstretched length of 20 m. One end of the cord is attached to his ankles, and the other end is tied to the bridge railings at his feet.

The bungee jumper steps off the bridge. **Figure 3** shows a graph of the force acting on the bungee jumper due to the cord, as a function of the vertical distance travelled by the bungee jumper, for part of the jump. Points A and B are labelled on the graph.

Figure 3

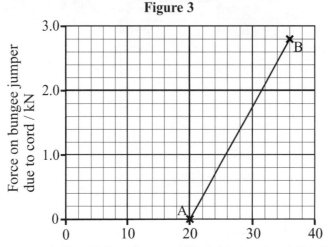

6.1 The elastic bungee cord remains slack until point A. The mass of the bungee jumper is 65 kg. Using the principle of conservation of energy, calculate the speed of the bungee jumper at point A. You may assume that there is zero air resistance, and that the mass of the bungee cord is negligible compared to the mass of the bungee jumper.

speed = ... ms^{-1}
(3 marks)

6.2 Between points A and B, the elastic bungee cord is stretched to a length greater than 20 m, and the vertical velocity of the bungee jumper decreases. Describe the energy transfers that occur between points A and B.

....

....
(1 mark)

6.3 Calculate the work done by the bungee cord on the jumper between points A and B.

work done = ... J
(1 mark)

Score

Examiners love to throw an unfamiliar context into a question. This can seem pretty daunting at first, but don't panic — they'll always give you enough information to answer the question. Take a deep breath, and jot down everything you're told in the question. Then you'll be in a good position to consider which equations or concepts you'll need to help you on your merry way.

15

Materials — 1

There's lots of fun (or at least practice) to be had with questions on wires, graphs and the good ol' Young modulus in this section. Have a go at these questions to stretch your brain and see what you're made of.

For each of questions 1-4, give your answer by ticking the appropriate box.

1   Which of the following statements about the elastic limit of a material is correct?

    A   The elastic limit is the point at which a material starts to stretch without additional load. ☐

    B   A graph of tensile stress against tensile strain is always linear up to the elastic limit. ☐

    C   The elastic limit is the maximum force that can be applied to an elastic material before it breaks. ☐

    D   If a material is stretched up to its elastic limit and released, it will return to its original shape. ☐

(1 mark)

2   Which of the following are the correct units for the Young modulus of a material?

    A $Pa\,kg^{-1}$ ☐

    B $N\,m^{-2}$ ☐

    C $Pa\,m^{2}$ ☐

    D $N\,m^{2}$ ☐

(1 mark)

3   A monkey hangs vertically from a light uniform rope attached to the ceiling. The weight of the monkey, W, causes the rope to extend elastically by 0.1 m. What is the spring constant of the rope?

    A $10W\,Nm^{-1}$ ☐

    B $0.1W\,Nm^{-1}$ ☐

    C $0.01W\,Nm^{-1}$ ☐

    D $0.05W\,Nm^{-1}$ ☐

(1 mark)

4   A spring stretched elastically has an extension of x and stores elastic strain energy E.
How far must the spring be stretched elastically in total so that it stores elastic strain energy $2E$?

    A x^{2} ☐

    B $\sqrt{2}\,x$ ☐

    C $\sqrt{2x}$ ☐

    D $2x$ ☐

(1 mark)

5 A student does an experiment to determine the lifting force exerted by a helium balloon using the equipment shown in **Figure 1**.

Figure 1

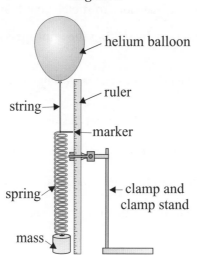

5.1 The length of the spring before the helium balloon was attached was 10 cm.
Attaching the helium balloon caused the spring to stretch elastically.
The student measures the new length of the spring to be 11.5 cm using the marker.
The spring has a spring constant of $0.50 \, \mathrm{N \, m^{-1}}$.
Calculate the lifting force on the spring caused by the balloon.

force = ... N

(1 mark)

5.2 Explain **one** way the student could change the experiment to reduce the percentage uncertainty in her length measurement.

....

....

....

....

(2 marks)

5.3 The balloon is inflated with helium until it has a radius of 9.5 cm.
The density of helium is $0.164 \, \mathrm{kg \, m^{-3}}$. Estimate the mass of helium contained in the balloon.

mass = ... kg

(2 marks)

6 A manufacturer uses a machine to test the properties of a uniform 2.0 m length of rope. The machine exerts increasing amounts of force on the piece of rope, while measuring the extension of the rope. The machine then gradually decreases the force and continues to measure the extension off the rope.

Figure 2 shows a graph of the force applied and the extension of the rope recorded by the machine during the test.

Figure 2

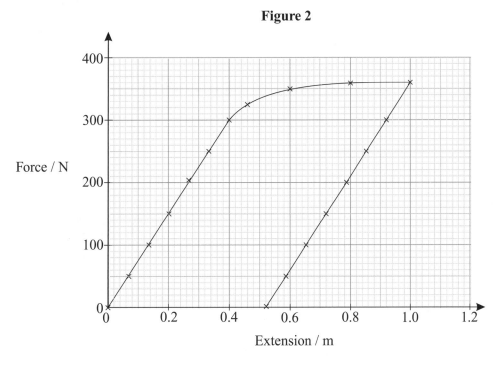

6.1 Estimate the energy stored in the rope at the limit of proportionality.

energy stored = ... J
(2 marks)

6.2 Calculate the spring constant of the rope.

spring constant = ... Nm⁻¹
(1 mark)

6.3 Once the force is removed, it is found that the rope has been permanently stretched. Calculate the work done to cause this permanent deformation.

work done = ... J
(2 marks)

There are loads of things examiners can ask you about force-extension graphs, so make sure you're really comfortable with interpreting them. Remember, if force and extension are directly proportional, the object is obeying Hooke's law — the gradient is equal to the stiffness constant and the area under the graph is equal to the elastic strain energy stored in the object.

Score

14

Materials — 2

1   A student carries out an experiment to determine the Young
modulus of a material using the equipment shown in **Figure 1**.

Figure 1

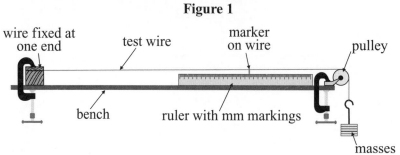

The student measures the diameter of the wire using a vernier caliper.
The student measures and records the extension of the wire each time a 100 g
mass is added to the wire. He calculates the tensile stress and tensile strain of the wire for each
mass added. He repeats this process for each mass added to the wire until the wire breaks.
Figure 2 shows a graph of tensile stress against tensile strain for the wire.

Figure 2

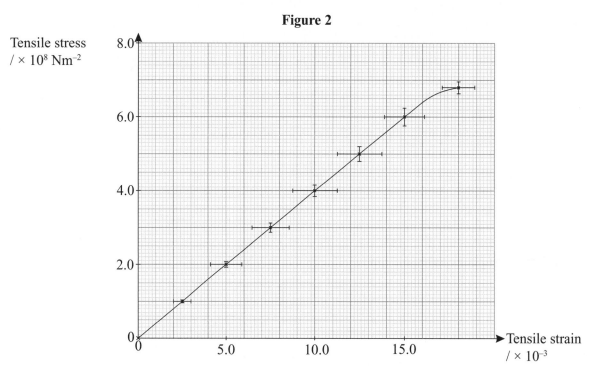

1.1 Use **Figure 2** to calculate the Young modulus of the material.
Include the percentage uncertainty in your answer.

Young modulus = ... Nm⁻² ± .... %

(4 marks)

1.2 State and explain **one** change the student could make to their experiment that could decrease the uncertainty in the student's tensile stress results.

....

....

....

....
(2 marks)

1.3 The student suggests the Young modulus of a cable made from multiple identical wires would be higher than that of a single wire. Is the student correct? Explain your answer.

....

....
(1 mark)

1.4 Show that, whilst a wire obeys Hooke's law, the energy per unit volume it stores is equal to the area under a stress-strain graph for that wire.

....

....

....

....

....

....

....
(2 marks)

1.5 When strain measured 15.0×10^{-3}, the wire was 1.024 m long and had a cross-sectional area of $3.8 \times 10^{-7} \, m^2$. Calculate the total energy stored by the wire at this point.

energy = ... J
(3 marks)

1.6 Describe the difference between the limit of proportionality and the elastic limit of a material.

....

....

....
(1 mark)

2　**Figure 3** shows the stress-strain graphs for two rods made from materials X and Y.

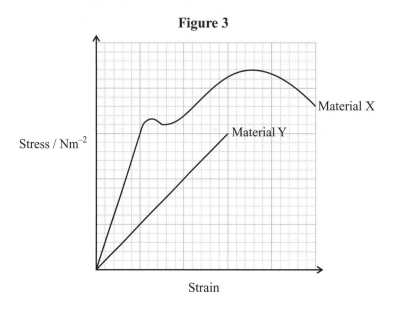

Figure 3

Stress / Nm^{-2}

Material X

Material Y

Strain

2.1　Another rod is made from material W.
Material W is stiffer than Material X and has a lower ultimate tensile stress than material Y.
On **Figure 3**, sketch a possible stress-strain graph for the rod of material W.

(2 marks)

2.2　One of the materials is used to make the body of a car. Car bodies are designed to deform in a crash to help minimise the energy transferred to the passengers.
By comparing the properties of materials W, X and Y,
suggest and explain which material is most suitable for this use.

....

....

....

....

....

....

....

....

....

....

....

....

(6 marks)

3   A 1.0 kg rod of alloy X is fired into a target at high speed.

3.1   The rod has a kinetic energy of 18 kJ just before it collides with the target.
The rod undergoes a maximum compressive strain of 5.0%.
When strain is at its maximum, 45% of the rod's initial kinetic energy is stored as elastic potential energy.
The energy per unit volume stored in the rod = ½ × stress × strain.
Alloy X has a density of 8000 kgm^{-3}. Calculate the Young modulus of alloy X.

Young modulus = ... Nm^{-2}

(4 marks)

3.2   **Figure 4** shows a rectangular bar of another alloy placed between two walls.
The tensile stress in the bar is 0 Pa. The Young modulus of the alloy is 200 GPa.
When heated, the bar would increase in length by Δl m if it was unrestricted.
Instead the bar remains the same length but experiences a tensile stress
equal to the stress it would require to extend the bar by Δl.

Figure 4

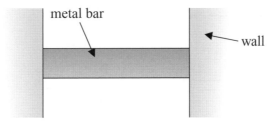

The temperature change (ΔT) and the extension of the bar are related by the equation:

$$\Delta l = \alpha \Delta T l$$

where $\alpha = 1.3 \times 10^{-5}$ K^{-1} and l is the original length of the bar.
Calculate the tensile stress of the metal bar when it is heated from 293 K to 523 K.

tensile stress = ... Pa

(3 marks)

Electricity — 1

There's more to electricity than just $R = V \div I$. Have a go at this electrifying section of questions to make sure you know your e.m.f.s from internal resistances, your resistivity from resistance and your LEDs from thermistors.

For each of questions 1-4, give your answer by ticking the appropriate box.

1 The diagram shows the current flowing in and out of a junction in a circuit. What is the current through the branch marked X?

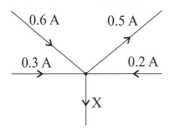

A	0.2 A	**B**	0.6 A
C	1.6 A	**D**	1.1 A

(1 mark)

2 Which graph shows how the power of a fixed resistor changes with current?

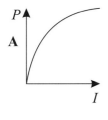 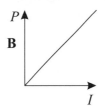 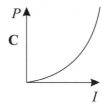 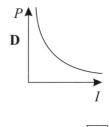

A		**B**	
C		**D**	

(1 mark)

3 A hairdryer contains a heating element with a resistance of 57.5 Ω. The hairdryer is connected to the mains at 230 V. How much energy is transferred by the heating element when the hairdryer is switched on for 50 s?

A	660 000 J	**B**	46 000 J
C	760 000 J	**D**	38 000 000 J

(1 mark)

4 A length of copper wire has a resistance of 60.0 nΩ. The wire has a length of L and a cross-sectional area A. The wire is stretched so that the length is now equal to $1.25L$, and the cross-sectional area is $0.80A$. What is the resistance of the stretched wire?

A	93.8 nΩ	**B**	38.4 nΩ
C	60.0 nΩ	**D**	1.56 nΩ

(1 mark)

5   A student investigates a series of wires. Each wire is made from a different material. The student does not know which material each wire is made from.

The student investigates the resistivity of the wires to determine which material each wire is made from. **Table 1** shows the wire materials and their resistivities at room temperature.

Table 1

Material	Resistivity at room temperature / Ωm
Lead	2.1×10^{-7}
Copper	1.7×10^{-8}
Molybdenum	5.3×10^{-8}
Tantalum	1.3×10^{-7}

5.1 State the material in **Table 1** that would be the best choice for use as electrical wiring. Explain your answer.

....

....

....

(3 marks)

5.2 The student carries out an experiment to investigate how the resistance of each wire varies with length. **Figure 1** shows how resistance varies with length for one wire, wire A.

Figure 1

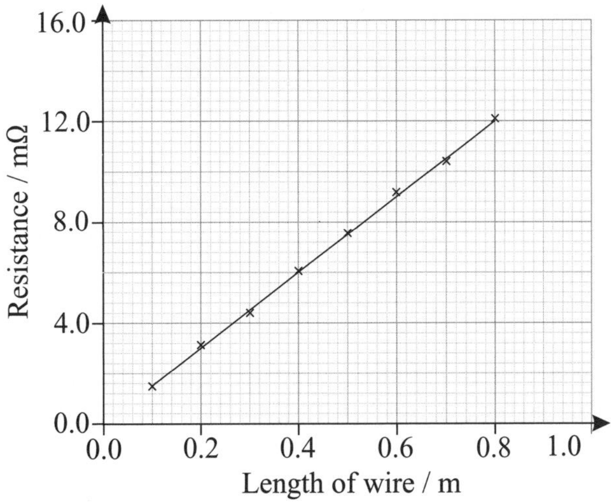

The cross-sectional area of wire A throughout the experiment is 1.4×10^{-5} m^2.
Determine which material wire A is made from.

material = ...

(3 marks)

6   **Figure 2** shows an LED connected in a circuit with a variable power supply.

Figure 2

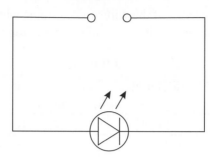

6.1   The potential difference supplied by the variable power supply is increased until the LED lights up.
The value at which the LED first lights up is 0.50 V. The current through the LED at this voltage is 2.50 A.
Calculate the energy transferred by the LED at this voltage and current when it is lit up for exactly 1 minute.

energy = ... J

(2 marks)

6.2   Explain why your answer to 6.1 is a minimum energy that is transferred to the LED to light it for 1 minute.

....

....

(1 mark)

6.3   The power dissipated by the LED in the forward bias direction at 3 V is 5 W. Explain why the power
dissipated by the LED in the reverse bias direction at 3 V will be significantly lower than this.

....

....

....

(2 marks)

6.4   A potential difference of 2.0 V is supplied by the variable power supply. The resistance of the LED is now
0.5 Ω. Calculate the number of charge carriers that flow through the LED during exactly 1 minute.

Each charge carrier has a charge
equal to the elementary charge, e.

number of charge carriers = ...

(3 marks)

Score

18

Electricity — 2

1   A student investigates the properties of a cell using the circuit shown in **Figure 1**.

Figure 1

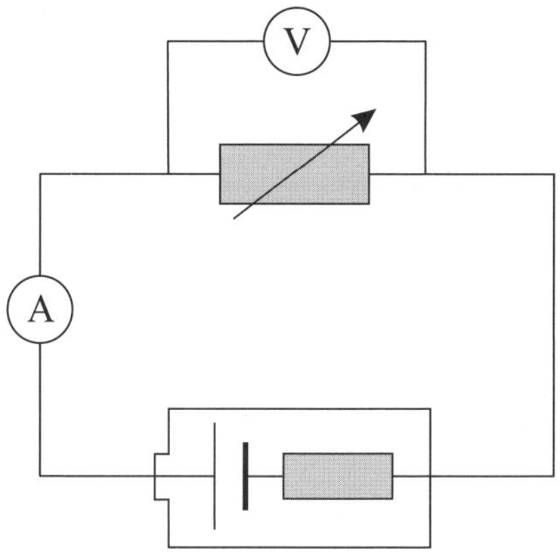

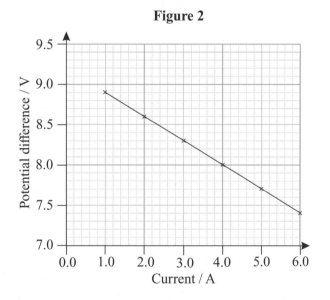

Cell

The student uses a variable resistor to change the current flowing through the circuit. He records values of the potential difference and current. A graph of the results is shown in **Figure 2**.

Figure 2

1.1 Determine the internal resistance of the cell.

internal resistance = ... Ω
(2 marks)

1.2 Determine the e.m.f. of the cell.

e.m.f. = ... V
(1 mark)

1.3   The difference between the e.m.f. and the terminal potential difference is often called the 'lost volts'.
Calculate the lost volts when the current through the circuit is 5.0 A.

lost volts = ... V

(1 mark)

1.4   Calculate the work done by the cell when it transfers a total of 80.0 C of charge in exactly 20 seconds
at a constant rate.

work done = ... J

(2 marks)

1.5   The student repeats the experiment using a cell with the same e.m.f. but a higher internal resistance.
He plots a graph of potential difference against current of his results.
State and explain the difference(s) you would expect there to be between this graph and **Figure 2**.

....

....

....

(1 mark)

1.6   The student checks his result for the e.m.f. of the cell by connecting a high-resistance voltmeter directly
across the cell. Explain why the voltmeter the student uses needs to have a high resistance.

....

....

....

(2 marks)

1.7   The student replaces the cell in the circuit with a different cell with an internal resistance of 0.50 Ω.
He also replaces the variable resistor with a fixed resistor. The cell transfers 5.0 J of energy for every
0.40 C of charge that flows through it. Calculate the resistance of the fixed resistor given that the current
flowing through the circuit is 0.80 A.

resistance = ... Ω

(3 marks)

2 **Figure 3** shows a temperature-sensing circuit. The cell has negligible internal resistance.

Figure 3

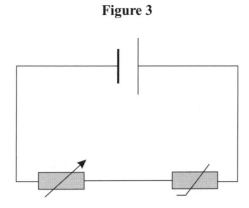

2.1 The cell supplies energy to the circuit at a rate of 2.4 Js⁻¹. Calculate the potential difference across the variable resistor when the resistance of the variable resistor is 9.0 Ω and the resistance of the thermistor is 6.0 Ω.

potential difference = ... V

(3 marks)

The circuit has a filament lamp added to it to create a temperature-sensing circuit for a freezer.
When the temperature falls below a certain temperature, the filament lamp in the circuit lights up.

2.2 On **Figure 3**, draw the position of the filament lamp in the circuit. Explain how the circuit operates.

....

....

....

(3 marks)

2.3 Another cell with negligible internal resistance is added to the circuit in series.
State and explain the effect this will have, if any, on the behaviour of the lamp as the temperature varies.

....

....

....

(2 marks)

2.4 State and explain how the brightness of the filament lamp would be different if the cells had an internal resistance that was not negligible.

....

....

(1 mark)

3 A student is investigating an unknown circuit component, component L. They construct a series circuit containing component L, a fixed resistor, a switch and a cell that supplies a constant e.m.f.

Figure 4 shows a graph of how the total charge that had passed through component L changed with time once the circuit was switched on.

Figure 4

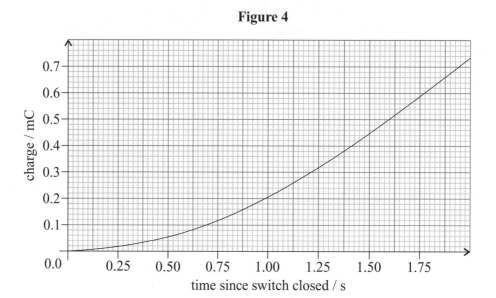

charge / mC

time since switch closed / s

3.1 At a time of 0.90 s after the switch was closed, the potential difference across the fixed resistor was 0.40 µV. Calculate the resistance of the resistor.

resistance = ... Ω

(3 marks)

3.2 Component L is a device called an inductor. It consists of a coil of insulated copper wire.
The turns on the coil are arranged side-by-side, touching each other.
The coil is 2.0 cm long, and made from a length of wire that has a total length of 1.40 m.
The straight length of wire has a resistance of 0.12 Ω. The resistivity of copper is 1.7×10^{-8} Ωm.
Estimate the number of turns on the coil.

number of turns = ...

(3 marks)

Score

27

Electricity — 3

1   **Figure 1** shows a circuit including four resistors, labelled A to D.

Figure 1

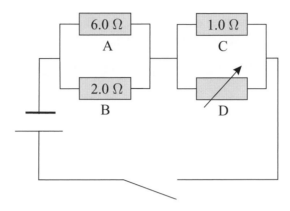

1.1   The circuit is powered by an 11.5 V cell. You may assume that the internal resistance of the cell is negligible. Calculate the total resistance of the circuit in **Figure 1** when the switch is closed and the resistance of the variable resistor is 4.0 Ω.

resistance = ... Ω
(3 marks)

1.2   Calculate the total current through the circuit.

current = ... A
(1 mark)

1.3   Calculate the energy transferred to resistor B during 64 seconds.

energy transferred = ... J
(3 marks)

1.4 Describe what happens to the combined resistance of resistors C and D as the resistance of the variable resistor is increased.

....

....

....

(2 marks)

1.5 The cell is replaced with a new cell with an e.m.f of 8.0 V, in which the internal resistance is no longer negligible. Calculate the internal resistance of the cell when it supplies 25.0 W of power to the circuit. The variable resistor remains at 4.0 Ω.

internal resistance = ... Ω

(2 marks)

1.6 When the switch is open, the potential difference across the cell is 8.0 V and when it is closed it is 7.6 V. Explain why these values for the potential difference are different.

....

....

(1 mark)

2 Magnetic Resonance Imaging (MRI) uses very large magnetic fields to create an image of the internal structures of the human body. The patient lies within a ring-shaped scanner, at room temperature, which contains a lighting system to help the patient feel less claustrophobic. **Figure 2** shows the temperature-resistivity graph of three types of wire made from different materials being considered for use in an MRI scanner.

Figure 2

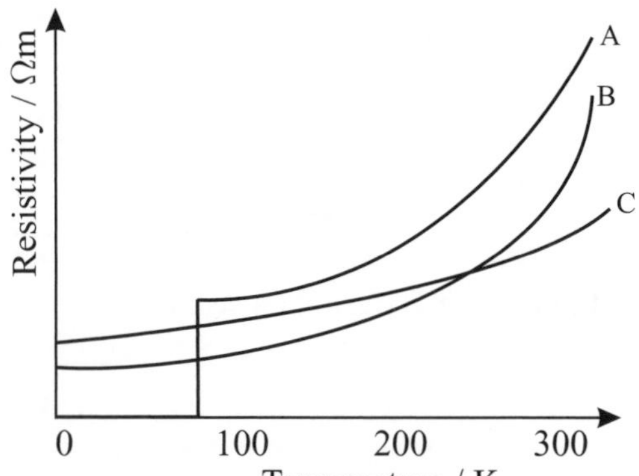

2.1 One of the wires is made from a superconducting material. Identify which material is the superconductor. Explain your answer.

....

....

....

(2 marks)

2.2 Discuss which of the three types of wire shown in **Figure 2** is most suitable for each of the following applications within the MRI scanner:
1. An electromagnet used to produce extremely strong magnetic fields.
2. The wires used in the lighting circuits inside the scanner at room temperature.

....

....

....

....

....

....

....

....

....

....

....

....

(6 marks)

2.3 The properties of a fourth wire, D, are being investigated for use in the MRI scanner. At room temperature, the wire has a resistivity of 2.3×10^{-8} Ωm. The wire has a diameter of 0.50 mm. Calculate the length of wire needed to produce a resistance of 0.050 Ω.

length = ... m

(3 marks)

2.4 Superconducting materials can also be used in power cables to transmit large amounts of electricity. Explain how the use of superconducting materials reduces energy losses in the power cables.

....

....

(1 mark)

EXAM TIP
In the exam you might be given quite complex circuits with a combination of components in series and parallel. If you're finding a circuit tricky to get your head around, just take your time and work out which bits of the circuit are relevant to the question you're trying to answer.

Score

24

Further Mechanics — 1

As surely as a pendulum swings back to its midpoint, we've returned to mechanics. Now we're tackling motion in the thrilling flavours of 'circular' and 'simple harmonic'. Time to see if you're in resonance with the physics of it all.

For each of questions 1-4, give your answer by ticking the appropriate box.

1   A teacher wants to illustrate the effects of resonance by showing that a wine glass can smash if driven by the right sound wave. She connects a signal generator to a loudspeaker and places it 50 cm from the glass. Which **one** of the following could **not** improve the likelihood of the glass smashing?

   A   Place the glass closer to the loudspeaker.   ☐

   B   Increase the degree of damping by using a clamp and stand to hold the glass in place.   ☐

   C   Vary the frequency of the sound produced by the loudspeaker.   ☐

   D   Wait for a period of time after the loudspeaker is turned on.   ☐

(1 mark)

2   A ruler is clamped to the edge of a bench. The end of the ruler is displaced downwards by 2.5 cm and released. The ruler oscillates with simple harmonic motion at a frequency of 4.0 Hz. At time t, the end of the ruler is at a distance of 0.20 cm from the midpoint of the oscillation, and the amplitude of the oscillation has been reduced by 80% due to the effects of damping. What is the speed of the end of the ruler at time t?

   A 0.50 ms^{-1} ☐   B 0.0072 ms^{-1} ☐

   C 0.13 ms^{-1} ☐   D 0.12 ms^{-1} ☐

(1 mark)

3   A bucket is tied to a length of rope and filled with water.
A student holds the end of the rope and swings the bucket in a horizontal circle.
The bucket has a small hole in the bottom, so water is gradually lost from the bucket over time.
Assuming the centripetal force is constant over time, which **one** of the following statements is correct?

   A   The centripetal acceleration remains constant with time.   ☐

   B   The centripetal acceleration is inversely proportional to the distance from the centre of the circle.   ☐

   C   The linear speed of the bucket increases over time.   ☐

   D   The linear speed of the bucket remains constant over time.   ☐

(1 mark)

4   A simple pendulum is made of a mass mounted onto a rod. It oscillates at a frequency f.
By what factor would the frequency of the pendulum change if the distance between the mass and the pendulum's pivot doubled, assuming the pendulum rod has negligible mass?

   A $\sqrt{2}$ ☐   B 2 ☐

   C $\frac{1}{4}$ ☐   D $\frac{1}{\sqrt{2}}$ ☐

(1 mark)

5 The oscillation of a simple pendulum approximates that of simple harmonic motion.
Figure 1 shows three different positions in the oscillation of a simple pendulum. The displacement of the bob from the midpoint of the oscillation (point B) is at a maximum magnitude at points A and C.

Figure 1

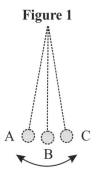

5.1 State the condition necessary for an object to move with simple harmonic motion.

....

....

(1 mark)

5.2 On the axes in **Figure 2**, sketch how the kinetic energy (E_k), gravitational potential energy (E_p) and the sum of both ($E_k + E_p$) each vary during one complete oscillation of the pendulum in **Figure 1**.

Figure 2

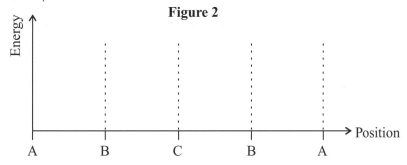

(3 marks)

5.3 A displacement-time graph for the simple pendulum is shown in **Figure 3**.
Sketch a velocity-time graph and an acceleration-time graph on the axes in **Figure 3**.
Label the y-axes with the values of any maxima and/or minima.

Figure 3

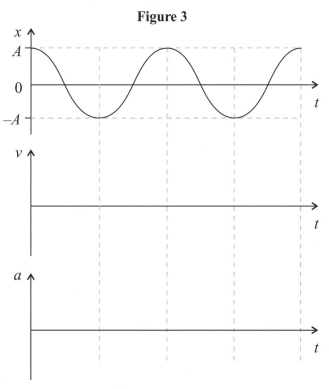

(4 marks)

A grandfather clock uses a simple pendulum like the one in **Figure 1** to keep an accurate track of time. The seconds hand of the clock moves forward exactly one second each time the pendulum moves from A to C, and another second each time it moves from C to A.

5.4 Determine the length of a pendulum in a grandfather clock that would accurately tell the time. The average gravitational field strength (g) at the Earth's surface is 9.81 ms^{-2}.

length = ... m

(1 mark)

The pendulum is lightly damped. As a result, the clock needs to be wound up once a week.

5.5 Suggest **one** potential cause of light damping in the pendulum.

....

....

(1 mark)

5.6 Explain why damping doesn't affect the clock's ability to accurately tell the time.

....

....

....

....

(2 marks)

5.7 A grandfather clock has a pendulum of the length determined in part 5.4.
It is used to tell the time at the Earth's equator, where $g = 9.78$ ms^{-2}.
The clock was set to exactly the right time at 18:00:00 on a Monday evening.
Determine the time displayed by the clock at 18:00:00 the following Monday.

time = ...

(3 marks)

6 During the final stage of a wash cycle, an undamped washing machine increases the rotational frequency of the rotating drum from 0 to 1250 revolutions per minute (rpm). The rotating drum has a diameter of 35 cm.

6.1 Calculate the maximum linear speed that the clothes in the washing machine could reach during the final stage of the wash cycle.

linear speed = ... ms^{-1}

(2 marks)

Between the rotational frequencies of 600 and 900 rpm, the washing machine can be observed to vibrate. The amplitude of these vibrations are plotted against rotational frequency in **Figure 4**.

Figure 4

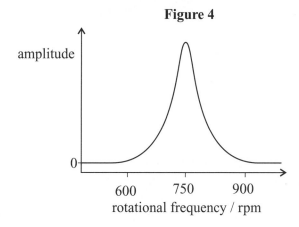

6.2 Explain the shape of the graph shown in **Figure 4**.

....

....

....

(2 marks)

6.3 Newer models of the washing machine are heavily damped. Describe what you would expect the amplitude profile to look like in newer models compared to that in **Figure 4**.

....

....

(1 mark)

6.4 Damping is incorporated into the design of many everyday objects. For example, a set of supermarket weighing scales is damped to reduce the variation in weight measurements when food is put on the scales. State and explain the degree of damping that is most suitable for a set of supermarket weighing scales.

....

....

(2 marks)

Mechanics questions can involve calculations that deal with some pretty awkward numbers. In these cases, don't round any values in the middle of a calculation, as this will cause your final answer to be inaccurate. However, you must round your final answer to an appropriate number of significant figures (s.f.s) — it should match the value used in the calculation with the fewest s.f.s.

Score

26

Further Mechanics — 2

1   A student is investigating the behaviour of a mass-spring system.
Figure 1 shows the experimental set-up used.

Figure 1

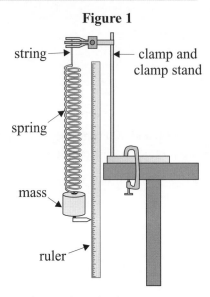

The student uses the following experimental method:

1.   Weigh the mass (*m*) on a set of scales, and attach it to the spring.
2.   Pull the mass 20 cm below the equilibrium position, then release it and simultaneously start
     the stopwatch. Stop the stopwatch when the mass has completed five full oscillations.
3.   Repeat the timing of five full oscillations twice more, and calculate the mean of these three readings.
     Then divide this value by five to obtain the period (*T*) of the oscillation.
4.   Repeat the procedure with five different masses.

Table 1 shows the results of the experiment.

Table 1

m / kg	T / s (to 2 d.p.)	Uncertainty in T / s	T^2 / s^2 (to 2 d.p.)	Uncertainty in T^2 / s^2 (to 2 d.p.)
0.200	0.24	0.06		
0.400	0.35	0.06	0.12	0.04
0.600	0.42	0.06	0.18	0.05
0.800	0.44	0.06	0.19	0.05
1.000	0.54	0.06	0.29	0.06
1.200	0.59	0.06		

1.1   Determine the missing values in **Table 1**.

0.200 kg: T^2 = ... ± .... s^2

1.200 kg: T^2 = ... ± .... s^2

(3 marks)

1.2 On the grid below, plot a graph of T^2 against m, including error bars.

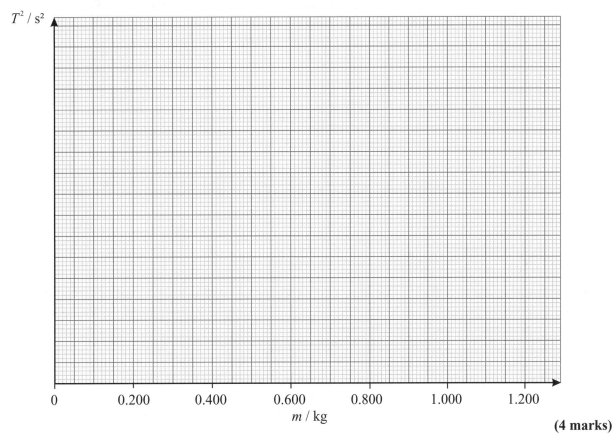

T^2 / s²

0   0.200   0.400   0.600   0.800   1.000   1.200

m / kg

(4 marks)

1.3 The student has read that a mass oscillating on a spring obeys the equation $T = 2\pi\sqrt{\frac{m}{k}}$.
Explain how the graph drawn in part 1.2 supports this relationship.

....

....

....

(2 marks)

1.4 Using the graph drawn in part 1.2, determine the spring constant, k, of the spring used in the experiment.
Calculate the percentage uncertainty in this value.

$k =$ .... Nm⁻¹ ± .... %

(5 marks)

1.5 Suggest and explain **one** way in which the experimental method could be improved to reduce
the uncertainty in the spring constant value.

....

....

....

(2 marks)

2   A bobsleigh team are testing a new track. **Figure 2** and **Figure 3** outline the layout of the final corner of the track. **Figure 2** shows the corner from above, and **Figure 3** shows a cross-section of the track as seen from the bobsleigh team's perspective.

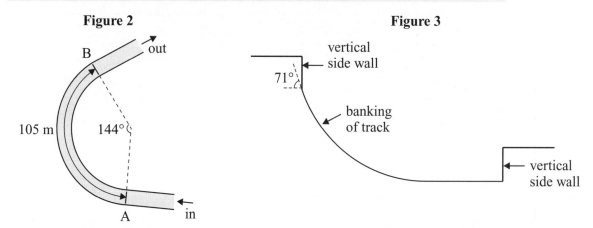

Figure 2   Figure 3

The corner can be modelled as part of a circle, as illustrated in **Figure 2**. The height of the track remains constant between points A and B. The bobsleigh team enters and travels around the final corner of the track at a speed of 31 ms^{-1}. The bobsleigh travels around the corner on the banked side of the track, shown in **Figure 3**, at a constant angle to the horizontal.

Calculate how much faster the bobsleigh could theoretically travel when travelling around the final corner without crashing into the side wall. Give your answer as a percentage of the speed the bobsleigh team went. You may assume that the friction and air resistance acting on the bobsleigh are negligible.

You may need to use the identity: $\tan(\theta) = \dfrac{\sin(\theta)}{\cos(\theta)}$.

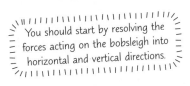

You should start by resolving the forces acting on the bobsleigh into horizontal and vertical directions.

maximum theoretical speed = ...% faster

(6 marks)

Score

22

EXAM TIP   If you're struggling to answer a mechanics question in the exam, the best thing to do is to draw a quick diagram — this will make the problem easier to visualise. You can then label it with the key information from the question, and with any other variables that are relevant.

Thermal Physics — 1

Maybe you get a giddy thrill from gas laws. Perhaps your heart starts racing when you consider kinetic theory. Possibly, you're just a big fan of moles. Whatever bakes your cake, I reckon that this is the ideal section for you.

For each of questions 1-4, give your answer by ticking the appropriate box.

1 Which of the following statements about Brownian motion is **not** true?

    A Particles displaying Brownian motion follow a random, zigzagging path. ☐

    B Brownian motion is the result of many collisions with fast moving molecules. ☐

    C Only particles suspended in a liquid display Brownian motion. ☐

    D Brownian motion provides evidence in support of kinetic theory. ☐

                                                                      (1 mark)

2 Which of the following is **not** a simplifying assumption of kinetic theory?

    A Between collisions, the particles of an ideal gas must move in straight lines. ☐

    B The time interval between an ideal gas particle's collisions must be much smaller than the duration of the collisions. ☐

    C The particles of an ideal gas must obey Newton's laws of motion. ☐

    D The particles of an ideal gas must undergo perfectly elastic collisions ☐

                                                                      (1 mark)

3 For an ideal gas, which of the following pairs of variables are directly proportional, when all other variables are held constant?

    A Pressure and volume ☐

    B Temperature and root mean square speed of the gas particles ☐

    C Number of moles and temperature ☐

    D Temperature and total internal energy ☐

                                                                      (1 mark)

4 At a temperature of exactly 300 K, a sample of ideal gas occupies a volume of 1.8 m^3. Whilst maintained at a constant pressure of 1.0×10^5 Pa, the gas is gradually cooled to 275 K. How much work is done on the gas as it cools?

    A 15 000 J ☐

    B 25 000 J ☐

    C 18 000 J ☐

    D 17 000 J ☐

                                                                      (1 mark)

5   The apparatus shown in **Figure 1** is used to investigate Boyle's law.

Figure 1

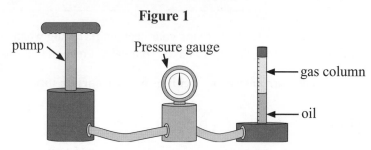

pump   Pressure gauge   gas column

oil

5.1   The pump is used to decrease the volume of the gas column. This process is carried out gradually so that the gas column maintains a constant temperature. Describe the energy transfers to and from the gas column as its volume decreases at a constant temperature.

....

....

....

(2 marks)

As the volume of the gas column decreases, the student takes measurements of the length of the gas column and of its pressure. The student's measurements are recorded in **Table 1**.

Table 1

length / cm	pressure / kPa	$\dfrac{1}{\text{pressure}}$ / kPa^{-1}
20	100	
18	111	
16	125	
14	143	
12	167	
10	200	

5.2   Complete **Table 1** by filling in the final column. Give each value to **two** significant figures.

(1 mark)

5.3   Using **Figure 2**, draw a graph of $\dfrac{1}{\text{pressure}}$ against length. Include a line of best fit on your graph.

Figure 2

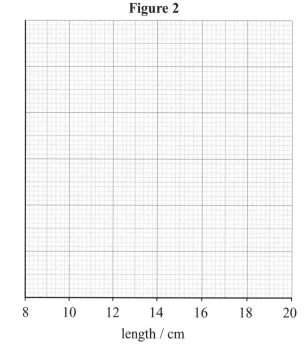

$\dfrac{1}{\text{pressure}}$ / kPa^{-1}

length / cm

(3 marks)

5.4 The vessel in which the gas column is contained is cylindrical with a radius of 1.2 cm. The gas is maintained at a temperature of 293 K. Use the graph you have drawn in **Figure 2** to calculate the number of moles of gas in the column.

moles = ...
(3 marks)

5.5 The temperature at which the gas is maintained is increased to 303 K and the experiment is repeated. Using the axes provided in **Figure 3**, sketch **two** lines showing how the volume of the gas varies with pressure at both 293 K and 303 K. Clearly label each line with the corresponding temperature.

Figure 3

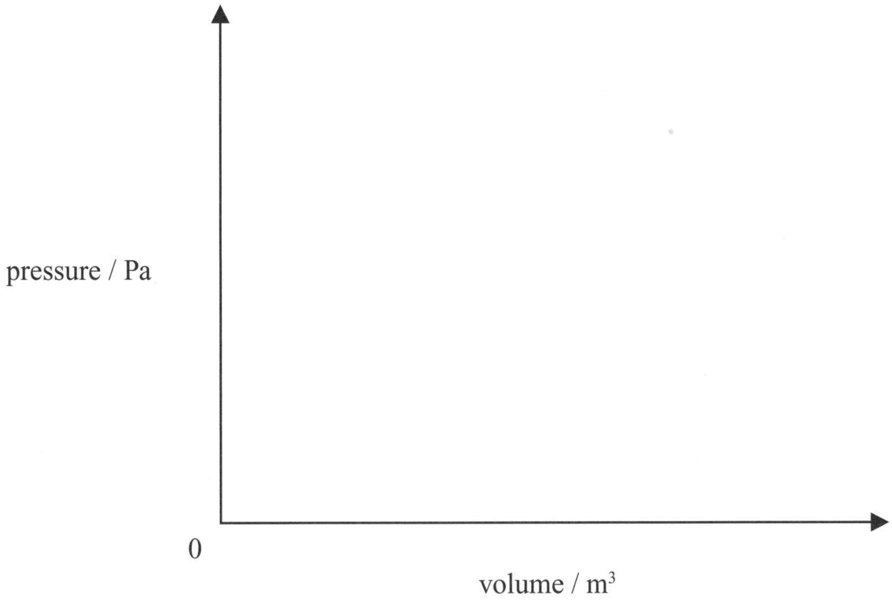

pressure / Pa

0

volume / m³

(2 marks)

5.6 The vessel in which the gas column is contained is replaced with an almost identical cylindrical column. The only difference between the two columns is that the replacement column has a smaller radius. Comment on how the change will affect the resolution with which the volume of the gas column can be measured.

....

....

....
(1 mark)

Thermal Physics — 2

1   **Figure 1** shows a container that contains a freely movable
    piston. The total volume of gas in the container is 10.0 m³.

Figure 1

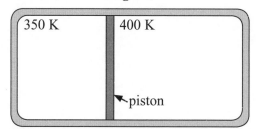

1.1 The container's chambers each contain 3.5 moles of the same ideal gas. One chamber has a temperature of
     350 K and the other has a temperature of exactly 400 K. No heat can pass through container's walls or the
     piston. Given that the piston is stationary, calculate the volume of the 400 K chamber.

volume = ... m³

(3 marks)

1.2 Identify the chamber in which the atoms collide with the walls more frequently. Justify your answer.

....

....

(1 mark)

1.3 The piston is removed without altering the system's internal energy and the gas from the chambers
     is allowed to mix completely. By calculating the mixture's final temperature, determine whether the
     mixture's final temperature will be the average of the two starting temperatures.

(2 marks)

1.4 As a result of removing the piston, the average kinetic energy of the particles that were initially in the
     350 K chamber increases, whilst the average kinetic energy of the particles that were initially in the 400 K
     chamber decreases. Explain how this exchange of energy takes place.

....

....

....

(1 mark)

2   **Figure 2** shows a graph of temperature against total internal energy
for a 1.0 kg sample of pure water as it is heated.

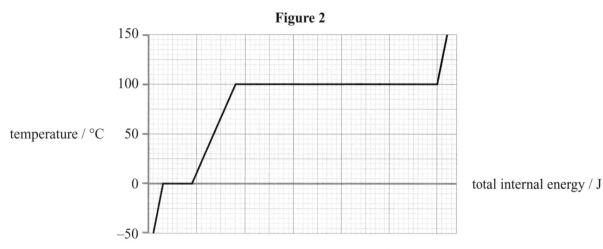

Figure 2

2.1   Given that the specific latent heat of vaporisation for water is 2.3×10^6 J kg^{-1},
use **Figure 2** to determine the specific latent heat of fusion for water.

specific latent heat of fusion = ... J kg^{-1}
(2 marks)

2.2   Use **Figure 2** to determine whether the water molecules' average kinetic energy
or the water molecules' average potential energy increases by a greater amount
as the sample's temperature is increased from –50°C to 150°C. Explain your answer.

....

....

....
(2 marks)

2.3   Using **Figure 2**, identify which of water's states has the greatest specific heat capacity.
Explain your answer.

....

....
(2 marks)

2.4   A 3.5 kg brick is heated to 50.0 °C and placed into an insulated tank containing 10.0 kg of water at a
temperature of 20.0 °C. After some time, the brick and the water reach a stable temperature of 22.0 °C.
Given that the specific heat capacity of water is 4.2 kJ kg^{-1} K^{-1}, calculate the specific heat capacity of the
brick in kJ kg^{-1} K^{-1}. Assume no heat energy is transferred to the tank.

specific heat capacity = ... kJ kg^{-1} K^{-1}
(2 marks)

3   An engineer is designing a hairdryer.

3.1   Inside the hairdryer a fan is used to draw a continuous flow of air over a 1100 W heating element.
In order to be safe for use, the air expelled by the hairdryer must not exceed a temperature of 60.0 °C.
The heating element has an efficiency of 0.76 and the specific heat capacity of air is $1.00 \text{ kJ kg}^{-1}\text{K}^{-1}$.
You may assume that typical room temperature is 23.0 °C.
Calculate, in units of kg s^{-1}, the minimum air flow rate at which the hairdryer is able to operate safely.

air flow rate = ... kg s^{-1}
(2 marks)

3.2   Calculate the minimum volume of air the hairdryer needs to expel each second in order to operate safely.
Assume the expelled air is an ideal gas with a molar mass of 29.0 g mol^{-1} and a pressure of 1.00×10^5 Pa.

volume = ... m^3
(2 marks)

3.3   Calculate the root mean square speed of the expelled air molecules' random motion.
Assume that the expelled air is an ideal gas with a molar mass of 29.0 g mol^{-1},
at a temperature of 60.0 °C and a pressure of 1.00×10^5 Pa.

root mean square speed = ... ms^{-1}
(2 marks)

4 Kinetic theory is used to predict the behaviour of ideal gases.

4.1 Explain **one** way in which the development of the kinetic theory of ideal gases differed from the development of the ideal gas law.

....

....

....

(1 mark)

4.2 **Figure 3** shows an atom of mass m moving with velocity u inside a cubic container with sides of length l.

Figure 3

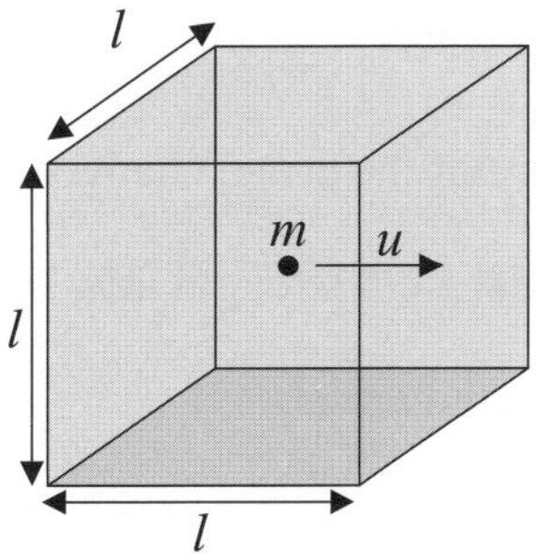

With **Figure 3** as your starting point, derive the following equation for the pressure of an ideal gas.

$$pV = \frac{1}{3} Nm(c_{rms})^2$$

(6 marks)

EXAM TIP

If you really want to ace your exam, then you need to get used to recognising familiar concepts in new and unfamiliar settings. If a question leaves you feeling overwhelmed, look out for key phrases (like 'continuous flow') which can tell you what a question is really all about.

Score

28

Gravitational and Electric Fields — 1

Two of the most fundamental fields in physics — one scintillating section. If inverse square laws, charged particles and equipotentials send your spirits into orbit, then boy, have we got a treat in store for you...

For each of questions 1-4, give your answer by ticking the appropriate box.

1   The diagram shows a drone flying parallel to the surface of the Earth.

Which of the following statements is correct?

A   The gravitational potential energy of the drone changes as it moves along line AB.   ☐

B   The magnitude of the gravitational field strength at A is different to the magnitude at B.   ☐

C   The line AB is a gravitational equipotential.   ☐

D   The magnitude of the gravitational force on the drone changes as it travels along line AB.   ☐

(1 mark)

2   A satellite is orbiting the Earth at a radius r, with an orbital period of T. The satellite is knocked out of its orbit and settles into a new stable orbit at a radius equal to $1.40r$. What is the orbital period of the new orbit?

A $1.25T$ ☐   **B** $1.66T$ ☐

C $2.74T$ ☐   **D** $1.96T$ ☐

(1 mark)

3   A rocket is being launched from the surface of a planet. The planet has a mass of M kg. To escape the gravitational field of the planet, the rocket must travel at a speed of v ms^{-1}. Which of the following is the correct expression for the radius of the planet, r?

A $r = vGM$ ☐   **B** $r = \dfrac{GM}{2v^2}$ ☐

C $r = \dfrac{v^2}{2GM}$ ☐   **D** $r = \dfrac{2GM}{v^2}$ ☐

(1 mark)

4   The diagram shows two positively charged point charges, Q_1 and Q_2. The charge on Q_1 is 9 times the charge on Q_2.

Q_1 ⊛ ——————————— d ——————————— ⊛ Q_2

At what distance along the line from Q_1 would the net electrostatic force on a test charge be zero?

A $0.33d$ ☐   **B** $0.25d$ ☐

C $0.75d$ ☐   **D** $0.67d$ ☐

(1 mark)

5   The electric potential at a distance of 5.00×10^{-14} m from the centre of a nucleus is 2650 kV.

5.1   Calculate the charge of the nucleus. Ignore the effect of any negatively-charged electrons.

charge = ... C

(1 mark)

5.2   The nucleus splits into two individual nuclei, A and B, as shown in **Figure 1**.

Figure 1

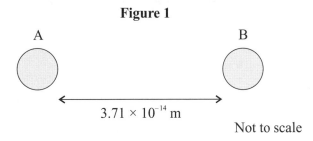

A   B

3.71×10^{-14} m

Not to scale

Nucleus A has a charge of 5.76×10^{-18} C and a radius of 6.32×10^{-15} m.
When the edges of the nuclei are 3.71×10^{-14} m apart, the force between them is 181 N.
Calculate the radius of nucleus B.

radius = ... m

(2 marks)

6   Read the following passage and answer the questions that follow.

Different types of charged particle can be identified based on their path of motion through a uniform electric field. A particle detector made of a series of charged parallel plates is shown from above in **Figure 2**. The plates in each set are 5.0×10^{-3} m apart and have a potential difference of 10 V across them. A voltmeter is connected across each set of plates to monitor their potential difference.

Figure 2

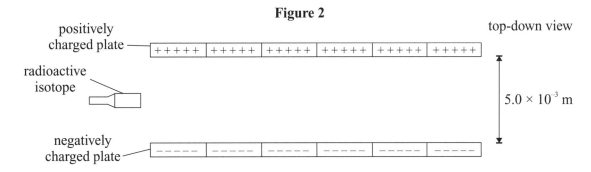

positively charged plate

top-down view

radioactive isotope

5.0×10^{-3} m

negatively charged plate

5   A scientist positions a radioactive isotope at one end of the series of plates, as shown in **Figure 2**. The scientist monitors the potential difference across each set of charged plates. When a charged particle collides with a plate, the particle's charge is added to the charge on the plate. The scientist would then be able to observe a fluctuation in potential difference on one of the voltmeter's readings, and deduce some of the properties of the radiation emitted by the isotope.

10   It can be assumed that all particles emitted from the radioactive isotope are emitted at the same speed.

6.1 Describe and explain the path that an alpha particle would take through the detector.

....

....

....

....

....

(3 marks)

The potential difference across each set of plates in the detector is proportional to the charge on the plates.

6.2 An electron and a positron have the same mass, and an equal but opposite charge. Explain why both factors make it impossible for the particle detector in **Figure 2** to distinguish between these particles.

Remember, the positron is the antiparticle of the electron.

....

....

....

....

....

....

....

....

....

....

(6 marks)

6.3 The plates are rotated by 90° so that the negative plates are located directly above the positive plates. The distance between the plates remains the same. Calculate the potential difference that would need to be placed across the charged plates in order for a positron to pass straight through the particle detector without being deflected due to gravity.

potential difference = ... V

(3 marks)

Gravitational and Electric Fields — 2

1   A geostationary satellite with a mass of 2200 kg is about to be launched into a synchronous orbit. The orbit will have an orbital radius of 42 200 km about the centre of the Earth.

1.1   State **one** use of geostationary satellites, and explain why the synchronous nature of its orbit around Earth is useful for this purpose.

....

....

....

(2 marks)

1.2   Explain why a satellite uses very little fuel once it has reached its intended orbit.

....

....

(1 mark)

1.3   Calculate the speed the satellite needs to travel at in its orbit to maintain an orbital radius of 42 200 km.

speed = ... ms^{-1}

(2 marks)

1.4   The gravitational potential of the satellite changes by 5.3×10^7 Jkg^{-1} as it is launched from the Earth's surface into the synchronous orbit. By considering the energy of the satellite, calculate the initial speed that the satellite would need to be launched at to enter and remain in a synchronous orbit around Earth. You may assume that frictional forces acting on the satellite are negligible, that there is no change in the satellite's mass during the launch and that the satellite is travelling perpendicular to Earth's radius when it reaches the synchronous orbit. Ignore any effects produced by the rotation of the Earth.

speed = ... ms^{-1}

(4 marks)

Satellites at the end of their operational lives are often moved into a 'graveyard' orbit to reduce the risk of a collision with another satellite.

Figure 1 is a graph showing how the Earth's gravitational field strength, g, varies with radial distance, r, from the centre of the Earth.

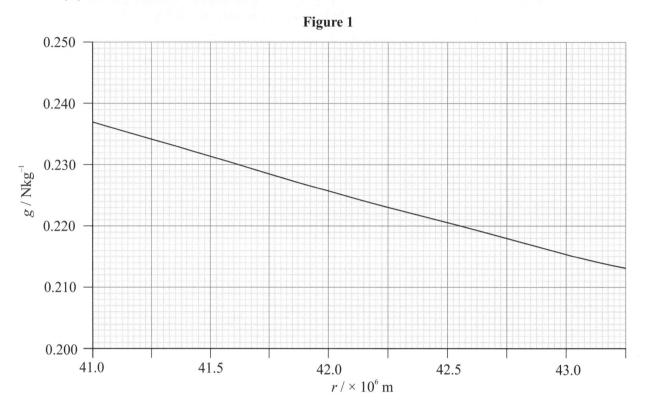

Figure 1

1.5 When the geostationary satellite is no longer useful, it will be moved to a graveyard orbit with a radius of 42 500 km. Use **Figure 1** to estimate the change in gravitational potential experienced by the satellite as it is moved from the synchronous orbit to the graveyard orbit.

Change in gravitational potential = ... Jkg⁻¹
(2 marks)

2 Electric charge builds up in a storm cloud, giving the base of the cloud a negative charge. The distance between the base of the cloud and the ground is 1.66 km. The electric field between the cloud and the ground can be modelled as a uniform electric field with a field strength of 20.0 kNC⁻¹, as shown in **Figure 2**. When sufficient electric charge has built up, the cloud discharges by transferring some of its charge to the ground in a lightning strike.

Figure 2

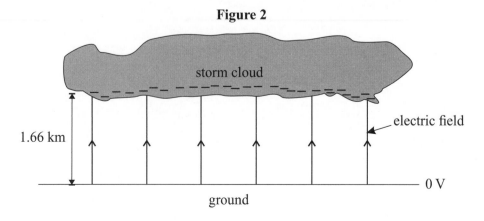

2.1 A lightning strike transfers 5.0×10^8 J of energy to the ground.
Calculate the amount of charge transferred from the cloud to the ground during the lightning strike.

charge = ... C
(2 marks)

2.2 **Figure 3** shows a storm cloud moving over a tower.

Figure 3

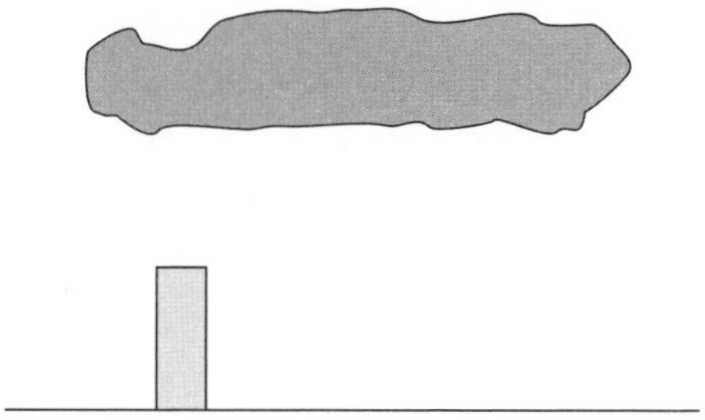

Explain why the electric field beneath the cloud is not uniform.

....

....

....
(1 mark)

The exact mechanism for the build-up of charge in storm clouds is unknown. One hypothesis is that the charge builds up due to collisions between snow crystals and soft hail particles called 'graupel'. This can cause the snow crystals to gain a positive charge, and the graupel to gain a negative charge. The graupel falls to the ground from inside the cloud.

2.3 A graupel particle has a mass of 1.04×10^{-4} kg, and a charge of -1.7×10^{-12} C. Compare the magnitude of the gravitational and electrostatic forces acting on the graupel particle. Use your answer to justify whether the charge on a storm cloud will have a noticeable effect on the graupel falling from the storm cloud.

....

....

....

....

....

....
(3 marks)

EXAM TIP Make sure you pay close attention to the units given in the question. It's a really common mistake to forget to convert a variable to SI units, especially when you're under pressure in the exam. So if you get a few minutes at the end of an exam, this is one thing that's worth checking.

Score

17

Gravitational and Electric Fields — 3

1 Eris is a dwarf planet in our solar system. The mass of Eris was determined by examining the orbit of its moon, Dysnomia. The orbit of Dysnomia around Eris can be assumed to be circular.

Dysnomia has an orbital period of 15.77 days.
The orbital radius of Dysnomia about Eris is 3.735×10^7 m.

1.1 Show that the speed of Dysnomia is inversely proportional to the square root of the radius of its orbit.

(2 marks)

1.2 Calculate the mass of Eris.

mass = ... kg
(3 marks)

1.3 Explain why scientists cannot determine the mass of Dysnomia from observing its orbit.

....

....
(1 mark)

Eris' orbit around the Sun is highly elliptical, as shown in **Figure 1**. Points A and B mark the positions where the distance between Eris and the centre of the Sun is at its maximum and minimum values respectively. The maximum distance between Eris and the Sun over the course of its orbit is 1.46×10^{13} m.

Figure 1

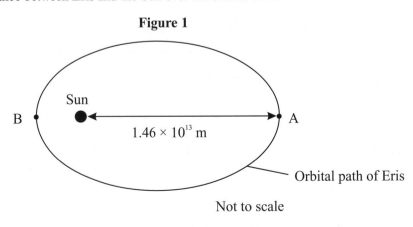

Not to scale

1.4 The difference in the gravitational potential of Eris between points A and B is 1.38×10^7 Jkg^{-1}. Calculate the distance between the centre of Eris and the centre of the Sun when Eris is at point B. The mass of the Sun is 1.99×10^{30} kg.

distance = ... m

(3 marks)

---

2 **Figure 2** shows two charged spheres on insulating rods. The left-hand sphere has a charge of 0.11 μC and the right-hand sphere has a charge of –0.11 μC.

2.1 Draw lines between the two spheres on the diagram to represent equipotentials.

Figure 2

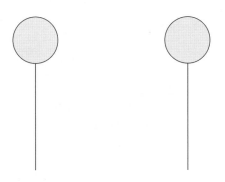

(1 mark)

2.2 The centres of the two spheres are initially 7.0 cm apart. 0.34 mJ of work is then done against the electric field to move the left-hand sphere further to the left. Calculate the magnitude of the force that acts between the two spheres after the left-hand sphere is moved.

force = ... N

(3 marks)

A different charged sphere is attached to a rigid insulating rod that has a 90° bend in it. The end of the rod is attached to a platform that is fixed to the top of a mass balance. Parallel plates are placed above and below the sphere to create a uniform electric field, as shown in **Figure 3**. The parallel plates are 20 cm apart.

Figure 3

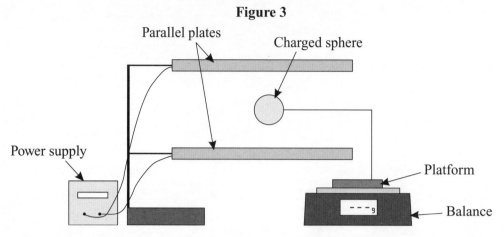

The balance is zeroed before the sphere and rod are attached to the platform. The potential difference between the plates is increased and the mass measured on the balance is recorded. The results are shown in **Figure 4**.

Figure 4

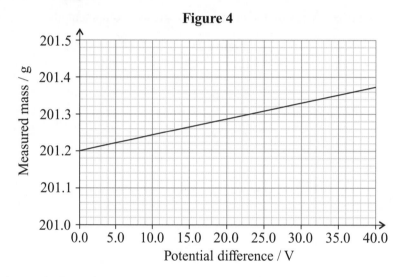

2.3 Calculate the charge on the sphere.

charge = ... C

(3 marks)

You should know where you are with straight line graphs by now. If you get faced with one in the exam, just look at the two quantities on the axes and find an equation that links them together with the one you need to find. However novel and weird the equation might be, once you've rearranged it into that comforting old graph format, $y = mx + c$, you'll be coming up roses.

Score

16

Capacitors — 1

Next up, some electrifying questions on capacitors. Prepare to be quizzed on capacitance, charging and discharging capacitors, permittivity, dielectrics and the (not so) mysterious time constant.

For each of questions 1-4, give your answer by ticking the appropriate box.

1 What does the area under a graph of charge against potential difference for a capacitor represent?

A The capacitance of the capacitor. ☐

B Time that the capacitor has been charging. ☐

C The energy stored by the capacitor. ☐

D The permittivity of the capacitor's dielectric. ☐

(1 mark)

2 A 12 V potential difference is applied to a capacitor. The capacitor stores 144 μC of charge on each plate. What is the capacitance of the capacitor?

A 12 μF ☐

B 12 F ☐

C 1728 F ☐

D 1728 μF ☐

(1 mark)

3 Which of the following is equivalent to the charge stored by a capacitor?

A The gradient of a graph of current against time for the capacitor. ☐

B The area under a graph of current against time for the capacitor. ☐

C The gradient of a graph of potential difference against time for the capacitor. ☐

D The area under a graph of potential difference against time for the capacitor. ☐

(1 mark)

4 A 20.0 μF capacitor is discharged through a 60.0 kΩ resistor.
The initial potential difference across the capacitor is 8.0 V.
Determine the potential difference across the capacitor after 1.2 seconds.

A 6.8 V ☐

B 5.1 V ☐

C 2.9 V ☐

D 0.0080 V ☐

(1 mark)

5 A parallel plate capacitor is made up of two plates, each with an area of 0.40 m². The plates are separated by a 5.0 cm air gap. The relative permittivity of air is 1.0.

5.1 Determine the capacitance of the capacitor.

capacitance = ... F

(1 mark)

5.2 The capacitor is charged using a 20.0 V power supply. Calculate the maximum energy stored by the capacitor.

maximum energy = ... J

(1 mark)

5.3 The area of the capacitor plates is halved and the distance between the plates is doubled. Explain what effect, if any, this will have on the capacitance of the capacitor.

....

....

....

....

(2 marks)

6 A 100.0 nF capacitor stores a maximum of 7.2×10^{-6} J of energy. The capacitor is fully charged.

6.1 Calculate the charge stored on each plate of the capacitor.

maximum charge = ... C

(2 marks)

The capacitor is discharged through a fixed resistor.

6.2 The time taken for the charge on the plates to halve is 8.0 ms. Determine the resistance of the fixed resistor.

resistance = ... Ω

(2 marks)

6.3 Determine the charge on the capacitor 4.0 ms after it has begun discharging.

charge = ... C

(2 marks)

7   A student makes a capacitor from tin foil and paper, shown in **Figure 1**.

The paper acts as a dielectric and completely fills the gap between the two plates.
The tin foil sheets each have an area of exactly 400 cm^2.
The student measures the distance between the plates to be 0.40 mm.

Figure 1

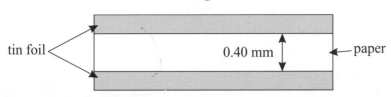

7.1 The student connects the capacitor in a circuit. He measures the maximum capacitance of the capacitor to be 3.27 nF. Calculate the relative permittivity of paper.

relative permittivity = ...
                                                        (2 marks)

7.2 The capacitor would have a lower capacitance if the paper was removed and replaced by a vacuum.
Explain how dielectrics increase the capacitance of capacitors.
Your answer should include information about the polarisation of the particles in the capacitor.

....

....

....

....

....

....

....

....

....

....

....

....

....

                                                        (6 marks)

EXAM TIP You'll only be given the equations for the charge on a charging and discharging capacitor in the exam data booklet, not those for potential difference and current. The equations for charge and potential difference are basically the same, just replace Q with V and Q_o with Vo, and Bob's your uncle — there's another two equations you don't need to learn. Win.

Score

22

Capacitors — 2

1   **Figure 1** shows a cylindrical capacitor made from cardboard tubes connected to a power supply.

The outer surface of each tube is covered in aluminium foil, and each roll of foil acts as a capacitor plate.
The length of the capacitor can be adjusted by moving the smaller tube inside the larger tube.
The capacitor has an inner radius of a metres and an outer radius of b metres.

Figure 1

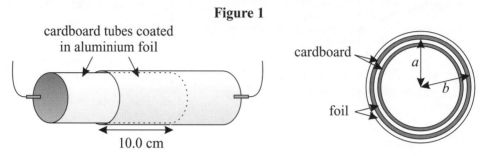

A student is told that the capacitance per unit length of the capacitor is given by:

$$\frac{C}{L} = \frac{2\pi\varepsilon_0\varepsilon_r}{\ln\left(\frac{b}{a}\right)}$$

where C is capacitance in F, L is the length in m, ε_0 is the permittivity of free space in Fm^{-1},
and ε_r is the relative permittivity of the material between the plates.

1.1   The cardboard tubes have a relative permittivity of 2.5. The inner radius of the capacitor
is 5.0 cm, and the outer radius is 6.0 cm. Determine the maximum capacitance that
can be achieved when the capacitor is in the position shown in **Figure 1**.

capacitance = ... F

(2 marks)

1.2   The student charges the capacitor through a 1.2 MΩ resistor by applying a 25 V
potential difference across the capacitor when it is in the position shown in **Figure 1**.
Calculate the time taken for the potential difference across the capacitor to reach 14 V.

time taken = ... s

(3 marks)

1.3   Describe an experiment to investigate how the capacitance of the capacitor varies with length in order to
confirm the equation. Your answer should include how to minimise the uncertainty in the results.

....

....

....

....

....

....

....

....

....

....

....

(6 marks)

2 A student is investigating the behaviour of a capacitor as it is discharged through a 20.0 kΩ resistor. **Figure 2** shows a graph of the student's results.

Figure 2

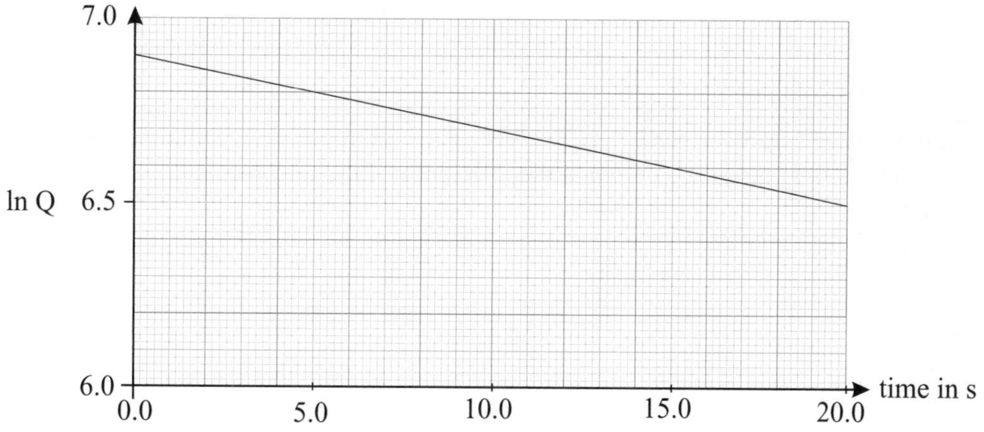

2.1 Determine the time constant of the capacitor from **Figure 2**.

time constant = ... s

(3 marks)

2.2 The initial current through the capacitor is 1.2 mA. Determine the current through the circuit after 8.0 s.

current = ... A

(2 marks)

2.3 Determine the time taken for the charge on the capacitor to reach 40% of its maximum capacity.

time taken = ... s

(3 marks)

EXAM TIP

The capacitor equations that contain an exponential are some of the trickiest. Make sure you've brushed up on your log and exponential rules so you can rearrange these equations in any way your heart desires. It could grab you some nice marks in the exam.

Score

19

Magnetic Fields — 1

Ever noticed how Fleming's left hand rule looks a bit like a finger-gun? Flemming's wonder rule is just one of the fascinating facts you'll need to answer these questions on magnetic fields, forces, transformers and so much more...

For each of questions 1-4, give your answer by ticking the appropriate box.

1   Which of the following is Faraday's law?

   A   Induced emf is always in such a direction as to oppose the change that caused it.   ☐

   B   Induced emf is directly proportional to the rate of change of flux linkage.   ☐

   C   The force on a moving charge in a magnetic field is always at 90° to its direction of travel.   ☐

   D   The force on a moving charge in a magnetic field is always opposite to its direction of travel.   ☐

(1 mark)

2   The input power of a transformer is 184 210 kW. The output potential difference is 125 kV and the output current is 1.4 kA. What is the efficiency of the transformer?

   A   85%   ☐

   B   90%   ☐

   C   95%   ☐

   D   98%   ☐

(1 mark)

3   The graph shows the oscilloscope trace of an ac source with an average power of 9.00 W. What is the rms voltage of the source?

   A   1.5 V   ☐

   B   13 V   ☐

   C   3.0 V   ☐

   D   6.1 V   ☐

current / A

2.4

1.2

0   time / s

- 1.2

- 2.4

(1 mark)

4   The diagram shows the top of a square loop in a magnetic field. The magnetic flux through the loop is 8.66×10^{-3} Wb. The current through the loop is 2.0 A. Which of the following is the size of the force felt by a vertical side of the loop?

   A   0 N   ☐

   B   0.33 N   ☐

   C   3.3 N   ☐

   D   33 N   ☐

top-down view

6.0 cm

30°

loop

(1 mark)

5 Some students are investigating factors that affect the force on a current-carrying wire in a magnetic field.

One student investigates how the size of the current through the wire affects the force on it.
Figure 1 shows an aerial view of the student's apparatus, and his experimental method is described below.
The wire is clamped to ensure the section of wire between the magnets remains stationary and in the same alignment to the magnetic field throughout the experiment.

Figure 1

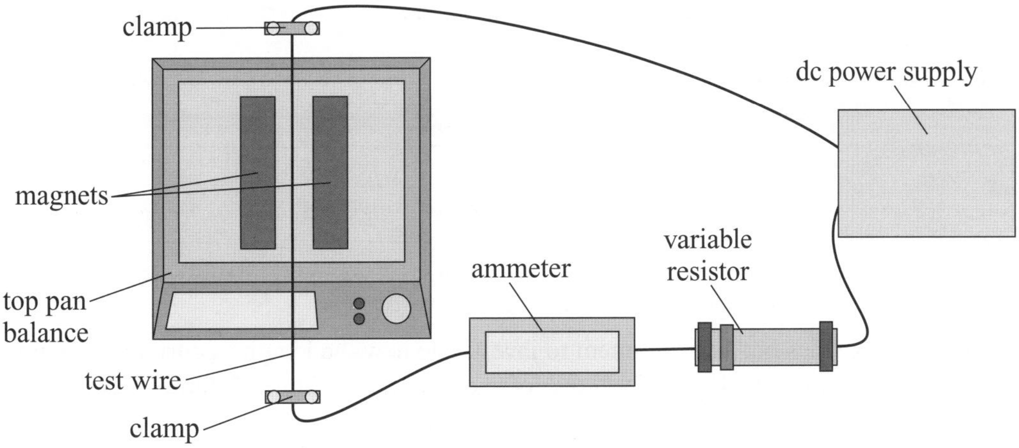

Method:

1. Set up the apparatus as shown in **Figure 1**.
2. Measure and record the length of the wire between the magnets.
3. Zero the balance. Turn on the power supply.
4. Record the current shown on the ammeter and the mass shown on the balance.
   Adjust the variable resistor to change the current through the wire
5. Repeat step 4 for a number of different values of current.
6. Calculate the force on the wire for each current using the mass reading and the equation $F = mg$.

Table 1 shows an incomplete table of the student's results.

Table 1

Current / A	Mass / g	Force / N
0.00	0.0	0.000
1.47	1.8	0.018
2.94	3.5	0.034
4.41	5.3	0.052
5.88	7.1	

The magnets produce a uniform magnetic field with a strength of 80 mT. The uncertainty in all the mass values is ±0.1 g. The length of the wire measured to be in the uniform magnetic field is 0.15 m

5.1 Using **Table 1**, calculate the force on the wire when it carried a current of 5.88 A.
Determine whether this result agrees with the force on the wire that would be predicted by theory.

(3 marks)

5.2 Suggest and explain **two** alterations the student could make to his apparatus or experimental method to improve the accuracy of his results.

....

....

....

....

....

....

....

....

(2 marks)

Another student carries out an experiment to investigate how the length of current-carrying wire that is perpendicular to a magnetic field affects the force on the wire. **Figure 2** shows a graph of her results.

Figure 2

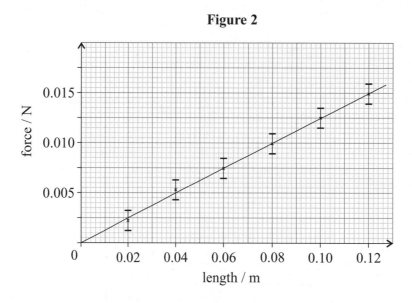

5.3 During the experiment, the current through the wire was kept at a constant value of 2.5 A.
Using **Figure 2**, determine the magnetic flux density of the magnetic field used in this experiment, and the uncertainty in this value.

magnetic flux density = ... ± .... T

(4 marks)

6   Cyclotrons are used to accelerate particles such as protons for a number of applications.

6.1   Briefly describe how a cyclotron works.

....

....

....

....

....

....

....

....

(4 marks)

Figure 3 shows a proton moving inside a region of a cyclotron.

Figure 3

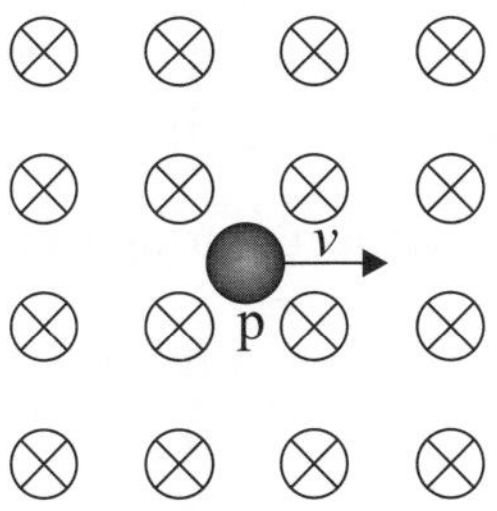

The magnetic field has a flux density of 0.38 T. The proton travels at a speed of 1.2×10^7 ms^{-1}.

6.2   Draw the direction of the force acting on the proton due to the magnetic field on **Figure 3**
and calculate the size of the proton's acceleration.

acceleration = ... ms^{-1}

(2 marks)

6.3   The proton leaves the cyclotron 1.5 m from its centre.
Determine the kinetic energy of the proton when it leaves the cyclotron.

kinetic energy = ... J

(3 marks)

EXAM TIP

In the exam, you may need to interpret magnetic field diagrams. Make sure you're familiar
with the conventions for drawing fields, e.g. what the arrows on the field lines represent.
You'll need to keep this in mind for gravitational and electric fields too.

Score

22

Magnetic Fields — 2

1   A student decides to investigate how the radius of a current-carrying test coil affects the strength of the magnetic field produced near its centre. The apparatus used is shown in **Figure 1**.

Figure 1

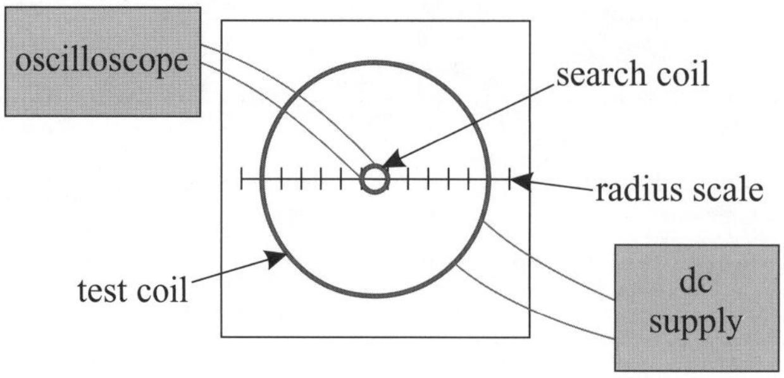

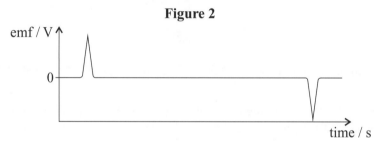

The student carried out the following method:

1.   Place the test coil in position, so that the search coil is at its centre.
2.   Turn on the power supply and record the peak emf value displayed on the oscilloscope when the supply is turned on.
3.   Turn off the power supply.
4.   Change the radius of the test coil, keeping the number of turns constant. Repeat steps 2-3 for a range of test coils with different radii.

Figure 2 shows the oscilloscope trace produced during steps 2 and 3 of one test.

Figure 2

1.1   Explain the shape of the trace shown in **Figure 2**.

....

....

....

....

(2 marks)

The student found that the larger the radius of the test coil, the smaller the induced emf.
The time taken for the emf to be induced in the search coil was the same throughout the experiment.

1.2   Using the information above, describe the relationship between the strength of the magnetic field produced near the centre of the test coil and the test coil's radius. Explain your answer.

....

....

....

....

(2 marks)

The student replaces the test coil in **Figure 1** with a solenoid that produces a uniform magnetic field in its centre. She uses this equipment to investigate how the induced emf in the search coil changes as it is rotated in the uniform magnetic field at a steady rate. She monitors how the induced emf changes with the angle between the normal to the search coil and the magnetic field as she rotates the search coil.

Figure 3 shows the positions of the search coil when the student records a minimum and maximum magnitude of emf.

Figure 3

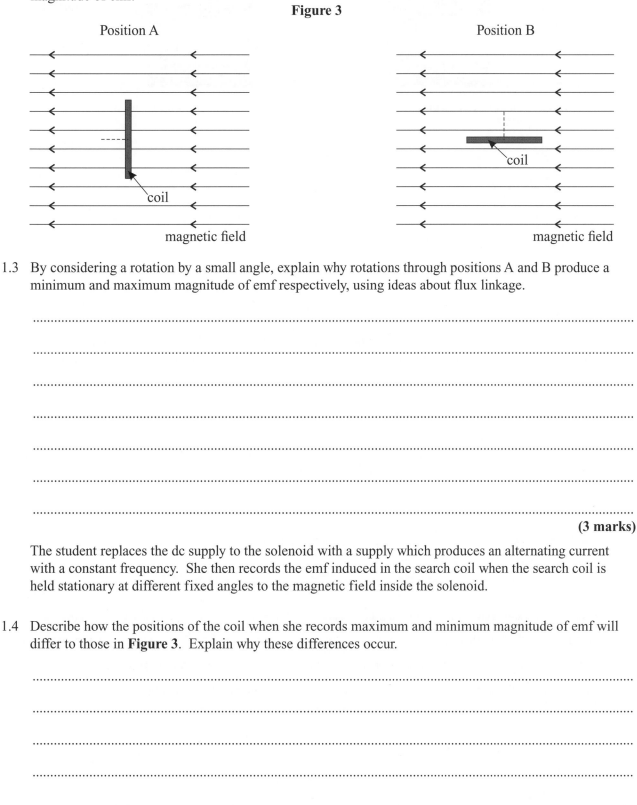

1.3 By considering a rotation by a small angle, explain why rotations through positions A and B produce a minimum and maximum magnitude of emf respectively, using ideas about flux linkage.

....

....

....

....

....

....

....

(3 marks)

The student replaces the dc supply to the solenoid with a supply which produces an alternating current with a constant frequency. She then records the emf induced in the search coil when the search coil is held stationary at different fixed angles to the magnetic field inside the solenoid.

1.4 Describe how the positions of the coil when she records maximum and minimum magnitude of emf will differ to those in **Figure 3**. Explain why these differences occur.

....

....

....

....

....

....

....

(3 marks)

2 Transformers are used to change the potential difference of electricity in the UK national grid.

Figure 4 shows two different transformer designs, A and B.
The transformers have different cores but are otherwise identical.

Figure 4

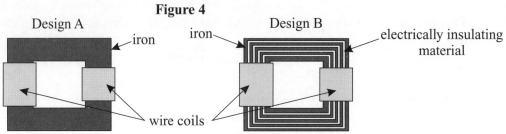

2.1 State which transformer design you would expect to be most efficient. Explain your answer.

....

....

....

....

....

....

(3 marks)

Two transformers, X and Y, are supplied with the same input power and have output voltages of 275.0 kV and 400.0 kV respectively. Transformer X is 98.67% efficient, and has an output current of 1200.0 A. Transformer Y has an output current of 830.0 A.

2.2 Determine the efficiency of transformer Y.

efficiency = ... %

(3 marks)

A section of overhead cable runs parallel to a second, identical cable. Both carry a 1200 A current. The magnetic field strength around a current-carrying cable is given by $B = \dfrac{\mu_0 I}{2\pi r}$, where μ_0 is the permeability of free space in Hm^{-1}, I is the current in A and r is the distance from the centre of the cable in m.

2.3 Determine the force per unit length felt by the second cable, due to the first cable.
Assume that the cables are always a constant distance of 5.2 m apart.

force per unit length = ... Nm^{-1}

(3 marks)

3 A square coil, consisting of 25 turns, has a side length of 2.2 ± 0.1 cm, as shown in **Figure 5**. It is placed into a uniform magnetic field, such that the angle between the field and the normal to the coil is 45°.

Figure 5

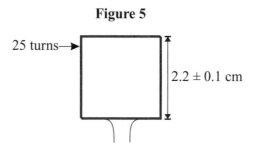

25 turns→

2.2 ± 0.1 cm

3.1 The flux linkage of the coil is 7.0 ± 0.1 mWb.
Calculate the magnetic flux density of the magnetic field, and the percentage uncertainty in this value.

magnetic flux density = ... T ± .... %

(3 marks)

The coil is connected to a circuit, and spun at a constant angular speed.
While being spun at this speed, it generates an rms voltage of 0.11 ± 0.01 V across the circuit.

3.2 Assuming the system has negligible internal resistance, determine the angular speed of the coil in $rad\,s^{-1}$.
Calculate the percentage uncertainty in this value and comment on the accuracy of the result.
Suggest **one** way to improve the accuracy.

angular speed = ... $rad\,s^{-1}$

uncertainty = ... %

....

....

....

(5 marks)

EXAM TIP

Be careful when dealing with the angles of coils in magnetic fields. Remember, the angle between a coil and a magnetic field is measured from the normal of the plane of the coil, not the plane of the coil itself. Be sure you're measuring angles from the right place, and check that your answers make sense in the context of what you know about electromagnetic induction.

Score

27

Nuclear Decay and Half-Life — 1

Blimey there's a lot to learn about radiation. Get started with some questions about nuclear decay and half-life...

For each of questions 1-5, give your answer by ticking the appropriate box.

1   Which of the following correctly describes the relationship between nuclear radius, R, and nuclear density, ρ?

   A $R \propto \rho$ ☐   **B** $\dfrac{1}{R^3} \propto \rho$ ☐

   C $R^2 \propto \rho$ ☐   **D**   They are independent of each other.   ☐

(1 mark)

2   Which of these graphs shows the correct relationship between the number of neutrons, N, against the atomic number, Z, of stable nuclei?

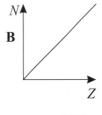 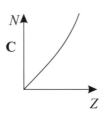 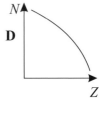

   A ☐   **B** ☐   **C** ☐   **D** ☐

(1 mark)

3   A sample initially contains 10 000 radioactive nuclei. The decay constant for the radioactive isotope is 2.5×10^{-4} s^{-1}. How many nuclei will decay in 20 seconds?

   A   5   ☐   **B**   9950   ☐

   C   50   ☐   **D**   100   ☐

(1 mark)

4   The intensity of gamma radiation detected x cm from a source is 144 cps. Estimate the count rate that would be detected $0.5x$ cm from the source using the same detector. Assume the count rate due to background radiation is negligible.

   A   12 cps   ☐   **B**   288 cps   ☐

   C   20 736 cps   ☐   **D**   576 cps   ☐

(1 mark)

5   The graph shows the natural log of the activity of a radioactive isotope sample against time. What is the decay constant for the isotope?

   A   0.20 s^{-1} ☐

   B   0.30 s^{-1} ☐

   C   0.60 s^{-1} ☐

   D   1.2 s^{-1} ☐

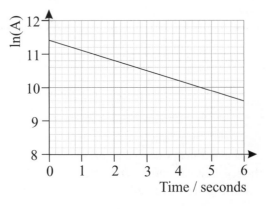

(1 mark)

6 A student is investigating the radiation produced by three separate sources. **Figure 1** shows the student's apparatus.

Figure 1

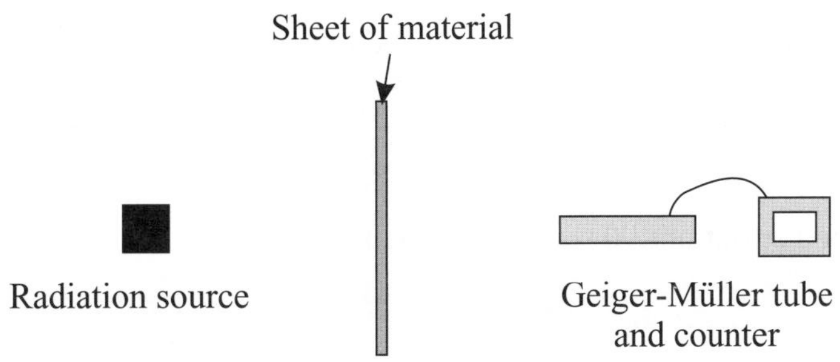

Sheet of material

Radiation source

Geiger-Müller tube and counter

6.1 The student collects data for the count rate of the different samples.
Explain how the student should correct these measurements for background radiation.
Explain how this will help improve the student's results.

....

....

....

(2 marks)

6.2 State **two** sources of background radiation.

1. ....

2. ....

(2 marks)

6.3 State and explain **two** safety precautions the student should follow when carrying out this experiment.

1. ....

....

....

2. ....

....

....

(2 marks)

Table 1 shows the data collected by the student, corrected for background radiation.

Table 1

Radioactive source	Count rate (cps)			
	No Barrier	Thin paper	2 cm thick aluminium sheet	2 cm thick lead sheet
Strontium-90	250	248	1	0
Caesium-137	121	119	8	3
Dubnium-262	160	20	15	0

6.4 Determine the type or types of radiation produced by the caesium-137 sample. Explain your answer.

....

....

....

....

(2 marks)

6.5 Suggest **one** use for a strontium-90 source. Explain your answer.

....

....

....

(2 marks)

The student then removes the sheets of material and uses the equipment to measure the count rate over time for the dubnium-262 source. **Figure 2** shows a graph of their results, corrected for background radiation.

Figure 2

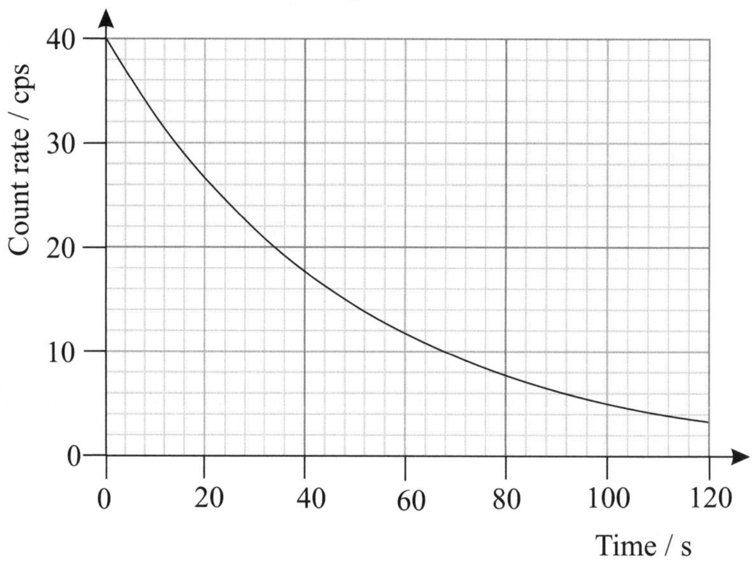

6.6 Determine the decay constant of dubnium-262.

decay constant = ... s^{-1}

(2 marks)

6.7 Initially, the sample contained 2.0 g of the radioactive isotope.
Calculate the number of radioactive nuclei in the sample after 210 seconds.

number of radioactive nuclei = ...

(2 marks)

7   A scientist creates 5.0 g of the artificial element neptunium-236.
The element is radioactive. It has a half-life of 1.5×10^5 years.

7.1 Calculate the initial activity of the neptunium-236 sample.

activity = ... Bq

(3 marks)

Neptunium-236 has three possible decay modes. **Table 2** shows the decay modes,
the products of these types of decay and the probability of each one occurring.

Table 2

Decay mode	Probability of occurrence	Decay product
Alpha	0.002	protactinium-232
Beta	0.125	plutonium-236
Electron capture	0.873	uranium-236

7.2 Describe the process of electron capture.

....

....

....

(2 marks)

7.3 Calculate the time taken for 2.5 g of uranium-236 to be created from the 5.0 g of neptunium-236.

time = ... s

(4 marks)

In the exam, you could be asked to suggest which of a number of radioactive sources is best
suited to a given application. Don't panic if it's a use that you've not come across before.
Just think about the properties of the source, such as half-life, penetrating power and how
dangerous it is, and look at how these factors link to the use you're being asked about.

Score

28

Nuclear Decay and Half-Life — 2

1 Cobalt-60 is an artificial, radioactive isotope. It has a half-life of 5.3 years.

1.1 State the mathematical relationship between the half-life of a radioactive isotope and the probability that an unstable nucleus will decay per second.

....

....

(1 mark)

Figure 1 shows how cobalt-60 decays to nickel-60, which is a stable isotope.

Figure 1

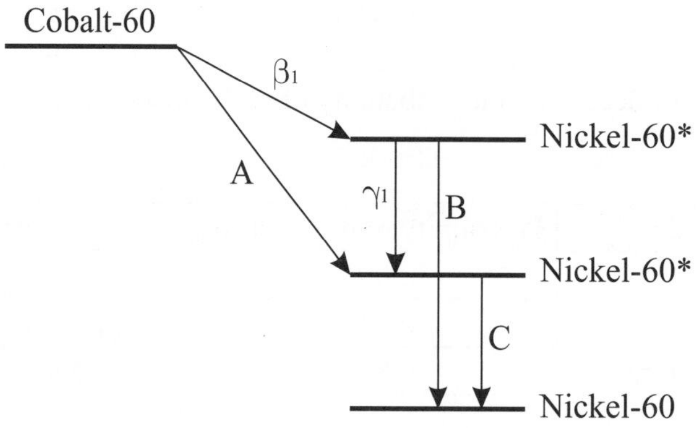

The * symbol indicates an excited nuclear state.

The energy values on the diagram are as follows: A = 1.48 MeV, B = 2.50 MeV, C = 1.33 MeV.

1.2 Some of the decay processes shown in **Figure 1** lead to an excited nuclear state. Explain what is meant by an excited nuclear state.

....

....

(1 mark)

1.3 Determine the energies of γ_1 and β_1.

γ_1 energy = ... MeV

β_1 energy = ... MeV

(2 marks)

1.4 Suggest a use of cobalt-60. Explain your answer.

....

....

....

....

(2 marks)

2   Radium is a radioactive element first discovered by Marie and Pierre Curie. They used the radiation emitted from radium-226 to define the unit the curie (Ci). 1 curie = 3.7×10^{10} decays per second.

2.1   A sample of 3.2×10^{22} radium-226 atoms has an activity of 12 Ci.
Determine the decay constant for radium-226.

decay constant = ... s^{-1}
(2 marks)

2.2   Radium-226, a solid at room temperature, decays to radon-222 which is a colourless and odourless radioactive gas at room temperature. Radon-222 has a half-life of 3.8 days and decays via alpha decay. Compare the dangers of exposure to samples of radium-226 and radon-222, assuming each sample initially has the same number of atoms of each element.

....

....

....

....

....

....
(3 marks)

2.3   During the decay of radium-226, nuclear equilibrium of radon-222 can occur, at which the rates of production and decay of radon-222 are equal, so the number of radon-222 atoms remains constant. Determine the number of radon-222 atoms that must be present in the sample in part 2.1 for this nuclear equilibrium to occur.

number of atoms = ...
(3 marks)

3   A 20th century plate is coated with a glaze that contains uranium-238. A scientist measures the activity of the plate to be 980 Bq. The decay constant of uranium-238 is 4.9×10^{-18} s^{-1}.

3.1   Calculate the number of radioactive uranium nuclei in the plate.
Assume that all of the radiation emitted from the plate is due to the decay of uranium-238 nuclei.

number of nuclei = ...
(1 mark)

3.2 Calculate the half-life of uranium-238. Give your answer in years.
Given that the activity of uranium-238 in the plate when it was newly made is known, use your answer to explain why measuring the current activity of the plate could not be used to date it.

half-life = ... years

....

....

....

(2 marks)

Potassium-argon dating is a method used to determine the age of rocks. Potassium-40 is a radioactive isotope, which decays 89.1% of the time into calcium-40 and 10.9% of the time into argon-40. Argon is inert, so once produced it stays unchanged within rocks. To date a rock, a small sample is melted and its argon and potassium levels are measured. The equation below is then used to determine the age of the sample.

$$t = \frac{T_{1/2}}{\ln 2} \ \ln \left(\frac{K + \frac{Ar}{0.109}}{K} \right)$$

$T_{1/2}$ is the half life of potassium-40, K is the number of potassium-40 nuclei remaining in the sample and Ar is the number of argon-40 nuclei found in the sample.

3.3 A rock sample contains 5.0×10^{-2} mol of potassium-40 and 4.6×10^{-6} mol of argon-40. The half-life of potassium-40 is 1.25×10^9 years. Calculate the age of the rock sample.

age = ... s

(3 marks)

3.4 Starting from $N = N_0 e^{-\lambda t}$, derive the equation used to determine the age of a sample using potassium-argon dating. You can use the relationship $-\ln(a \div b) = \ln(b \div a)$.

(3 marks)

Scattering and Gamma Rays

1 If a gamma ray has enough energy, it can be converted into a particle-antiparticle pair through a process called pair production.

1.1 Determine whether a gamma ray with an energy of 1.1 MeV could produce an electron-positron pair.

(1 mark)

1.2 A gamma ray that has an energy of 3.6×10^{-11} J is converted into a different particle-antiparticle pair. The particle and antiparticle are each produced with a kinetic energy of 1.0×10^{-12} J. Determine the mass of the particle created.

mass = ... kg

(2 marks)

2 Describe an experiment that could be used to investigate the relationship between the intensity of gamma radiation and the distance from a gamma source. Your answer should include a diagram of the apparatus that should be used, the measurements that should be taken and the expected results. Include any safety precautions that would need to be taken.

....

....

....

....

....

....

....

....

....

....

(6 marks)

3 Read through the following passage and answer the questions that follow it.

Determining the nuclear radius.

In 1909, Rutherford's scattering experiment investigated the structure and size of atoms.
It led to the discovery that atoms contain within them a tiny nucleus which contains most of
the atom's mass. Rutherford's team estimated the radius of this nucleus by calculating the distance
of closest approach. This involved firing alpha particles towards a gold nucleus and determining
5   how close they got to the nucleus using the equation:

$$E_k = \frac{Q_{gold} Q_{alpha}}{4\pi\varepsilon_0 r}$$

Where E_k is the kinetic energy of the alpha particle, Q_{gold} and Q_{alpha} are the charges of the gold nucleus and
the alpha particle, ε_0 is the permittivity of free space, and r is the distance of closest approach. The closest
calculated distance determined an upper limit (maximum possible value) on the radius of a gold nucleus.
10   Later, other scientists used electron scattering to determine nuclear radii. The diffraction patterns
produced by firing a beam of electrons at different materials were studied. They showed the relation:

$$\sin\theta = \frac{1.22\lambda}{2R}$$

where θ is the angle of the first minimum of the diffraction pattern, λ is the de Broglie wavelength of the
electrons, and R is the radius of the nucleus. From these results, a relationship between the mass (nucleon)
15   number of an atom and its nuclear radius was discovered:

$$R = R_0 A^{1/3}.$$

Where R is the radius of the nucleus, R_0 is a constant and A is the mass number of the nucleus.
This relationship was also evidence for nuclear material having a constant density.

3.1 Briefly describe Rutherford's scattering experiment and explain how it led to the discovery of the nucleus.

....

....

....

....

(3 marks)

3.2 Given that the kinetic energy of an alpha particle used in the experiment was 7.7 MeV, use the equation on
line 6 to calculate the upper limit of the nuclear radius determined by Rutherford's team (line 9).
The charge on a gold nucleus is +79e.

radius = ... m

(2 marks)

3.3 Determine the radius of a gold nucleus using the relationship stated on line 16.
A gold nucleus has a nucleon number of 197. R_0 is equal to 1.4×10^{-15} m.

radius = ... m

(1 mark)

3.4 Show how the relationship on line 16 shows that nuclear material has a constant density.

(2 marks)

A beam of high-energy electrons is fired through a thin foil of beryllium-9 to determine its radius using electron scattering. The electrons produce a diffraction pattern on a fluorescent screen.
Figure 1 shows a graph of the electron intensity on the screen against the angle from the horizontal.

Figure 1

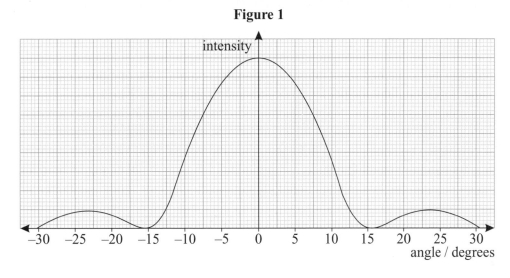

3.5 The electrons in the beam had a de Broglie wavelength of 1.28×10^{-15} m.
Use **Figure 1** and the equation on line 12 to calculate the radius of a beryllium-9 atom.

radius = ... m

(3 marks)

3.6 Use your answer to 2.5 to calculate the density of nuclear material. Assume the mass of a nucleon = 1.0 u.

density = ... kgm⁻³

(2 marks)

Nuclear Fission and Fusion

1   Nuclear fission is used to generate electricity in a thermal nuclear reactor.

1.1   State what is meant by the critical mass of nuclear fuel.

....

(1 mark)

1.2   Describe the function of both the coolant and the control rods in a thermal nuclear reactor.

....

....

....

(2 marks)

1.3   Suggest a material that could be used in the control rods in a thermal nuclear reactor.

....

(1 mark)

1.4   Some people may be concerned about the safety of nuclear power. Describe **three** measures taken within nuclear power stations to limit the risk to employees and the general public.

....

....

....

....

....

....

(3 marks)

1.5   Suggest why, despite the risks, nuclear power is one of the main methods by which electricity is generated in the UK.

....

....

....

(1 mark)

2   Moderators in thermal nuclear reactors are used to reduce the speed of neutrons produced by nuclear fission until they become 'thermal neutrons'.

2.1   Explain what would happen to the nuclear chain reaction within a reactor if the moderator was removed.

....

....

(2 marks)

2.2 Describe how a moderator slows down neutrons in a nuclear reactor.

....

....

....

(1 mark)

2.3 State **one** factor that affects how efficient a material would be as a moderator.

....

....

(1 mark)

One of the nuclear fission reactions that occurs in the reactor is shown below:

$$_{0}^{1}n + _{92}^{235}U \longrightarrow _{56}^{141}Ba + _{36}^{92}Kr + 3_{0}^{1}n$$

Table 1 shows the rest energies of the product nuclei involved in the reaction.

Table 1

Product	Rest energy in MeV
$_{56}^{141}Ba$	1.3165×10^5
$_{36}^{92}Kr$	8.5888×10^4

The uranium-235 nucleus has a rest energy of 2.196×10^5 MeV and is at rest immediately before the reaction. Of the energy released in the reaction, 152.00 MeV is transferred to the kinetic energy of the product nuclei, 25.000 MeV of energy is released as electromagnetic radiation, and the remaining energy is transferred to the kinetic energy of the product neutrons

2.4 Using the data above and in **Table 1**, calculate the kinetic energy of a neutron emitted in the fission reaction in MeV. Assume that each product neutron has the same kinetic energy, and that the kinetic energy of the thermal neutron is negligible.

kinetic energy = ... MeV

(2 marks)

3 **Figure 1** shows the mass number of atoms plotted against their average binding energy per nucleon.

Figure 1

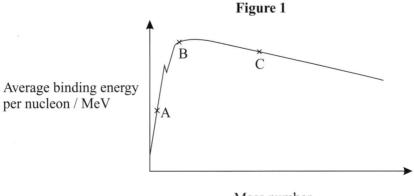

Average binding energy per nucleon / MeV

Mass number

3.1 State what is meant by the binding energy of a nucleus.

....

....
(1 mark)

3.2 Determine which of the atoms labelled A - C on **Figure 1** will release energy when it undergoes fusion. Explain your answer.

....

....
(1 mark)

3.3 Calculate the binding energy per nucleon for a boron-10 atom, $^{10}_{5}B$, in electron volts.
Boron-10 has a nuclear mass of 10.01294 u.

binding energy per nucleon = ... eV
(3 marks)

3.4 Boron-10 can be produced by either a single beta-minus decay from beryllium-10 or by a single beta-plus decay from carbon-10. Carbon-10 has a nuclear mass of 10.01685 u and beryllium-10 has a nuclear mass of 10.01353 u. Determine which beta particle would have a higher velocity. Explain your answer.

....

....

....

....

....
(3 marks)

3.5 Nuclear fusion is the source of energy for the Sun. One fusion process that occurs is shown below:

$$^{3}He + {}^{3}He \rightarrow {}^{1}H + {}^{1}H + {}^{4}He + energy$$

Determine the amount of energy released by the process shown above. The mass of a hydrogen atom is 1.00783 u, the mass of a helium-3 atom is 3.01603 u and the mass of a helium-4 atom is 4.00260 u.

energy = ... J
(2 marks)

> **EXAM TIP**
> There are two ways to do calculations that involve binding energy and mass defects. The first way is to use the equation $E = mc^2$. Another way is to remember that binding energy = mass defect (in terms of u) × 931.5 MeV. You'll get slightly different answers, but both ways are correct. Whatever method you go for, make sure all your quantities are in the correct units.

Score

24

Astrophysics — 1

From detecting objects with telescopes, to analysing observations and modelling the Universe, astrophysics is no small undertaking. Give these questions a go, and see if you're ready to shine bright in the exam.

1   Fomalhaut is a class A star, located 7.7 parsecs from Earth.

1.1   State the element responsible for the strongest absorption lines observed in the spectrum of light from Fomalhaut.

....

(1 mark)

1.2   Fomalhaut has an apparent magnitude of 1.16. Calculate the absolute magnitude of Fomalhaut.

absolute magnitude = ...

(2 marks)

1.3   **Figure 1** shows the axes of a Hertzsprung-Russel (H-R) diagram.
Plot Fomalhaut on **Figure 1**. Use **Figure 1** and your knowledge of the H-R diagram to determine whether Fomalhaut is likely to be a main sequence star, a red giant or a white dwarf.

Figure 1

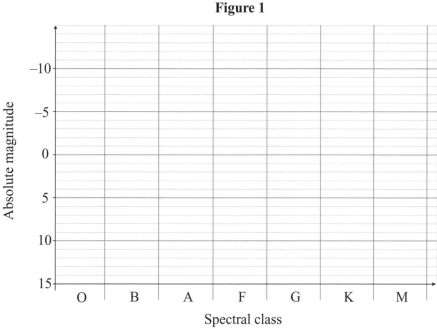

....

(2 marks)

1.4   Dagon is an exoplanet that was discovered orbiting around Fomalhaut.
Explain **one** observation which may indicate the presence of an exoplanet orbiting a distant star.

....

....

....

....

(2 marks)

124

2   An astronomer is using a refracting telescope to observe the night sky.
     A diagram of the lenses in the refracting telescope in normal adjustment
     is shown in **Figure 2**. The principal focus of both lenses is labelled F.

Figure 2

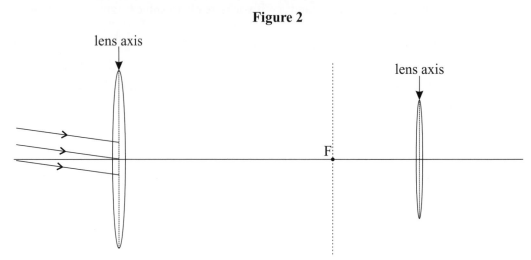

2.1 Complete the ray diagram in **Figure 2** to show what happens to the light as it passes through the telescope.
                                                                                                            (2 marks)

2.2 Give **one** limitation of a refracting telescope.

     ....

     ....
                                                                                                            (1 mark)

     The objective lens of the telescope has a diameter of 0.2 m and a focal length of 1.65 m.
     The eyepiece lens has a diameter of 0.02 m and a focal length of 0.15 m.

2.3 Calculate the magnification of the telescope.

                                               magnification = ...
                                                                                                            (1 mark)

2.4 The astronomer wants to observe a binary star system located 1.6×10^{18} m from Earth.
     The two binary stars are separated by a distance of 2.7×10^{11} m. The astronomer detects light from the
     stars with wavelength of 570 nm. Determine whether the telescope will be able to resolve the two stars.

     ....

     ....
                                                                                                            (3 marks)

3   Quasars are very bright astronomical objects that have undergone large red shifts.

3.1   Explain what is meant by red shift, and state the primary cause of red shift of distant astronomical objects.

....

....

....

(2 marks)

3.2   Quasar L is 3.68 Gpc from Earth. Estimate the recessional velocity of quasar L in ms^{-1}.
Assume that Hubble's constant = 72.0 km s^{-1} Mpc^{-1}.

recessional velocity = ... ms^{-1}

(2 marks)

3.3   Explain why this recessional velocity cannot be used in the red shift equation $z = -\dfrac{v}{c}$ to calculate the red shift of quasar L.

....

....

(1 mark)

3.4   Quasar L is found to have a red shift of 3.91.
Quasar L emits infrared radiation with a wavelength of 1.5×10^{-5} m.
Calculate the wavelength of this radiation when it reaches Earth.

wavelength = ... m

(2 marks)

3.5   Quasar L has a power output of approximately 3.8×10^{40} W.
Another quasar, quasar X, has a power output of approximately 1.5×10^{39} W.
The intensity of light received on Earth from quasar L is 2.3 times greater than the intensity of light received from quasar X. Estimate the distance of quasar X from Earth in parsecs.

distance = ... pc

(2 marks)

EXAM TIP

In the Astrophysics exam you may be asked to draw a ray diagram, e.g. to illustrate how a telescope works. Make sure you have a sharp pencil for your exam, and draw any rays carefully and clearly. All the rays you draw should be straight, fine lines that can be easily distinguished from one another, and have arrows to show the direction of the light.

Score

23

Astrophysics — 2

1 Type 1a supernovae occur in binary star systems, where one of the stars is a white dwarf.

1.1 Sketch the light curve of a typical type 1a supernova on **Figure 1**.

(1 mark)

Figure 1

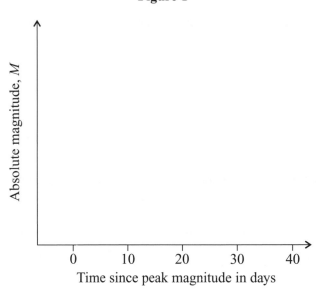

1.2 Explain how it is possible to accurately calculate the distance of a type 1a supernova from Earth from observations of its brightness.

....

....

....

....

....

....

....

....

(3 marks)

1.3 A particular white dwarf has a black body curve that peaks at a frequency of 880 THz. Estimate the temperature of the white dwarf.

temperature = ... K

(2 marks)

2   Some supernovae are produced as part of the life cycle of massive stars.
When this occurs, they emit powerful bursts of gamma rays.

2.1   A supernova occurs 2.75 kpc from Earth. At a distance of 10.0 pc from the supernova, the gamma ray
burst has an intensity of I. Estimate the intensity of the gamma rays when they reach Earth, in terms of I.

intensity = ... I

(2 marks)

The supernovae of the most massive stars can leave behind a black hole.

2.2   Scientists believe that the Milky Way has a supermassive black hole at its centre with a Schwartzchild
radius of 1.3×10^{-6} ly. Calculate the mass of this supermassive black hole.

mass = ... kg

(2 marks)

2.3   Some supermassive black holes can cause quasars to form.
We observe quasars mainly as bright radio sources.
Describe the structure of a quasar and explain why they are seen as bright radio sources.

....

....

....

....

....

....

(3 marks)

2.4   Explain why quasars are some of the most distant objects that can be observed.

....

....

....

....

(2 marks)

3 The William Herschel telescope is a large reflecting telescope, located in Spain. It detects visible light using a Cassegrain arrangement.

Figure 2 shows an incomplete ray diagram of the Cassegrain arrangement. Two incident rays have been partially drawn.

Figure 2

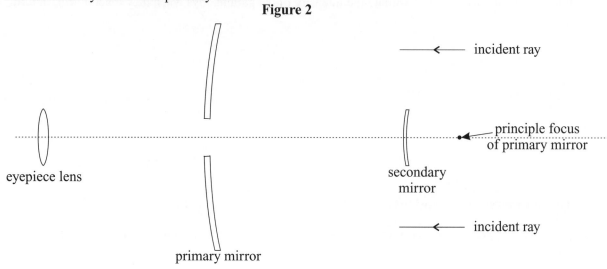

3.1 By continuing the incident rays, complete **Figure 2** to show how the rays reach the eyepiece lens.

(2 marks)

Most terrestrial reflecting telescopes are designed to detect either visible light or radio waves.

3.2 Explain the similarities and differences between reflecting telescopes designed to detect visible light and reflecting telescopes designed to detect radio waves. Your answer should include reference to their position, structure and relative resolving and collecting powers.

....

....

....

....

....

....

....

....

....

....

....

....

....

....

....

....

(6 marks)

4 The three most commonly occurring types of star are main sequence stars, red giants and white dwarfs.

4.1 Suggest why the core of a red giant is larger than the white dwarf it will produce.

....

....

....

....

....

(2 marks)

Figure 4 shows the cooling curve of a white dwarf.

Figure 4

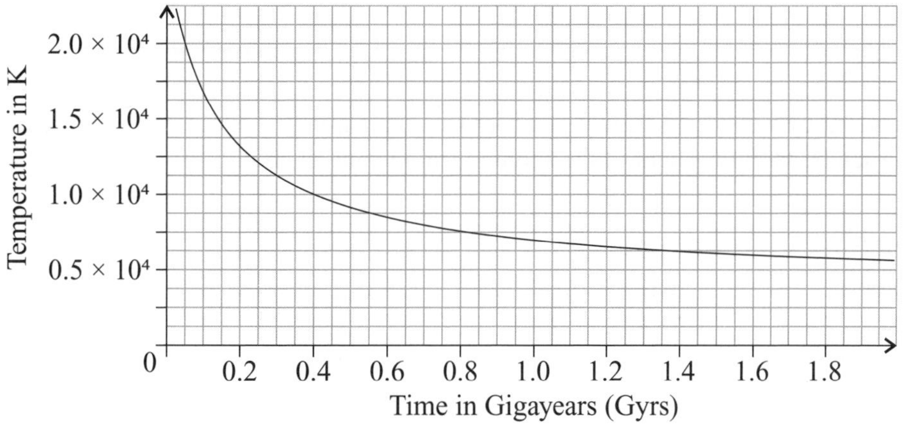

4.2 The white dwarf has a radius of 6.4×10^6 m.
Calculate the power output of the white dwarf at 0.8 Gyrs on the cooling curve.

power output = ... W

(3 marks)

4.3 When a white dwarf cools to a very low temperature, it will become a black dwarf. It is predicted to take at least 10^{15} years for a white dwarf to become a black dwarf. Given that the Hubble constant is equal to 2.1×10^{-18} s^{-1}, explain why scientists believe there are no black dwarfs in the Universe.

....

....

(2 marks)

EXAM TIP

Some questions may use skills you've learnt in the course applied to new and unfamiliar examples. For instance, something you've learnt about detecting exoplanets could be applied to detecting binary stars. Think about the similarities between the question and scenarios you've met on your course to help you work out how to answer the question.

Score

30

Medical Physics — 1

From internal body scans to the specs on your face — it's pretty amazing how much physics gets used in medicine. Physics is basically a hero. Have a go at these questions to test how much you know.

1   An endoscope is used to see inside the body during surgery. It consists of two bundles of optical fibres, one that illuminates the body parts, and one that transmits an image of the body parts to the surgeon.

1.1   Describe how light is transmitted through optical fibres to illuminate the inside of the body.

....

....

....

....
(2 marks)

1.2   Describe what is meant by a coherent bundle of fibres and explain why it is necessary to use a coherent bundle of fibres when transmitting light to the surgeon from inside the body.

....

....

....
(2 marks)

1.3   State **one** way in which the use of endoscopes has improved surgical procedures.

....

....

....
(1 mark)

2   A patient is diagnosed with hypermetropia by his optician.

2.1   Describe what is meant by hypermetropia.
In your answer, include where the image is formed by the eye and the possible causes of this condition.

....

....

....

....

....
(4 marks)

2.2   The patient is given spectacles to fix the defect in his vision.
Each lens in the spectacles has a power of 2.5 D. Calculate the focal length of each lens.

focal length = ... m
(1 mark)

2.3 **Figure 1** shows an incomplete ray diagram of light being focussed by one of the lenses.
Complete the diagram to show the formation of an image of a real object O.

Figure 1

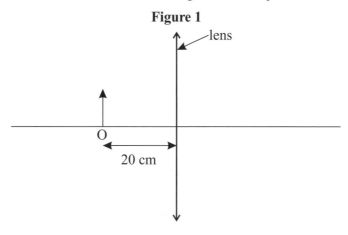

(2 marks)

3 A patient is undergoing a series of examinations of their heart.
Figure 2 shows an electrocardiogram for the patient.

Figure 2

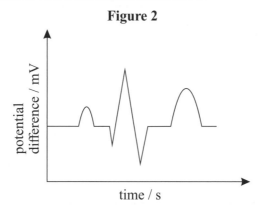

3.1 Label the P, QRS and T stages on the electrocardiogram in **Figure 2**.
Describe the behaviour of the patient's heart during the three stages.

....

....

....

....

(4 marks)

The patient then receives an ultrasound scan of the heart, known as an echocardiogram.

3.2 The average density of cardiac tissue in the heart wall is 1.05 g cm^{-3}. The walls of the heart have an
average thickness of 1.0 cm. It takes 6.4 μs for the ultrasound wave to travel through the wall of the heart.
Calculate the acoustic impedance of cardiac tissue.

acoustic impedance = ... kgm^{-2}s^{-1}
(2 marks)

3.3 Immediately before reaching the heart, the ultrasound waves travel through the surrounding tissue, which has an acoustic impedance of 1.4×10^6 kgm^{-2}s^{-1}. Calculate the percentage of the incoming ultrasound waves that are reflected when the ultrasound pulse reaches the heart.

percentage reflected = ... %

(2 marks)

4 A patient is undergoing a Magnetic Resonance (MR) scan. A magnetic field with a gradient of magnetic field strength is applied across the patient, and pulses of radio waves are directed towards the body.

4.1 Describe how radio waves are used in an MR scan to produce images of the body.

....

....

....

....

....

....

(4 marks)

4.2 Discuss the advantages and disadvantages of MR scans compared to CT scans in terms of safety, convenience, and the quality of the images produced.

....

....

....

....

....

....

....

....

....

(6 marks)

EXAM TIP

Make sure you're comfortable with drawing ray diagrams — practise drawing ray diagrams for both types of lens, and for when the object is either side of the principal focus. Always make sure you draw them in pencil — it can be easy to make mistakes under exam pressure and it can get confusing if you have to scribble out lines that have been incorrectly drawn in pen.

Score

30

Medical Physics — 2

1 Technetium-99m (Tc-99m) is a radioactive isotope that can be used as a medical tracer.

1.1 Explain why Tc-99m is produced on-site in hospitals.

....
(1 mark)

The gamma rays produced by medical tracers can be detected by a gamma camera, shown in **Figure 1**.

Figure 1

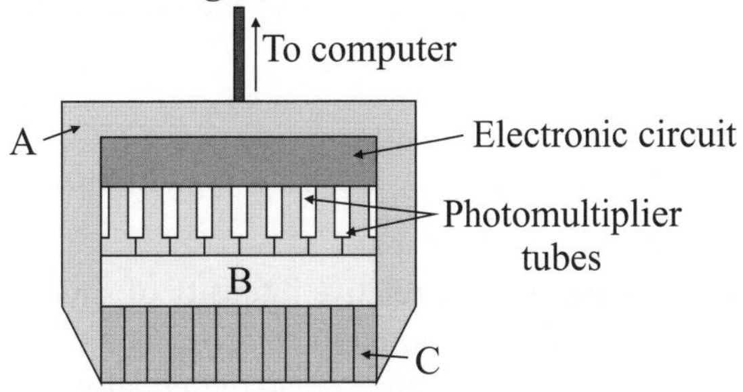

1.2 Name the parts of the gamma camera in **Figure 1** labelled A, B and C.

A ....

B ....

C ....
(2 marks)

1.3 Describe the function of the photomultiplier tubes within the gamma camera.

....

....

....
(2 marks)

1.4 A Tc-99m tracer has an effective half-life of 4.8 hours. Calculate the biological half-life of Tc-99m.

biological half-life = ... hours
(2 marks)

1.5 Describe the difference between physical half-life and biological half-life, and explain why it is important to consider them both when selecting a tracer.

....

....

....

....

....
(3 marks)

2 Human hearing can be represented by an equal loudness curve.
Figure 2 shows two equal loudness curves, A and B.
Curve A represents a normal equal loudness curve.

Figure 2

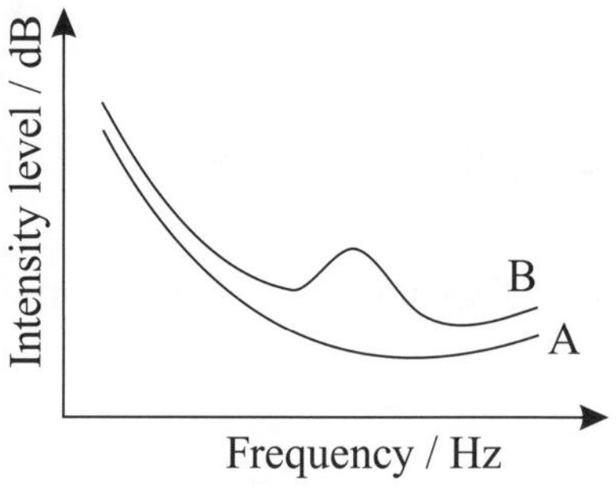

2.1 Curve B is the equal loudness curve for someone with hearing loss.
State the cause of the person's hearing loss.

....
(1 mark)

2.2 The relative intensity of a sound can be measured using the dB or dBA scale.
Explain the advantage of using the dBA scale over the dB scale to monitor human hearing.

....

....
(1 mark)

A decibel meter is used to measure the relative intensity of sound produced by a washing machine.
The intensity level of the sound is measured to be 55 dB at a distance of 1.5 m from the machine.
The sound waves produced by the machine spread out equally in all directions.

2.3 Calculate the total power of the sound emitted by the washing machine.

power = ... W
(4 marks)

3 In an ultrasound scan, high frequency sound waves are generated and directed into the body. These waves are then reflected off boundaries in the body, before being detected outside the body and converted into an image.

3.1 Piezoelectric crystals such as lead zirconate titanate (PZT) are used to generate and detect ultrasound waves.
Describe the process of generating and detecting ultrasound waves using PZT crystals. In your answer,
include a description and explanation of the thickness of the crystals that should be used in the device.

....

....

....

....

....

....
(5 marks)

3.2   A-scans and B-scans are two types of ultrasound scan. Describe and compare A-scans and B-scans.

....

....

....

....

....

....

....

(5 marks)

4   **Figure 3** shows an X-ray tube.

Figure 3

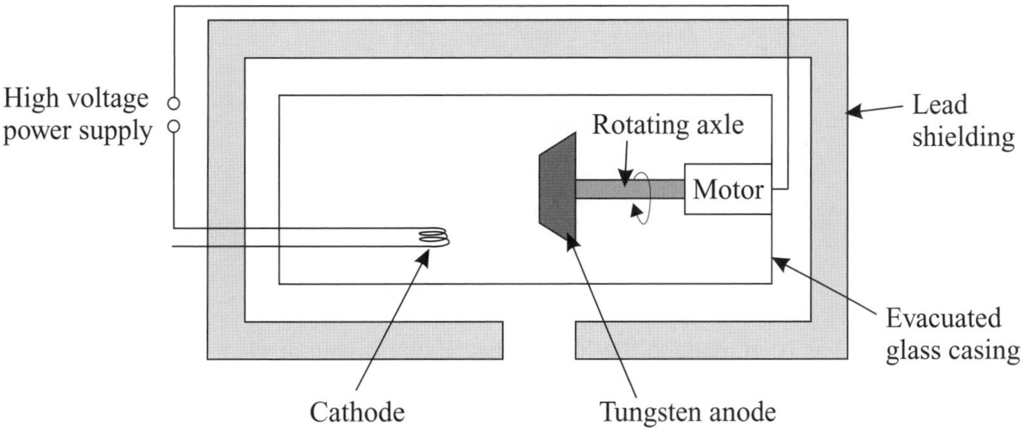

4.1   X-rays are produced by two different mechanisms in X-ray tubes.
With reference to **Figure 3**, describe both mechanisms of X-ray production that occur in the X-ray tube.
Comment on any labelled components which allow for more efficient X-ray production.

....

....

....

....

....

....

....

....

....

(6 marks)

4.2 X-rays with an intensity of 2.0×10^5 Wm^{-2} are incident on the lead shielding.
The lead shielding is 3.0 mm thick. The half-value thickness of the lead for the X-ray beam is 0.25 mm.
Calculate the intensity of the X-rays immediately after they have travelled out of the lead shielding.

intensity = ... Wm^{-2}

(2 marks)

Figure 4 shows the energy spectrum of X-rays produced in the X-ray tube.
Curve A is the original X-ray spectrum and curve B is an X-ray spectrum
after the properties of the X-ray tube have been altered.

Figure 4

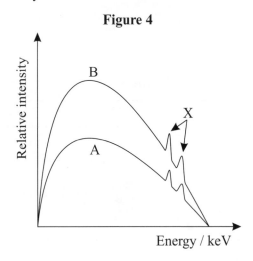

4.3 State the change that has been made to the X-ray tube. Explain your answer.

....

....

....

(2 marks)

4.4 Explain the origin of the double peak labelled X that appears in both energy spectra.
Explain why these peaks appear at the same position in the energy spectra.

....

....

....

....

....

....

(3 marks)

 EXAM TIP Examiners love to ask you about different imaging methods. Make sure you know how they all weigh up when it comes to risks, patient convenience, the quality of images and what the images show. And if you're asked to compare two methods, remember to give points about both — don't get carried away talking about one without saying how it measures up to the other.

Score

39

Engineering Physics — 1

From spinning wheels to refrigerators, engineering physics is all about mechanical motion and transferring energy. So fire up those mental engines, and let's get the ball rolling on your revision with these questions.

1   A bicycle manufacturer is testing a new bike wheel. The bike wheel has a radius of 310 mm and a mass of 1.8 kg. It is attached to an axle, and placed in a stand, as shown in **Figure 1**.

Figure 1

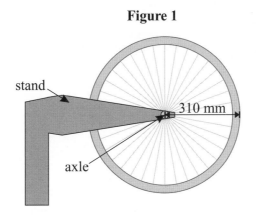

The manufacturer uses a motor to provide a fixed torque to the axle, which produces a constant clockwise angular acceleration of 2.9 rad s⁻². The torque is applied until the wheel reaches a desired angular velocity, and then the motor is switched off.

1.1 Calculate the time the torque must be applied for to accelerate the wheel from rest to an angular velocity of 32.3 rad s⁻¹ clockwise.

time = ... s

(1 mark)

1.2 Calculate the rotational kinetic energy of the wheel with an angular velocity of 32.3 rad s⁻¹. You may assume the wheel is a ring with its mass concentrated around the outside edge, and the moment of inertia of the axle is negligible. The moment of inertia of a ring with mass m and radius r is given by $I = mr^2$.

rotational kinetic energy = ... J

(2 marks)

1.3 After the motor is switched off, a resultant torque from air resistance and friction brings the wheel to rest. The manufacturer records that the wheel undergoes 52.4 rotations before coming to rest. Calculate the magnitude of the average angular deceleration of the wheel.

angular deceleration = ... rad s⁻¹

(2 marks)

1.4 Calculate the average magnitude of the frictional torque acting on the wheel.

frictional torque = ... Nm

(1 mark)

The bike manufacturer also produces wheels for competitive indoor cycling races.
These wheels are solid cylinders, with the same radius and mass as the traditional bike wheel in **Figure 1**.
They are made of a material with a uniform density.

1.5 Explain why the solid wheel may perform better than the traditional bike wheel in **Figure 1**.

....

....

....

....

....

....

....

(3 marks)

2 A record player comprises a turntable driven by a motor. To play a record, it is placed on
the turntable and a needle on a lever is lowered onto its surface, as shown in **Figure 2**.

Figure 2

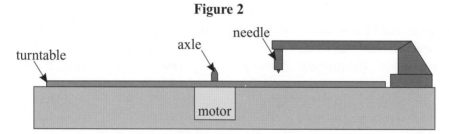

The turntable is a solid disc, with a mass of 0.50 kg and a radius of 32 cm.
When switched on, the motor applies a constant torque of 0.12 Nm to the turntable.
The turntable experiences a frictional torque at the axle which is initially zero, but increases proportionally
to the angular velocity of the turntable. The moment of inertia of a solid disc is given by $I = \frac{1}{2}mr^2$.

2.1 Calculate the initial angular acceleration of the turntable.

angular acceleration = ... $\mathrm{rad\,s^{-2}}$

(2 marks)

2.2 Sketch a graph on the axes below to show the angular displacement of the turntable after it is switched on. Explain the shape of the graph.

....

....

....

....

....

....

(4 marks)

A record is placed on the turntable.
The friction between the turntable and record is sufficiently high that the record will not slip.
The turntable spins at a constant angular speed of 33.3 revolutions per minute.
The frictional torque at the axle is 5.0×10^{-3} Nm. The motor applies a constant torque
equal to the frictional torque so that the turntable maintains a constant angular speed.

2.3 Calculate the energy dissipated by the frictional torque in ten minutes.

energy = ... J

(2 marks)

The needle is lowered into the spiral-shaped groove on the top of the record, so that it moves
towards the centre of the record as the record plays. The needle applies a constant frictional force.

2.4 Explain how the torque on the turntable due to the needle changes as the record plays.

....

....

....

(1 mark)

3 Three students are using different methods to estimate the useful power output (the power used to drive the wheels) of a car with a 6-cylinder 4-stroke petrol engine.

One uses a theoretical indicator diagram for the petrol engine cylinder, and another uses an actual indicator diagram showing the *p-V* behaviour in one of the engine's cylinders. These are shown in **Figure 3**.

Figure 3

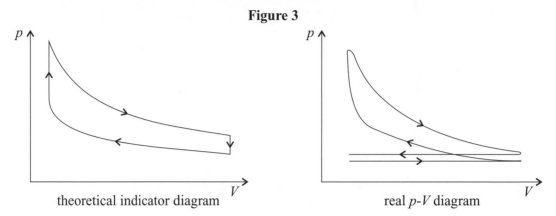

theoretical indicator diagram   real *p-V* diagram

The third student uses a device called a dynamometer to measure the energy required to decelerate the car to rest. The values obtained by each of the students are shown in **Table 1**.

Table 1

Method	Description	Power calculated / kW
1	theoretical indicator diagram	334.2
2	real *p-V* diagram	305.2
3	dynamometer	298.5

Describe how each method can be used to determine power, and compare the validity of the different values calculated as estimates of the useful power output. Explain the sources of any discrepancies between the power values calculated.

....

....

....

....

....

....

....

....

....

....

(6 marks)

EXAM TIP Remember, a crucial thing in physics is modelling systems. Often we have to start from an idealised version of a system, and slowly add complications to match how things really work. And the exams love asking about how this perfect world differs from reality. Think about how these models help us make predictions and why these predictions might not quite work out.

Score

24

Engineering Physics — 2

1 An Otto cycle is an idealised description of the thermodynamic behaviour of a piston in a four-stroke petrol engine, which assumes that the compression and expansion each consist of an adiabatic process followed immediately by a constant-volume process.

Figure 1 shows a *p-V* diagram of the Otto cycle.

Figure 1

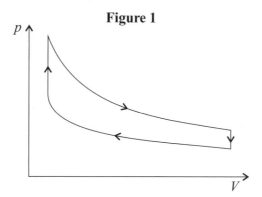

1.1 Explain why the expansion stroke of a real four-stroke petrol engine cannot involve a perfectly adiabatic expansion.

....

....
(1 mark)

The "compression ratio" describes the ratio of maximum to minimum volume, $\dfrac{V_{max}}{V_{min}}$, in a piston engine. The Otto cycle above has a compression ratio of 10.0.

1.2 Given that the fuel is at atmospheric pressure at the start of the compression stroke of an Otto cycle, calculate the pressure in a cylinder at the end of the compression stroke.
Atmospheric pressure = 1.0×10^5 Pa. Adiabatic constant of the fuel $\gamma = 1.4$.

pressure = ... Pa
(2 marks)

1.3 An Otto cycle, featuring adiabatic compression and expansion, can also be constructed for a diesel engine. Sketch the *p-V* diagram of an Otto cycle of a four-stroke diesel engine on **Figure 1**.
(2 marks)

2 An airtight refrigerator in a laboratory contains air at a pressure of 110 kPa. When switched on, the temperature of the air inside the refrigerator is lowered from 0.0 °C to −40.0 °C.

2.1 Calculate the pressure inside the refrigerator once the air has reached −40.0 °C.

pressure = ... Pa
(2 marks)

2.2 Sketch a *p-V* diagram for the cooling process, and label the initial and final pressures, on the axes below. State the amount of work done on the air during cooling.

(3 marks)

2.3 The refrigerator's maximum theoretical coefficient of performance is 3.1. Assuming the refrigerator runs at this coefficient of performance while maintaining a temperature –40°C, determine the temperature of the lab in degrees Celsius.

temperature = ... °C

(2 marks)

2.4 Explain why leaving the door of the refrigerator open is not an effective way of cooling down the laboratory.

....

....

....

....

....

(2 marks)

Figure 2

3 A research facility contains an experimental nuclear fusion reactor. The reactor runs in 'pulses', with each pulse lasting around 40 seconds.

The power consumption of the reactor during a pulse is shown in **Figure 2**. During a pulse, the reactor draws its power from flywheels.

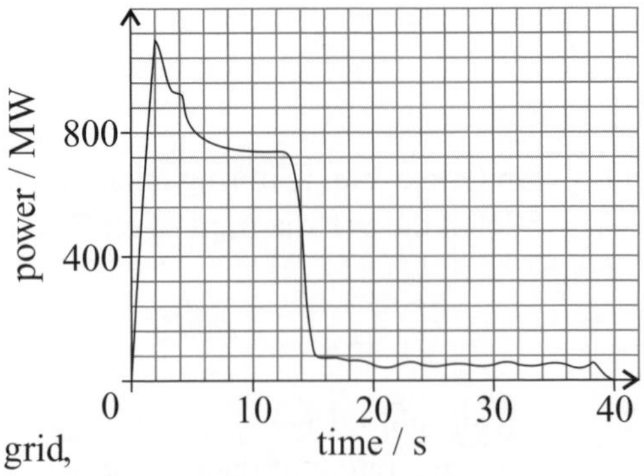

3.1 The maximum power that the reactor can draw from the national grid is 525 MW. State why the reactor cannot be directly powered by the national grid, and explain how flywheels can be used to power the reactor.

....

....

....

....

(2 marks)

3.2 A flywheel is rotating clockwise with 3.40×10^9 J of rotational kinetic energy.
The flywheel has a moment of inertia of 1.30×10^7 kg m^2.
It is connected to the driving wheel of the reactor and experiences an initial
decelerating torque which transfers energy to the mechanism at a rate of 400.0 MW.
Calculate the size of the decelerating torque.

torque = ... Nm

(2 marks)

Some engineers at the facility are looking to develop a system to store some of the residual energy in the
driving wheel when a pulse is finished. An engineer proposes the system shown in **Figure 3**.

Once a pulse has finished, the driving wheel is disconnected from the flywheel and attached with a
connecting rod to separate stationary flywheel, wheel A. This allows some of the kinetic energy of the
driving wheel after a pulse to be transferred to wheel A.

Figure 3

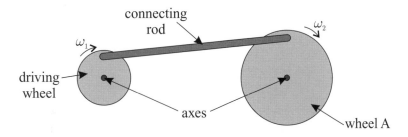

In the model system, wheel A has a moment of inertia of 5.09×10^{-2} kgm^2.
The driving wheel has a moment of inertia of 6.28×10^{-4} kgm^2.

Just before the wheel A is connected to the driving wheel,
the driving wheel is spinning with an angular speed of 12.0 rad s^{-1}.
After wheel A is connected, the driving wheel spins with an angular speed of 0.429 rad s^{-1}.
The connecting rod is assumed to have negligible mass.

3.3 Calculate the angular speed at which the wheel A will spin after it is connected.

angular velocity = ... rad s^{-1}

(3 marks)

4   An isobaric chamber is a closed container which maintains a constant internal pressure. **Figure 3** shows a heat pump that takes energy from a cold reservoir and transfers it to the gas inside an isobaric chamber.

Figure 3

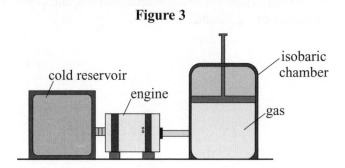

The heat pump is powered by a small engine which consumes 0.10 g
of propane gas per second as fuel, and has an efficiency of 0.60.
The gas in the isobaric chamber is initially at room temperature and atmospheric pressure.
After the heat pump has run for 15 s, the volume of gas in the isobaric chamber is 1.2 m³, and the
temperature of the gas is 493 K. The internal energy of the gas increases by 54 kJ during this time.

4.1 Calculate the coefficient of performance of the heat pump. Atmospheric pressure = 1.0×10^5 Pa.
Room temperature = 293 K. Calorific value of propane = 5.0×10^7 J kg⁻¹.

coefficient of performance = ...
(5 marks)

4.2 Explain why it is possible for a refrigerator to have a coefficient of performance greater than 1,
but it is impossible to have a heat engine with an efficiency greater than 1.

....

....

....

....

....
(2 marks)

Make sure you know the different types of engines inside and out, including their purpose,
processes and the equations that describe them. Some of the equations can look very similar,
so take care when you're doing calculations that you've chosen the correct one from the data
and formulae booklet. Check that your answers seem sensible for the situation.

Score

28

Turning Points in Physics — 1

The time's come to tackle relativity, as well as a load of other scientific breakthroughs from the last few hundred years. Make sure you're comfortable with the theories, maths and experiments in this section before starting.

1   A scientist uses a scanning tunnelling microscope to produce images of the surface of a metal.

1.1   Briefly describe how a scanning tunnelling microscope works.

....

....

....

....

....

(3 marks)

The scientist then uses transmission electron microscopy (TEM) to study the organisation of atoms in the metal. The spacing between the atoms is approximately 0.002 nm.

1.2   An electron gun is used to accelerate the electrons in a transmission electron microscope. In an electron gun, electrons are emitted when a metal cathode is heated. State the name of this process.

....

(1 mark)

1.3   Calculate the potential difference required to accelerate an electron from rest so that it has a de Broglie wavelength of 0.002 nm.

potential difference = ... V

(2 marks)

1.4   Explain whether the potential difference calculated in 1.3 would be an appropriate accelerating voltage to use in a transmission electron microscope to study the metal.

....

....

....

(1 mark)

1.5   In TEM, the image is produced from the diffraction patterns of electrons that have passed through a sample. Explain how increasing the accelerating potential difference would affect the image produced.

....

....

....

....

(2 marks)

2   Theories about the nature of light have changed over time.

2.1   Describe the theories of light put forward by Newton and Huygens.

....

....

....

....

(2 marks)

2.2   Describe an experiment which led to an acceptance of Huygens' theory and explain how it supported Huygens' theory.

....

....

....

....

....

(3 marks)

Scientists realised that the wave model of light could not always accurately predict how light behaved.

2.3   The photoelectric effect is a term that describes the emission of electrons from a metal when light is shone on it. Electrons are only emitted from the surface of a metal when the light shone on it is above a certain threshold frequency. Explain why the wave model of light failed to explain this behaviour.

....

....

....

....

(2 marks)

2.4   Describe the theory proposed by Planck which explained the photoelectric effect.

....

....

(1 mark)

2.5   Scientists now believe that light acts as both a wave and a particle.
Determine the momentum of a photon with a frequency of 6.5×10^5 Hz.

momentum = ... kgms^{-1}

(2 marks)

3 Hundreds of years ago, it was theorised that light needed a medium to travel through. This supposed medium is referred to as the luminiferous aether.

Scientists attempted to prove the existence of this medium and to measure its properties. In the late 1800s, Michelson and Morley devised an experiment to determine the motion of the Earth through the aether.

Figure 1 shows the Michelson-Morley interferometer they used in their investigation.

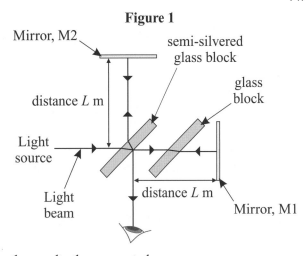

Figure 1

3.1 Describe Michelson and Morley's experiment, including the results they expected to see and the results that they achieved. Explain how their results were significant to our current understanding about the nature of light.

....

....

....

....

....

....

....

....

....

....

....

....

(6 marks)

3.2 The results of the Michelson-Morley experiment helped lead to the development of the theory of special relativity. One effect of special relativity is time dilation. Determine the speed at which an object would have to travel for its internal clock to measure 20% less time passing compared to a stationary observer.

speed = ... ms^{-1}
(2 marks)

EXAM TIP
Make sure that all the points you write about for levelled questions are relevant to the question. It might be tempting to waffle about vaguely related stuff that you know by heart, but it'll get you no dice with the examiner. Be strict with yourself about staying on-topic.

Score

27

Turning Points in Physics — 2

1 Cathode rays were discovered to be beams of electrons by J.J. Thomson in the 19th century. Thomson produced cathode rays and then deflected them into a circular path using a magnetic field.

1.1 Electron guns are used to generate and accelerate electrons. Determine the velocity of an electron after it has been accelerated from rest through a potential difference of 0.50 V.

velocity = ... ms^{-1}

(2 marks)

The charge to mass ratio of an electron is given by $\dfrac{Q}{m} = \dfrac{2V}{B^2 r^2}$, where Q is the charge of the electron, m is the mass of the electron, V is the accelerating potential difference, B is the magnetic field strength and r is the radius of the deflected path.

1.2 Derive the equation $\dfrac{Q}{m} = \dfrac{2V}{B^2 r^2}$.

(3 marks)

1.3 Thomson's work was built upon by many scientists, including Robert Millikan who determined the absolute charge of an electron in the early 20th century. Briefly describe the steps involved in Millikan's oil-drop experiment.

....

....

....

....

....

....

....

....

(4 marks)

2   A large number of experiments have been carried out that support the theory of special relativity.

In the 1960s, William Bertozzi investigated the speed and kinetic energies of electrons.
Figure 1 shows the behaviour he observed.

Figure 1

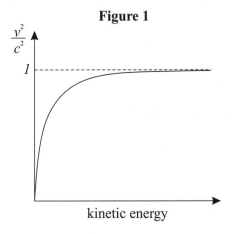

2.1   Describe how a graph of $\dfrac{v^2}{c^2}$ against kinetic energy would look based on Newtonian predictions,

and use it to explain how **Figure 1** supports ideas from special relativity.

....

....

....

....

....

(3 marks)

Muons are unstable particles created in the Earth's atmosphere when cosmic rays from the Sun
interact with the atmosphere. These muons have a mean lifetime of 2.2 μs at rest and they can travel
at speeds around $0.98c$. Due to their high speeds, muons are influenced by relativistic effects.

2.2   A muon is created 8.0 km above the Earth's surface. The muon travels to the Earth's surface at a speed of
$0.98c$ without decaying. Determine the distance travelled by the muon from the muon's reference frame.

distance travelled = ... km

(1 mark)

2.3   Explain how the detection at the Earth's surface of large numbers of muons created high in the Earth's
atmosphere is evidence of time dilation.

....

....

....

....

....

....

(3 marks)

3   In the 1840s, a scientist named Hippolyte Fizeau investigated the speed of light.
His experiment consisted of a beam of light shone through a rotating cogwheel and reflected
by a distant mirror. The reflected beam then travelled back through the cogwheel.

By adjusting the frequency at which the cogwheel rotated, Fizeau was able to allow a beam of light
through a gap between two cog teeth and then block the reflected beam with the adjacent cog tooth.
Fizeau calculated the speed of light in metres per second using $v = 4DNf$, where D is the distance from
the light source to the mirror, N is the number of teeth on the cogwheel and f is the frequency at which
the cogwheel rotates.

3.1   Derive the speed equation from Fizeau's experiment.

(3 marks)

Fizeau used a cog with 720 teeth that rotated at 12.6 rotations per second.
His mirror was 8633 m away from the cog.

Physicist James Clerk Maxwell predicted that the speed of light in metres per second
could be calculated using the equation below.

$$c = \frac{1}{\sqrt{\mu_0 \times \varepsilon_0}}$$

3.2   Calculate Fizeau's value of the speed of light and determine whether it was within
5% of Maxwell's value for the speed of an electromagnetic wave.

....

....

(2 marks)

It's all very good substituting numbers into an equation, but to derive an equation you really
need to understand what it means, and exactly what the quantities involved are. If you're really
stuck on a derivation, try writing out the initial equation and the final equation next to each
other. Circle any differences between them to figure out what substitutions need to be made.

Score

21

Mixed Questions — 1

One more section to go — and this one's a corker. These questions can test a mix of anything in sections 1-12, so make sure you've swotted up on everything from particles to nuclear physics before you give these a go.

For each of questions 1-4, give your answer by ticking the appropriate box.

1   Which of the following quantities is not always conserved when subatomic particles interact?

    A   Energy   ☐

    B   Lepton number   ☐

    C   Strangeness   ☐

    D   Baryon number   ☐

                                                                                   (1 mark)

2   An electric motor, connected to a 230 V supply, is used lift a 9.0 kg mass vertically upwards at a rate of 0.35 ms^{-1}. Assuming the motor is 100% efficient and resistive forces are negligible, what is the size of the current passing through the motor?

    A   0.91 A   ☐

    B   1.1 A   ☐

    C   0.13 A   ☐

    D   7.4 A   ☐

                                                                                       (1 mark)

3   **Figure 1** shows a uniform cube resting on an inclined plane. What minimum value must θ exceed for the weight of the cube to produce a moment and cause the cube to topple?

Figure 1

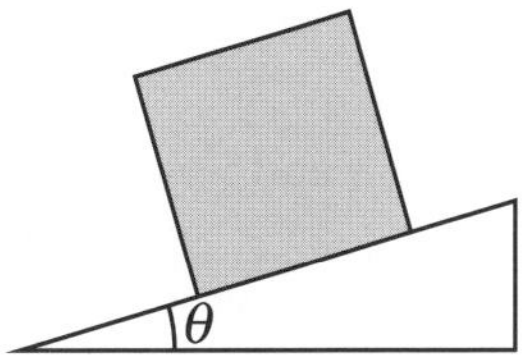

    A   30°   ☐   **B**   45°   ☐

    C   90°   ☐   **D**   60°   ☐

                                                                                 (1 mark)

4   A fixed resistor and a variable resistor, both initially with resistance R, are connected in series with a fixed voltage supply. By what factor does the voltage across the variable resistor change as its resistance is increased to $2R$?

    A   2   ☐

    B $\frac{4}{3}$ ☐

    C $\frac{3}{2}$ ☐

    D $\frac{2}{3}$ ☐

                                                                                     (1 mark)

5 A student is investigating the patterns created on a screen by monochromatic light when it is passed through a double-slit.

Figure 2 shows the set-up used for this experiment.

Figure 2

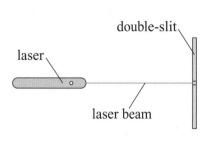

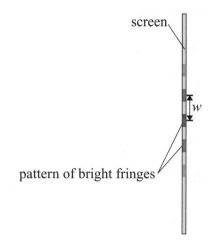

not to scale

A laser was used to shine monochromatic light through a double-slit, projecting a pattern onto a screen a fixed distance away. The spacing between adjacent fringes in the pattern, w, was recorded. The experiment was then repeated using double-slits with different slit separations, s.

5.1 Explain why bright fringes are formed on the screen when laser light passes through the double slit.

....

....

....

....

....

....

(4 marks)

5.2 **Table 1** shows the student's measurements of s and w.

Complete **Table 1** by calculating the missing values for $\frac{1}{s}$. Give your answers to 3 significant figures.

Table 1

s / m	w / m	$\frac{1}{s}$ / m^{-1}
2.00×10^{-4}	0.0088	
3.00×10^{-4}	0.0058	
4.00×10^{-4}	0.0044	
5.00×10^{-4}	0.0035	
6.00×10^{-4}	0.0029	
7.00×10^{-4}	0.0025	

(2 marks)

5.3 Using **Figure 3** and data from **Table 1**, draw a graph of w against $\frac{1}{s}$. Include a line of best fit.

Figure 3

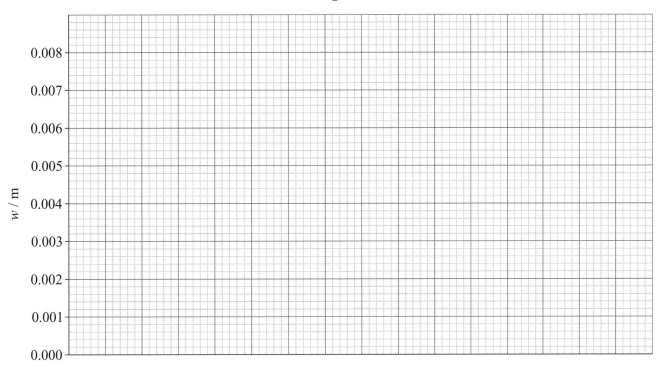

(3 marks)

The wavelength range of visible light is between 4.00×10^{-7} m and 7.00×10^{-7} m.

5.4 Use your graph to determine the maximum possible distance between the double-slit and the screen that would produce the results shown using monochromatic visible light.

maximum distance = ... m

(3 marks)

The screen had a frame made of aluminium. Aluminium has a work function of 6.53×10^{-19} J.

5.5 Calculate the maximum wavelength of light that could cause the emission of an electron from the aluminium frame via the photoelectric effect.

wavelength = ... m

(2 marks)

If you find yourself having to plot a graph, one of the first things you should do is to decide on a sensible scale for the axes. Looking at the range of values present in the data set can help you with this. Ideally your data set should span most of the space provided.

Score

18

Mixed Questions — 2

1   **Figure 1** shows a trick shot played on a miniature golf course.

Figure 1

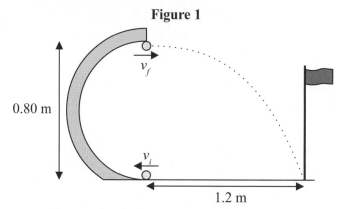

The golf ball, with mass 50.0 g, enters a semi-circular ramp with velocity v_i and leaves it with velocity v_f. Both velocities are directed horizontally and the ramp's height is 0.80 m. After leaving the ramp, the ball moves freely under gravity, landing in the hole, located 1.2 m from the base of the ramp.
You may assume the effects of resistive forces are negligible.

1.1   Calculate the magnitude of v_f.

$v_f =$ .... ms^{-1}
(2 marks)

1.2   Calculate the magnitude of v_i.

$v_i =$ .... ms^{-1}
(2 marks)

1.3   The time between the ball entering the ramp and the ball leaving the ramp is 0.37 s.
Calculate the magnitude of the average resultant force acting on the ball during this period.

average resultant force = ... N
(1 mark)

2   Read the passage, and answer the questions below.

Neutrinos are uncharged leptons that only interact via the weak interaction.
This makes them difficult to detect experimentally.

The anti-neutrino, its antimatter counterpart, was first discovered experimentally by the Cowan-Reines
neutrino experiment in 1956. The Cowan-Reines experiment was designed to look for a type of beta decay
5   known as inverse beta decay. In inverse beta decay, the following interaction takes place:

$$\bar{\nu}_e + p \longrightarrow n + e^+$$

To produce this interaction, antineutrinos were passed through two tanks containing cadmium chloride
dissolved in water. The antineutrinos interacted with the protons from the hydrogen atoms in the water.
This interaction could be detected by looking for distinct gamma ray emissions.

10   The positron produced by the interaction would quickly annihilate with an electron in the water, emitting
two gamma ray photons in opposite directions. The neutron produced in the interaction would be absorbed
by a cadmium nucleus, causing another gamma ray photon to be emitted. Detectors were set up around
the tank to detect these gamma ray emissions. For the inverse beta decay to have been considered detected,
the gamma photon emitted by a cadmium nucleus should be detected a few microseconds after the pair of
15   gamma photons produced by the annihilation.

During the experiment, antineutrinos were incident on one tank at a rate of 5×10^{13} antineutrinos per cm^2
each second. The rectangular face of the tank onto which the antineutrinos were incident had side lengths of
1.91 m by 1.37 m. The results of the experiment gave an approximate neutrino detection rate of 3 per hour.

2.1   Write a balanced equation of inverse beta decay (line 6) in terms of changing quark character,
and state the exchange particle involved in the interaction.

....

exchange particle = ...
(2 marks)

2.2   Assuming that the electron and positron have negligible kinetic energy immediately prior to their
annihilation (lines 10-11), explain why the gamma photons must be emitted in exactly opposite directions.

....

....

....
(2 marks)

2.3   Assuming the antineutrinos were incident across the entire face of the tank (line 16-18), estimate the
ratio of detected antineutrino interactions per second to the number of incident antineutrinos per second.
Using your result, comment on the likelihood of neutrinos undergoing particle interactions.

ratio = ...

....

....
(3 marks)

3   **Figure 3** shows a diagram of a set of electronic weighing scales.

Figure 3

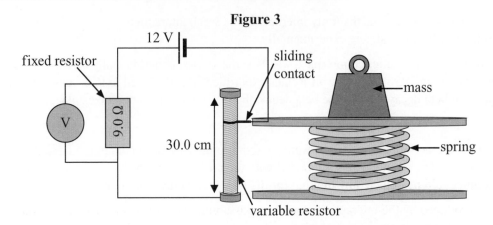

The circuit includes a variable resistor, the resistance of which is directly proportional to the height of its sliding contact. When no weight is applied to the weighing scales, the contact rests at the top of the variable resistor. As a result, the variable resistor is at its maximum resistance and the voltmeter reads 4.5 V. The voltage supply's internal resistance is negligible.

3.1 Calculate the variable resistor's maximum resistance.

resistance = ... Ω
(2 marks)

3.2 When a mass of 1.5 kg is placed on the weighing scales, the spring compresses, moving the contact downwards and increasing the reading on the voltmeter to 5.4 V.
Determine the value of the spring's spring constant.

spring constant = ... Nm^{-1}
(4 marks)

When doing calculation questions, it can really help to write down the variables you know and what you want to find out — that way it'll be easier to work out what equations you need. Remember, a question could get you to draw on a couple of entirely different topics, so don't just think about the equations in a single topic.

Score

18

Mixed Questions — 3

For each of questions 1-4, give your answer by ticking the appropriate box.

1 Which of the following describes Charles' law?

   A   The absolute temperature and volume of a gas are directly proportional at a constant pressure. ☐

   B   The absolute temperature and pressure of a gas are inversely proportional at a constant volume. ☐

   C   The pressure and volume of a gas are inversely proportional at a constant temperature. ☐

   D   The pressure and absolute temperature of a gas are directly proportional at a constant volume. ☐

(1 mark)

2 An electron enters a magnetic field, with a velocity, v, perpendicular to the field. The field has a magnetic flux density of 0.015 T. The electron experiences a force of 4.8×10^{-15} N due to the field. What is the magnitude of v?

   A 5.0×10^{-7} ms^{-1} ☐

   B 2.2×10^{-3} ms^{-1} ☐

   C 1.4×10^{3} ms^{-1} ☐

   D 2.0×10^{6} ms^{-1} ☐

(1 mark)

3 A 2200 μF capacitor stores 0.0352 C of charge. The distance between the capacitor's plates is 0.50 mm. What is the electric field strength between the capacitor plates?

   A 8.0×10^{-3} Vm^{-1} ☐

   B   0.15 Vm^{-1} ☐

   C   6.5 Vm^{-1} ☐

   D   32 000 Vm^{-1} ☐

(1 mark)

4 1506 J of energy is supplied to a 14.5 g sample of helium gas in a sealed container. The initial temperature of the gas was 275.0 K. The specific heat capacity of helium gas is 3157 Jkg^{-1}K^{-1}, and the mass of a helium atom is 4.00 u. What is the average kinetic energy of a helium atom in the sample after it is heated?

   A 1.2×10^{-20} J ☐

   B 6.4×10^{-21} J ☐

   C 4.2×10^{-21} J ☐

   D 5.7×10^{-21} J ☐

(1 mark)

5   A climber takes a flask containing 510 g of hot tea with her as she hikes up a mountain.

5.1   **Figure 1** shows the shape of Earth's surface in the area around the mountain.
On **Figure 1**, draw field lines to show the gravitational field, and draw and label one equipotential.

Figure 1

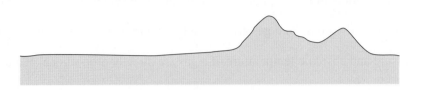

(1 mark)

The climber drinks some of the tea on the way up the mountain.
When she reaches the top, the temperature of the remaining tea has dropped to 6.0 °C.
The climber uses a portable gas stove to heat the remaining tea up again. 140 kJ of energy is supplied
by the stove to the tea to raise its temperature to its boiling point of 100.0 °C. 22 kJ of this energy is
transferred to the surroundings as heat. The tea has a specific heat capacity of 4200 Jkg^{-1}K^{-1}.

5.2   Calculate the mass of tea consumed by the climber on the way up the mountain.

mass = ... g

(2 marks)

The climber uses an altimeter to measure her altitude. **Figure 2** is a diagram showing the inner workings
of the altimeter. The capsule is a sealed container that contains a fixed amount of air and is able to expand
vertically. The top of the capsule is fixed, and the bottom of the capsule is connected to a mechanism that
controls the dial on the altimeter face. The lower the base of the capsule, the higher the reading on the dial.

Figure 2

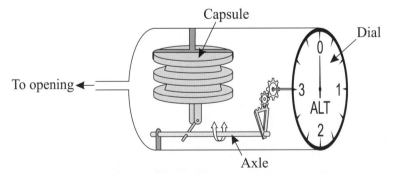

5.3   Air pressure decreases with altitude. Briefly explain how this enables an altimeter to display
an increase in altitude.

....

....

....

....

(2 marks)

6   **Figure 3** shows the inner workings of a torch that can be charged by shaking it back and forth.
A coil is fixed in the centre of the torch barrel. When a person shakes the torch,
the permanent magnet moves up and down the length of the barrel and through the coil.

Figure 3

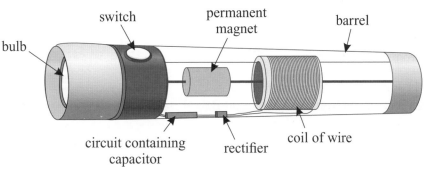

6.1   Suggest and explain **one** way in which the function of the torch would be affected if the coil
was instead directly connected to the bulb.

....

....

(1 mark)

6.2   A student using the torch notices that when they turn the torch so that the magnet falls through the coil,
it takes slightly longer to reach the bottom of the torch barrel than predicted for an object in free-fall.
Assuming air resistance and friction are negligible, explain why the magnet falls slower than predicted.

....

....

....

....

(2 marks)

The LED bulb in the torch will only light up while the potential difference across it is greater than 0.25 V.
The LED bulb can be assumed to have a constant resistance while it is lit.

6.3   The capacitor is fully charged to a potential difference of 2.2 V. The torch is immediately
switched on, causing the capacitor to discharge through the LED bulb. It takes
1.5 minutes for the potential difference across the capacitor to halve. Calculate the time
it will take for the LED bulb to go out after the torch has been switched on.

time = ... s

(2 marks)

Score

14

Mixed Questions — 4

Figure 1

1 Artificial satellites are man-made objects that must operate in space for long periods of time.

The satellite shown in **Figure 1** is orbiting Earth, and is moved from orbit A to orbit B.

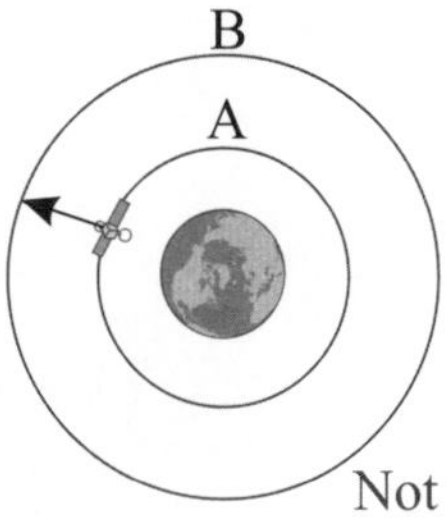

Not to scale

1.1 Explain why the linear speed of the satellite decreases when it is moved from orbit A to orbit B.

....

....

....

....

(2 marks)

1.2 When the satellite is in orbit B, it is at a gravitational potential of -8.94×10^6 Jkg^{-1} and completes one orbit in 26 hours. The satellite has a mass of 142 kg. Calculate the centripetal force acting on the satellite while it is in orbit B.

force = ... N

(3 marks)

Plutonium-238 ($^{238}_{94}$Pu) is an alpha-emitter that is used in many satellites as an energy source. It has a decay constant of 2.51×10^{-10} s^{-1} and each decay releases 5.593 MeV of energy.

1.3 Calculate the time it would take for 50.0 mg of plutonium-238 to release 250 kJ of energy.

time taken = ... s

(3 marks)

2 Fairground rides rely on the laws of physics to entertain people while keeping them safe.

2.1 **Figure 2** shows a ride in which a boat-shaped carriage swings back and forth about a pivot. The distance from the pivot to the centre of mass of the carriage is 22 m. The maximum displacement of the centre of mass from its rest position is 13 m. Estimate the maximum linear speed of the carriage.

Figure 2

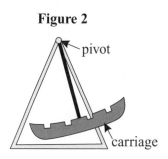

maximum speed = ... ms^{-1}

(3 marks)

Figure 3 shows a different ride that consists of a circular chamber which is rotated at high speeds. The frictional force, F_f, the weight of the rider, W, and the normal force, F_n, are labelled.

Riders enter the chamber and stand against the wall while the chamber is stationary. The chamber is then rotated with an increasing frequency. Eventually the floor moves downwards, leaving riders 'stuck' to the wall instead of falling to the ground.

The frictional force prevents a body from sliding up to a maximum value of:

$$F_f = \mu F_n$$

where μ is a constant called the coefficient of friction and F_n is the normal force.

Figure 3

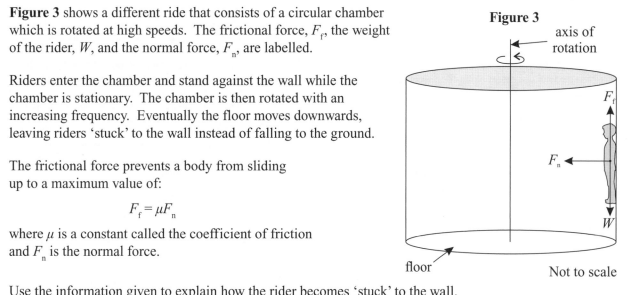

Not to scale

2.2 Use the information given to explain how the rider becomes 'stuck' to the wall.

....

....

....

....

....

....

....

....

....

(6 marks)

Diagrams are often provided with questions, but not always. It's tempting to save time by skipping it, but drawing a diagram can help to clarify what's going on. For example, it could help you think carefully about the directions in which different forces are acting on an object.

Score

17

Answers

Section One — Particles

Pages 3-6: Particles — 1

1   B *[1 mark]*
*Protons and neutrons are both hadrons and baryons. The nucleon number is
215, so there are 215 hadrons and 215 baryons in the nucleus.*

2   A *[1 mark]*
*Baryon number is not conserved in B, lepton number is not conserved in C and
charge is not conserved in D.*

3   D *[1 mark]*
*An up quark turns into a down quark in beta-plus decay and a W+ boson is
the exchange particle.*

4   D *[1 mark]*
*An antineutron has the same quark composition as a neutron, but with
antiparticles instead of particles.*

5.1   Neutron *[1 mark]*

5.2   Proton rest energy = 938.257 MeV
Number of protons in nucleus = 118
The total rest energy of 118 protons is:
$118 \times 938.257 = 110\ 714.326$ MeV
Neutron rest energy = 939.551 MeV
Number of neutrons in nucleus = 294 – 118 = 176
The total rest energy of 176 neutrons is:
$176 \times 939.551 = 165\ 360.976$ MeV
So the total rest energy of the constituent particles in an
oganesson-294 nucleus is:
$110\ 714.326 + 165\ 360.976 = 276\ 075.302$ MeV
So the nuclear binding energy of oganesson-294 is:
$276\ 075.302 – 274\ 059 = 2016.302$ MeV
= 2016 MeV (to nearest MeV)
*[3 marks for correct answer, otherwise 1 mark for calculating
the total rest energy of the protons and 1 mark for calculating
the total rest energy of the neutrons.]*

5.3 $^{294}_{118}\text{Og} \rightarrow\ ^{290}_{116}\text{Lv} +\ ^{4}_{2}\alpha$
[2 marks for all correct, otherwise 1 mark for either $^{290}_{116}Lv$ or $^{4}_{2}\alpha$]
*The nucleon number decreases by 4 and the proton number of the nucleus
decreases by 2.*

5.4   1 eV = 1.6×10^{-19} J
1 MeV = $(1.6 \times 10^{-19}) \times 10^{6} = 1.6 \times 10^{-13}$ J
Energy from one decay = $11.65 \times 1.6 \times 10^{-13} = 1.864 \times 10^{-12}$ J
1 kJ = 1000 J. Divide this by the energy from one decay to
calculate the amount of decays:
$1000 \div (1.864 \times 10^{-12}) = 5.36... \times 10^{14}$
So **5.4×10^{14} decays** are needed.
*[2 marks for correct answer, otherwise 1 mark for calculating
the energy produced by one decay correctly]*

6.1   Charge *[1 mark]*

6.2   Neutron *[1 mark]*. To conserve baryon number *[1 mark]*.

6.3   Muon neutrino/ν_μ *[1 mark]*. To conserve lepton number
[1 mark].

6.4   A neutron has a higher rest energy than a proton, so energy must
be supplied to a proton to turn it into a neutron *[1 mark]*.

6.5   Strangeness must be conserved in strong interactions *[1 mark]*.
The overall strangeness of 0 is conserved by creating one particle
with a strangeness of 1 and one particle with a strangeness of –1
[1 mark].

6.6   The conservation laws of baryon number and lepton number
mean that matter and antimatter must be created and destroyed in
equal amounts *[1 mark]*. Since there appears to be more matter
than antimatter, it implies that these conservation laws were not
followed during the formation of the universe *[1 mark]*.

7.1   Proton *[1 mark]* uud / up up down *[1 mark]*

7.2   Electron, muon and neutrino *[1 mark]*
*Only hadrons can experience the strong nuclear force and none of these
particles are hadrons.*

7.3   Exchange particles are particles that are transferred between two
particles when a force acts between them. *[1 mark]*

7.4   Positrons have the same mass and size of charge as electrons,
[1 mark] but have a positive charge instead of the electron's
negative charge *[1 mark]*.

7.5   There seemed to be a violation of the conservation of energy in
beta-minus decay. The missing energy was carried by (at that
time undetected) neutrinos *[1 mark]*.

Pages 7-10: Particles — 2

1.1   Beta plus / β^+ *[1 mark]*

1.2 $e^+ + e^- \rightarrow 2\gamma$ *[1 mark]*

1.3 $E_{min} = hf_{min} = 6.63 \times 10^{-34} \times 1.24 \times 10^{20}$
    $= \textbf{8.22} \times \textbf{10}^{-14}$ **J (to 3 s.f.)**
[2 marks for correct answer, 1 mark for correct substitution]

1.4   One photon does not have enough energy, because each photon
has an energy equal to only half the total rest energy of the
electron and positron together *[1 mark]*.

1.5   It is an electron capture process *[1 mark]*. One proton in the
nucleus captures an electron and turns into a neutron, emitting an
electron neutrino in the process *[1 mark]*.

1.6   Photons have no charge, so when particles are created from
photons the total charge of the created particles needs to be
equal to zero *[1 mark]*. A positron has a positive charge and
an electron has an equal negative charge, so they must both be
created at the same time for the total charge to be zero *[1 mark]*.

2.1   Mesons are particles containing a quark and an antiquark
[1 mark].

2.2   strange, up, up / suu *[1 mark]*. The total strangeness before
the interaction is 0. Strangeness is conserved, so the total
strangeness after the interaction must also be 0. There is an
antistrange quark in K+, so there must be one strange quark in
Σ^+ *[1 mark]*. The charge of the Σ^+ particle must be equal to 1,
and the strange quark has a charge of $-\frac{1}{3}$. The other two quarks
must therefore have a total charge of $+\frac{4}{3}$. This is only possible if
the two remaining quarks are up quarks, which have a charge of
$+\frac{2}{3}$ each *[1 mark]*.

2.3 π^0 *[1 mark]*

2.4 $\bar{s} \rightarrow \bar{u} + \mu^+ + \nu_\mu$ *[1 mark]*

2.5   Quarks have a baryon number of $+\frac{1}{3}$, antiquarks have a baryon
number of $-\frac{1}{3}$.
Baryon number before decay = $\frac{1}{3} + (-\frac{1}{3}) = 0$
Baryon number after decay = $\frac{1}{3} + (-\frac{1}{3}) + \frac{1}{3} + (-\frac{1}{3}) = 0$
[1 mark]

2.6   The weak interaction *[1 mark]*. Strangeness is not conserved in
the interaction, and the weak interaction is the only one in which
strangeness is not always conserved/K+ is a strange particle so it
must decay through the weak interaction *[1 mark]*.

3.1   Zero rest mass and zero charge *[1 mark]*

3.2   650 nm = 650×10^{-9} m. Calculate the energy of each photon:
$E = \dfrac{hc}{\lambda} = \dfrac{(6.63 \times 10^{-34}) \times (3.00 \times 10^{8})}{650 \times 10^{-9}} = 3.06 \times 10^{-19}$ J
200 mJ = 200×10^{-3} J
Number of photons produced each second
= energy delivered each second ÷ energy of one photon
= $(200 \times 10^{-3}) \div (3.06 \times 10^{-19})$
= $6.53... \times 10^{17} = \textbf{6.5} \times \textbf{10}^{17}$ **(to 2 s.f.)**
*[3 marks for correct answer, otherwise 1 mark for correct
substitution and 1 mark for correct calculation of E]*

3.3   E.g. Draw a large triangle between two points along the line of
best fit:

The Planck constant is equal to the gradient:

h = gradient = change in y ÷ change in x

$$= \frac{(5.2 \times 10^{-19}) - (2.8 \times 10^{-19})}{(7.8 \times 10^{14}) - (4.4 \times 10^{14})}$$

$$= 7.05... \times 10^{-34} = \textbf{7.1} \times \textbf{10}^{-34} \textbf{ Js (to 2 s.f.)}$$

The actual value of the Planck constant is 6.63×10^{-34} Js. 10% of this is 0.663×10^{-34} s. Add the two together to get the upper bound:

$(6.63 \times 10^{-34}) + (0.663 \times 10^{-34}) = 7.293 \times 10^{-34}$ Js

The scientist's value for the Planck constant is less than this, so her value is within 10% of the accepted value.

[1 mark for reading values from the graph correctly, 1 mark for correctly calculating the Planck constant from the graph, 1 mark for correctly calculating that the answer is within 10% of the accepted value]

4.1 X and Z. They have the same number of protons but a different number of neutrons *[1 mark]*.

4.2 mass of nucleus = mass of protons + mass of neutrons

$$= (3 \times 1.673 \times 10^{-27}) + (4 \times 1.675 \times 10^{-27})$$

$$= 1.1719 \times 10^{-26} \text{ kg}$$

charge of nucleus = 3 × charge of one proton

$$= 3 \times 1.60 \times 10^{-19} = 4.8 \times 10^{-19} \text{ C}$$

specific charge = charge ÷ mass

$$= (4.8 \times 10^{-19}) \div (1.1719 \times 10^{-26})$$

$$= 4.095... \times 10^{7} \text{ Ckg}^{-1}$$

$$= \textbf{4.10} \times \textbf{10}^{7} \textbf{ Ckg}^{-1} \textbf{ (to 3 s.f.)}$$

[3 marks for correct answer with unit, otherwise 1 mark for correctly calculating the mass of the nucleus and 1 mark for calculating the charge of the nucleus]

4.3 How to grade your answer:

Level 0: There is no relevant information. *[No marks]*

Level 1: It is mentioned that the strong force is attractive, and that the electromagnetic force between protons is repulsive, but there is little detail. Several errors with grammar, spelling and punctuation and there are problems with legibility. Answer lacks structure and information. *[1-2 marks]*

Level 2: There is a brief description of the attractive nature of the strong force on nucleons and how the strong force varies with distance. The repulsive electromagnetic force acting between protons is described. The ranges of the two forces are briefly compared. Only a few errors with grammar, spelling and punctuation. Answer has some structure and some problems with legibility. *[3-4 marks]*

Level 3: It is explained that the attractive strong force acts between all nucleons, whereas the repulsive electromagnetic force only acts between protons. The ranges of the two forces are compared, and the consequences of this on the stability of the nucleus are explained. Grammar, spelling and punctuation are used accurately and there is no problem with legibility. Answer is informative and well-structured. *[5-6 marks]*

Indicative content:

The strong force acts between nucleons.

Between 0.5 and 3 fm the force is attractive, so it holds the nucleons together.

Below 0.5 fm the strong force is repulsive, which stops the nucleons from moving closer towards each other.

The electromagnetic force only acts between protons because neutrons are not charged.

Protons are all positively charged, so the electromagnetic force causes them to repel each other.

The strong force between nucleons must be stronger than the electromagnetic repulsion between protons in order for the nucleus to remain stable.

In large nuclei, there is a large distance between many nucleons.

Beyond around 3 fm the strong force drops to zero.

This means that the strong force between nucleons with a large distance between them is very weak.

The electromagnetic force has a longer range, so the repulsion between protons is still relatively strong in large nuclei.

The greater the ratio of neutrons to protons in the nucleus, the smaller the repulsive electromagnetic force between the protons as they are further apart.

So for large nuclei to remain stable, they must have a greater number of neutrons than protons.

Pages 11-14: Particles — 3

1.1

Type of beta decay	Daughter nucleus	Particle emitted
Beta-minus	$^{40}_{20}\text{Ca}$	$^{0}_{-1}\text{e}$

[1 mark for correct daughter nucleus, 1 mark for correct particle emitted]

1.2 Antineutrino/$\overline{\nu}$ (or electron antineutrino, $\overline{\nu}_e$) *[1 mark]*

1.3 A down quark is changed into an up quark *[1 mark]* by the weak interaction *[1 mark]*.

1.4 The exchange particle in electromagnetic interactions is the virtual photon *[1 mark]*. Virtual photons are uncharged whilst the W$^-$ bosons have a negative charge *[1 mark]*. Virtual photons are massless whilst W$^-$ bosons have a large mass *[1 mark]*.

1.5 $^{40}_{18}Ar$ / argon-40 *[1 mark]*

1.6

[1 mark for correct particles drawn, 1 mark for straight lines and arrows drawn correctly, 1 mark for W$^+$ boson drawn coming from proton]

2.1 They will annihilate *[1 mark]*. Two photons will be produced *[1 mark]*.

2.2 The ν_e is emitted to conserve the lepton number for electrons, which is 0 on both sides of the equation *[1 mark]*. If a ν_μ was emitted instead, the lepton number for electrons on the right-hand side would be –1 and the lepton number for muons would be +1 *[1 mark]*.

2.3 Two $^1_1$H particles are used in equation 1.

One additional $^1_1$H particle is used in equation 2.

Equation 1 and equation 2 must occur twice in order to produce the two $^3_2$He nuclei needed in equation 3.

No $^1_1$H particles are used in equation 3, so the number of particles used is $2 \times (2 + 1) = 6$

Two $^1_1$H particles are produced in equation 3, so the net amount of particles required is $6 - 2 = 4$ *[1 mark]*

2.4 Protons are positively charged, so the electromagnetic force would cause the two protons in the diproton to repel each other, so the diproton would be unstable *[1 mark]*.

When one proton decays into an uncharged neutron, there will be no electromagnetic force acting between them and the nucleus will become more stable *[1 mark]*.

3.1 In beta plus decay, a proton changes into a neutron.

After each decay, the nucleon number remains the same but the charge decreases by 1. So the charge of the original nuclide is:

$25 + 1 + 1 = \textbf{27}$

And the nucleon number is **53**.

[1 mark for knowing that $^{53}_{25}Mn$ has a relative charge of 25, 1 mark for correct charge, 1 mark for correct nucleon number]

3.2 The quark composition of a neutron is up, down, down (udd).

Up quarks have a charge of $+\frac{2}{3}$ and down quarks have a charge of $-\frac{1}{3}$. So the total charge of a neutron is:

$+\frac{2}{3} + (-\frac{1}{3}) + (-\frac{1}{3}) = 0$

[1 mark for stating the quark composition of a neutron, 1 mark for calculating the total charge of a neutron correctly]

3.3

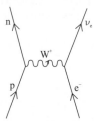

[1 mark for correct particles drawn, 1 mark for straight lines and arrows drawn correctly, 1 mark for W+ boson drawn coming from proton]

4.1 Alpha particles have a relatively short range *[1 mark]*

4.2 Momentum and energy are conserved in particle interactions *[1 mark]*. The total momentum and energy of the particles produced will be equal to the total momentum and energy of the gamma ray *[1 mark]*.

4.3 Energy is conserved, so:
energy after pair production
= rest energy of particles + kinetic energy of particles
= (2 × 0.510999) + (2 × 0.64) = 2.301998 MeV
energy before pair production = energy after pair production
So the energy of the gamma ray is 2.301998 MeV
1 eV = 1.60 × 10⁻¹⁹ J
So 2.301998 MeV = 2.301998 × 10⁶ × (1.60 × 10⁻¹⁹)
= 3.6831968 × 10⁻¹³ J

Rearrange $E = \frac{hc}{\lambda}$ for λ:
$$\lambda = \frac{hc}{E} = \frac{(6.63 \times 10^{-34}) \times (3.00 \times 10^{8})}{3.6831968 \times 10^{-13}}$$
= 5.40... × 10⁻¹³ m = **5.4 × 10⁻¹³ m (to 2 s.f.)**
[3 marks for correct answer, otherwise 1 mark for calculating the total energy after pair production and 1 mark for converting the energy of the gamma ray to J]

4.4 Gamma particles have no charge, so they will pass into the telescope and produce an electron and a positron without triggering the shield *[1 mark]*. If an electron and a positron pass into the telescope instead, the shield will be triggered to verify that they were not created inside the telescope by a gamma ray *[1 mark]*.

4.5 E.g. It cannot detect gamma rays with an energy less than 1.02 MeV/the rest energy of an electron and a positron *[1 mark]*.

Section Two — Electromagnetic Radiation and Quantum Phenomena

Pages 15-17: Electromagnetic Radiation and Quantum Phenomena — 1

1 B *[1 mark]*

2 C *[1 mark]*
The energy of the incident photon will be equal to the sum of the energies of the emitted photons, which can be found using E = hf.
$E_{incident} = h(f_1 + f_2)$
= 6.63 × 10⁻³⁴(1.51 × 10¹⁴ + 2.96 × 10¹⁵) = 2.06 × 10⁻¹⁸ J (to 3 s.f.)

3 A *[1 mark]*
First, you need to convert the work function into joules.
4.32 eV = 4.32 × 1.60 × 10⁻¹⁹ J = 6.912 × 10⁻¹⁹ J
Now you can use the equation $f_{threshold} = \phi \div h$ to find threshold frequency.
$f_{threshold}$ = (6.912 × 10⁻¹⁹) ÷ (6.63 × 10⁻³⁴) = 1.04 × 10¹⁵ Hz (to 3 s.f.)

4 D *[1 mark]*
$E = \frac{1}{2}mv^2$ and $\lambda = h \div (mv)$. Rearrange the de Broglie wavelength equation to make v the subject: $v = h \div (m\lambda)$. Substitute this into the kinetic energy equation:
$E = \frac{h^2}{2m\lambda^2}$. From this equation we see that doubling λ will have the effect of decreasing E by a factor of $2^2 = 4$.

5.1 E.g. below this threshold frequency photon energy (hf) is less than the metal's work function / Below this frequency the photon's energy is less than that required to break the electron's bonds and release it from the metal *[1 mark]*.

5.2 Photoelectrons are likely to lose energy in collisions as they leave the metal *[1 mark]*.

5.3 3.6 eV *[1 mark, allow 3.5-3.7 eV]*
The work function can be found by extending the line of best fit and seeing where it crosses the y-axis.

5.4 Convert work function into joules:
ϕ = 3.6 × 1.60 × 10⁻¹⁹ J = 5.76 × 10⁻¹⁹ J
Calculate $E_{k\,(max)}$:
$hf = \phi + E_{k\,(max)}$
$E_{k\,(max)} = hf - \phi$ = 6.63 × 10⁻³⁴ × 9.3 × 10¹⁴ − 5.76 × 10⁻¹⁹
= 4.059 × 10⁻²⁰ J
Now calculate v_{max}:
$E_{k\,(max)} = \frac{1}{2}m_e v_{max}^2$
$$v_{max} = \sqrt{\frac{2E_{k\,(max)}}{m_e}} = \sqrt{\frac{2 \times 4.059 \times 10^{-20}}{9.11 \times 10^{-31}}}$$
= 2.98... × 10⁵ ms⁻¹ = **3.0 × 10⁵ ms⁻¹ (to 2 s.f.)**
[2 marks for correct answer, otherwise 1 mark for correctly calculating $E_{k\,(max)}$]

5.5 $eV_s = E_k$, so $V_s = E_k \div e$ = (4.059 × 10⁻²⁰) ÷ (1.60 × 10⁻¹⁹)
= **0.253... V = 0.25 V (to 2 s.f.)** *[1 mark]*

If all your working is correct, but your answer is wrong because you've used a wrong answer from a previous question part, you may give yourself the marks for this question.

5.6 There will be no change *[1 mark]*.

6.1 How to grade your answer:
Level 0: There is no relevant information. *[No marks]*
Level 1: Answer provides a brief description of the stages of photon emission and absorption, but there is little detail. There is some attempt at explaining how optical brightener emits visible light when exposed to UV, though it lacks clarity. Several errors with grammar, spelling, punctuation and legibility. Answer lacks structure. *[1-2 marks]*
Level 2: Answer provides a description of most of the stages of photon emission and absorption as well as a partial explanation of how optical brightener emits visible light when exposed to UV. Only a few errors with grammar, spelling, punctuation and legibility. Answer has some structure. *[3-4 marks]*
Level 3: Answer provides a detailed and complete description of both photon emission and absorption as well as a clear explanation of how optical brightener emits visible light when exposed to UV. Grammar, spelling and punctuation are used accurately and there is no problem with legibility. The answer is structured in a way that makes it easy to follow. *[5-6 marks]*

Here are some points your answer may include:
Electrons in an atom or molecule can only exist at specific, discrete energy levels.
An electron can absorb a photon if the photon's energy is equal to the energy gap between two levels. This results in the excitation of the electron from the lower energy level to the higher energy level.
An excited electron can fall to a lower energy level by emitting a photon with energy equal to the difference between the two energy levels.
The molecule in the detergent absorbs a photon of ultra-violet light which has more energy than visible light, so the electron is excited to a high energy level.
The electron then returns to its ground state via two or more smaller transitions (a cascade). At each transition the electron emits a photon of visible light. The sum of the energies of the emitted photons equals the energy of the absorbed photon.

6.2 A high voltage is used to accelerate a small number of free electrons through the tube *[1 mark]*. These free electrons collide with atoms of the gas that fills the tube, resulting in some of the atoms becoming ionised or excited *[1 mark]*. As the excited atoms return to their ground state they emit a photon of UV light *[1 mark]*.

Pages 18-19: Electromagnetic Radiation and Quantum Phenomena — 2

1.1 Line emission spectra show that hot gases only emit photons of certain frequencies, and therefore energies *[1 mark]*. This suggests electrons in the atoms of the gas can only ever gain or lose energy in increments equal to these certain photon energies, which can be explained if they are moving between fixed energy levels *[1 mark]*.

1.2 Calculate photon energy:
$E = hf = 6.63 \times 10^{-34} \times 4.6 \times 10^{14} = 3.0498 \times 10^{-19}$ J
Convert to eV:
$(3.0498 \times 10^{-19}) \div (1.60 \times 10^{-19}) = 1.906... \text{ eV} = 1.9$ eV (to 2 s.f.)
This is the same energy as that required to move an electron to move from energy level 2 to 3, since $-1.5 - (-3.4) = 1.9$ eV

[2 marks for correct answer, otherwise 1 mark for correctly calculating photon energy in eV]

1.3 1.9 eV is the energy required to excite an electron from $n = 2$ to $n = 3$ and 10.2 eV is the energy required to excite an electron from $n = 1$ to $n = 2$ ($-3.4 - -13.6 = 10.2$) *[1 mark]*. Since the 1.9 eV radiation is associated with the transition from energy level 2 to 3, it can only be absorbed by an electron that is already excited to energy level 2 *[1 mark]*. And since the 10.2 eV radiation is associated with the transition from energy level 1 to 2, it will lead to more electrons occupying the 2nd energy level, increasing the rate at which 1.9 eV radiation is absorbed *[1 mark]*.

2.1 If light were a wave it would deliver a continuous stream of energy, capable of causing photoelectric emission regardless of frequency *[1 mark]*. However, no photoelectrons are emitted unless the frequency of the light incident on the surface exceeds a certain threshold frequency *[1 mark]*. Also, if light were a wave, delivering a continuous stream of energy, you would expect an increase in the light's intensity to lead to photoelectrons being emitted with greater K.E. *[1 mark]*. However, the maximum kinetic energy of the emitted electrons does not increase as the intensity of the light incident on the surface increases *[1 mark]*.

2.2 Much larger objects will have a much smaller de Broglie wavelength *[1 mark]*. No gaps exist that are small enough to match this wavelength and allow diffraction to occur *[1 mark]*.

2.3 Calculate the energy gained by a single electron:
$E = eV = 1.60 \times 10^{-19} \times 75 = 1.2 \times 10^{-17}$ J
Calculate the speed of an electron:
$E = \frac{1}{2}mv^2$
$v = \sqrt{\dfrac{2E}{m}} = \sqrt{\dfrac{2 \times 1.2 \times 10^{-17}}{9.11 \times 10^{-31}}} = 5.13... \times 10^6$ ms^{-1}
Calculate the de Broglie wavelength of an electron:
$\lambda = h \div (mv) = 6.63 \times 10^{-34} \div (9.11 \times 10^{-31} \times 5.13... \times 10^6)$
$= 1.41... \times 10^{-10}$ m
separation between adjacent carbon atoms
$\approx$ de Broglie wavelength of a diffracting electron
separation between adjacent carbon atoms
$\approx \mathbf{1.41... \times 10^{-10}}$ **m** $\approx \mathbf{1.4 \times 10^{-10}}$ **m (to 2 s.f.)**
[4 marks for correct answer, otherwise 1 mark for correctly calculating electron energy, 1 mark for correctly calculating electron velocity and 1 mark for correctly calculating de Broglie wavelength]

Section Three — Waves

Pages 20-23: Waves — 1

1 B *[1 mark]*

2 B *[1 mark]*
Use the equation d sin θ = nλ.
$d = (n\lambda) \div \sin\theta = (1 \times 750 \times 10^{-9}) \div \sin 30° = 1.5 \times 10^{-6}$ m

3 C *[1 mark]*
Since there are 2π radians in a full wave cycle, π ÷ 6 is only one twelfth of a full cycle. The full wavelength is given by 12 × 0.140 = 1.68 m. The period of a wave is given by T = 1 ÷ f. Also, rearranging c = f λ gives 1 ÷ f = λ ÷ c. So T = λ ÷ c = 1.68 ÷ 20.0 = 0.084 s.

4 C *[1 mark]*
Frequency is related to tension by the equation $f = \frac{1}{2l}\sqrt{\frac{T}{\mu}}$.
So, f is proportional to the square root of T.
Increasing T by 40% is equivalent to multiplying it by 1.4, which leads to frequency increasing by a factor of √1.4. √1.4 × 12.0 = 14.2 Hz to 3 s.f.

5.1 A stationary wave is the superposition of two progressive waves with the same frequency *[1 mark]*, that are moving in opposite directions *[1 mark]*.

5.2 E.g. measure and record the length of the string, l. Use the signal generator to gradually adjust the frequency of vibration until the first harmonic can be seen then record this frequency. Adjust l and repeat this process *[1 mark]*.

5.3 Calculate mass per unit length:
$\mu = m \div l = 2.0 \div 0.80 = 2.5$ gm^{-1}
Since we divide m by l to find μ, the percentage uncertainty in μ can be found by adding the percentage uncertainties in m and l.
percentage uncertainty in $m = (0.10 \div 2.0) \times 100 = 5\%$
percentage uncertainty in $l = (0.020 \div 0.80) \times 100 = 2.5\%$
So the percentage uncertainty in $\mu = 5 + 2.5 = 7.5\%$
absolute uncertainty in $\mu = 0.075 \times 2.5 = 0.1875$ gm^{-1}
$= 0.19$ gm^{-1} (to 2 s.f.)
$\boldsymbol{\mu = 2.5 \pm 0.19}$ **gm**$^{-1}$ **(to 2 s.f.)**
[3 marks for correct answer, otherwise 1 mark for correctly calculating μ and 1 mark for correctly calculating the % uncertainty in μ]

5.4 E.g. tension in the string *[1 mark]*.

6.1 A systematic error *[1 mark]*. It will lead to all measurements of the stationary waves' lengths being too small by a fixed amount *[1 mark]*.

6.2

[1 mark]
Sound waves are longitudinal, so vibrations will be parallel to the direction of the wave.

6.3

[2 marks for sketching a 0.75λ stationary wave and correctly labelling its nodes and anti-nodes, otherwise 1 mark for sketching a 0.75λ stationary wave]
A standing wave 0.75λ long will ensure a node at one end of the tube and an antinode at the other.

6.4 Calculate one wavelength:
$0.75\lambda = 63.75$
$\lambda = 63.75 \div 0.75 = 85$ cm
The third wave to form in the air column will be 1.25λ long.
$1.25\lambda = 1.25 \times 0.85 = \mathbf{1.06}$ **m (to 3 s.f.)**
[2 marks, otherwise 1 mark for correctly calculating the wavelength]
A standing wave 1.25λ long will mean there's a node at one end of the tube and an antinode at the other.

6.5 $c = f\lambda = 400 \times 0.85 = \mathbf{340}$ **ms**$^{-1}$ *[1 mark]*

6.6 The progressive waves that form a stationary wave travel and transmit energy in opposite directions, so they cancel out, meaning there is no net energy transfer *[1 mark]*.

Pages 24-26: Waves — 2

1.1 The superposition is where two waves cross each other and interfere *[1 mark]*. The resultant displacement at any point is equal to the vector sum of the individual displacements *[1 mark]*.

1.2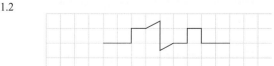

[2 marks — 1 mark for correct profile and 1 mark for correct position]

1.3 E.g.

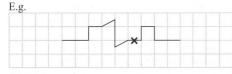

[1 mark]

You'd get a mark for placing a cross anywhere where the magnitude of the resultant displacement of the wave has decreased.

1.4 The piano tuner should strike the piano string and the tuning fork at the same time, then adjust the pitch of the piano string until the beat pattern can no longer be heard *[1 mark]*.

2.1 For constructive interference at the nth order maximum, the path difference between light from adjacent slits must be $n\lambda$.

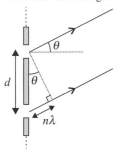

Using trigonometry on the right-angled triangle in the construction above, we find that the path difference between adjacent slits is also equal to $d \sin \theta$.

So, at the nth order maximum, $d \sin \theta = n\lambda$

[3 marks for correct derivation, otherwise 1 mark for correct construction and 1 mark for identifying that path difference must equal $n\lambda$]

2.2 Calculate slit separation:
$d = (1 \times 10^{-3}) \div 500 = 2.0 \times 10^{-6}$ m
Calculate wavelength using $d \sin \theta = n\lambda$
$\lambda = (d \sin \theta) \div n = (2.0 \times 10^{-6} \times \sin 24.8°) \div 2$
$= 4.194... \times 10^{-7}$ m $= 419.4...$ nm $= \mathbf{420}$ **nm (2 s.f.)**

[2 marks for correct answer, otherwise 1 mark for correctly calculating the slit separation]

2.3 The zero order maximum will be white *[1 mark]*. Higher order maxima will show all the colours of the visible spectrum, starting at violet on the side closest to the zero order maximum *[1 mark]*.

3.1 Polarisation is the process of making a wave oscillate in only one direction/plane *[1 mark]*.

3.2 Longitudinal waves can't be polarised as they only oscillate in a single direction (parallel to their direction of travel) *[1 mark]*. Transverse waves are capable of oscillating in any direction perpendicular to their direction of travel, so it is possible to polarise a transverse wave and make it only oscillate in one direction *[1 mark]*.

3.3 E.g. initially, no light can get through both lenses, as their transmission axes are perpendicular to each other *[1 mark]*. As the lens is rotated, an increasing amount of light may pass through. At 90° the transmission axes align and the amount of light passing through the lenses is at a maximum *[1 mark]*.

3.4 E.g. television signals are polarised *[1 mark]*.

Pages 27-30: Waves — 3

1.1 Light of a single wavelength *[1 mark]*

1.2 Light that originates from a single source will be coherent / will have a constant phase difference *[1 mark]*

1.3 Any two from: e.g. wear laser safety goggles *[1 mark]* / display warning signs *[1 mark]* / don't shine the laser towards a person *[1 mark]* / don't shine the laser towards a reflective surface *[1 mark]*.

1.4 Taking the initial measurement across a larger distance results in a smaller percentage error in the measurement, which leads to a smaller percentage uncertainty in the fringe width value *[1 mark]*.

1.5 $w = (\lambda D) \div s$
$D = (sw) \div \lambda = (1.0 \times 10^{-3} \times 1.1 \times 10^{-3}) \div (510 \times 10^{-9})$
$= \mathbf{2.15... \ m = 2.2 \ m}$ **(to 2 s.f.)** *[1 mark]*

2.1 $\sin \theta_c = n_3 \div n_2 = 1.46 \div 1.49 = 0.979...$
$\theta_c = \sin^{-1} 0.979... = 78.48° = \mathbf{78.5°}$ **(to 3 s.f.)**
[2 marks for correct answer, otherwise 1 mark for correctly calculating $\sin \theta_c$]

2.2 The maximum possible value of i occurs when the ray is incident on the core / cladding boundary at the critical angle.

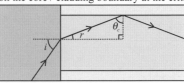

Since r and θ_c are angles in a right-angled triangle:
$r = 90° - \theta_c = 90° - 78.4...° = 11.5...°$
Use Snell's law: $n_1 \sin i = n_2 \sin r$
$\sin i = (n_2 \sin r) \div n_1 = (1.49 \times \sin 11.5...°) \div 1 = 0.297...$
$i = \sin^{-1} 0.297... = 17.3...° = \mathbf{17°}$ **(to 2 s.f.)**

[3 marks for correct answer, otherwise 1 mark for correct use of geometry to find angle of refraction and 1 mark for correctly calculating $\sin i$]

2.3 How to grade your answer:
Level 0: There is no relevant information. *[No marks]*
Level 1: A brief description and explanation of at least one type of signal degradation is given. There are several errors with grammar, spelling, punctuation and legibility. *[1 to 2 marks]*
Level 2: A description of the types of signal degradation is given, with a brief explanation of the causes of some of them. There may be a few errors with grammar, spelling, punctuation and legibility. *[3 to 4 marks]*
Level 3: A clear and well structured description of the types of signal degradation and a thorough explanation of their causes is given. Grammar, spelling and punctuation are used accurately and there is no problem with legibility. *[5 to 6 marks]*

Here are some points your answer may include:
Signals can be degraded by absorption, which is where energy from the wave is absorbed by the optical fibre. This leads to a reduction in the amplitude of the signal.
Signals can also be degraded by dispersion. There are two types of dispersion, modal and material.
Modal dispersion is caused by light rays entering the fibre at different angles, meaning that they take different paths along the fibre. This means that some light rays reach the end of the fibre faster than others.
Material dispersion is caused by different wavelengths of light travelling at different speeds in a material. This leads to some wavelengths of light reaching the end of the fibre faster than others.
Both types of dispersion lead to the signal becoming broader as it travels. This is called pulse broadening.

3.1 Waves that are coherent have the same wavelength and frequency and a fixed phase difference *[1 mark]*.

3.2 π radians / 180° *[1 mark]*
Point A is a minimum of the interference pattern, meaning maximum destructive interference is occurring, requiring a phase difference of π radians (180°).

3.3 Use Figure 3 to calculate fringe spacing:
fringe spacing, w = time taken by sound level meter to move between maxima × speed of the sound level meter
$w = 2.5 \times 0.25 = 0.625$ m
Calculate the sound's wavelength:
$w = (\lambda D) \div s$, so $\lambda = (ws) \div D = (0.625 \times 0.4) \div 10 = 0.025$ m
Calculate the speed of the sound waves:
$f = 13.5$ kHz $= 13\ 500$ Hz
$c = f\lambda = 13\ 500 \times 0.025 = 337.5$ ms^{-1} $= \mathbf{340}$ **ms^{-1} (to 2 s.f.)**
[3 marks for correct answer, otherwise 1 mark for correctly calculating fringe spacing and 1 mark for correctly calculating wavelength]

3.4 As frequency increases, fringe spacing will decrease *[1 mark]*. As the interference pattern contracts a second order maximum will come to occupy the position initially occupied by the first order maximum *[1 mark]*.

You could also have explained this in terms of how the change in frequency affects the wavelength, and how this affects the path difference and position of fringes.

3.5 For the second order maximum to reach the sound level meter, fringe spacing must halve *[1 mark]*.

Young's double slit formula is $w = (\lambda D) \div s$, so $w \propto \lambda$. The wave equation, $c = f\lambda$, shows that $\lambda \propto 1 \div f$.

As a result $w \propto 1 \div f$. So, for fringe spacing to halve, frequency must double to 27 kHz. *[1 mark]*.

This is beyond the upper limit of the sound level meter's range, so the student will not be able to measure the secondary peak in SPL *[1 mark]*.

Pages 31-33: Waves — 4

1.1 $n = c \div c_s$
$c_s = c \div n = (3.00 \times 10^8) \div 1.35 = 2.2222... \times 10^8$ ms^{-1}
$= 2.22 \times 10^8$ ms^{-1} (to 3 s.f.) *[1 mark]*

1.2 $\lambda_{sucrose} = c_s \div f = (2.22... \times 10^8) \div (5.0 \times 10^{14}) = 4.44... \times 10^{-7}$ m
$\lambda_{air} = c \div f = (3.00 \times 10^8) \div (5.0 \times 10^{14}) = 6.0 \times 10^{-7}$ m
$\Delta\lambda = \lambda_{air} - \lambda_{sucrose}$
$= (6.0 \times 10^{-7}) - (4.44... \times 10^{-7})$
$= 1.555... \times 10^{-7}$ m $= 155.5...$ nm $= \textbf{160 nm (to 2 s.f.)}$
[2 marks for correct answer, otherwise 1 mark for correctly calculating wavelength in sucrose and air]

1.3 E.g. calculate the refractive index that corresponds to a critical angle of 45°.
$\sin \theta_c = n_{air} \div n_{sucrose}$, so $n_{sucrose} = n_{air} \div \sin \theta_c$
$= 1 \div \sin 45° = 1.41...$ *[1 mark]*
A solution with a refractive index greater than 1.41... will have a critical angle smaller than 45°*[1 mark]*. The laser beam, which is incident at 45°, would be totally internally reflected by such a solution *[1 mark]*.
The solution's refractive index first exceeds 1.41... when its concentration is increased to 60% *[1 mark]*.

Alternatively you could calculate the critical angle for each of the solutions and observe that the 60% solution is the first with a critical angle less than 45°.

2.1 E.g. passing light through a polarising filter *[1 mark]*.

2.2 E.g. direct the unpolarised beam so that it reflects off the pane of glass and passes through the filter *[1 mark]*. Rotate the filter until the beam appears the dimmest *[1 mark]*. Adjust the beam's angle until its reflection is completely blocked when rotating the polarising filter — at this point the beam will be incident at Brewster's angle *[1 mark]*.

2.3 From Figure 2 it can be seen:
$\theta_B + 90° + r = 180°$
Rearrange this to find r: $r = 90° - \theta_B = 90° - 56.6° = 33.4°$
Use Snell's law and rearrange to find n_g:
$n_{air} \sin \theta_B = n_g \sin r$
$n_g = (n_{air} \sin \theta_B) \div (\sin r)$, $n_{air} = 1$.
$n_g = (\sin 56.6°) \div (\sin 33.4°) = 1.51... = \textbf{1.5 (to 2 s.f.)}$
[3 marks for correct answer, otherwise 1 mark for correctly calculating the angle of refraction, 1 mark for $n_{air} = 1$]

3.1 E.g.

[1 mark for a straight line of best fit passing through the origin]

3.2 $f = \dfrac{1}{2l}\sqrt{\dfrac{T}{\mu}}$

rearrange this equation into the form $y = mx + c$:
$\dfrac{1}{f} = 2l\sqrt{\dfrac{\mu}{T}}$

the gradient of the graph is given by:
$gradient = 2\sqrt{\dfrac{\mu}{T}}$

Rearrange this equation to make T the subject:
$T = \dfrac{4\mu}{gradient^2}$

From the graph, $gradient = \Delta y \div \Delta x$
$= 0.032 \div 1.00 = 0.032$ sm^{-1}
$T = (4 \times 1.5 \times 10^{-3}) \div 0.032^2 = 5.85...$ N $= \textbf{5.9 N (to 2 s.f.)}$
(Allow a line of best fit with a gradient between 0.031 sm^{-1} and 0.033 sm^{-1}, and values of T between 5.5 N and 6.2 N)
[3 marks for correct answer, otherwise 1 mark for correctly expressing tension in terms of gradient and 1 mark for correctly calculating the gradient]

3.3 $c = f\lambda$. For the first harmonic: $\lambda = 2l$
Substitute the second equation into the first: $c = 2fl$
Rearrange this equation into the form $y = mx + c$ to give:
$\dfrac{1}{f} = \dfrac{2l}{c}$

the gradient of the graph is given by: $gradient = \dfrac{2}{c}$

$c = 2 \div gradient = 2 \div 0.032 = 62.5$ ms^{-1} $= \textbf{63 ms}^{-1}$ **(to 2 s.f.)**
(Allow answers between $c = 61$ ms^{-1} and 63 ms^{-1})
[3 marks for correct answer, otherwise 1 mark for recalling $\lambda = 2l$ and 1 mark for correctly expressing wave speed in terms of gradient]

Section Four — Mechanics

Pages 34-36: Basics of Mechanics — 1

1 B *[1 mark]*
Speed tells you how fast — but not what direction.

2 D *[1 mark]*

3 B *[1 mark]*
Since the 3 N force and the 4 N force are at right angles, you can use Pythagoras's theorem to find the size of the resultant force F.
$F^2 = 3^2 + 4^2$, giving F = 5.

4 D *[1 mark]*
If x is the distance between the pivot and the 4 N weight, then for the moments caused by each weight to balance 4x = 12(6 - x). Solving this equation gives x = 4.5 m.

5.1 Moment = force × distance = $120 \times (0.40 \div 2)$
$= 120 \times 0.2 = \textbf{24 Nm}$ *[1 mark]*

5.2 couple *[1 mark]*

5.3 Since the turning force is supplied by a couple,
minimum turning force =
force provided by one hand × distance between forces
$160 = F \times 0.40$, so $F = 160 \div 0.40 = \textbf{400 N}$
[2 marks for correct answer, otherwise 1 mark for correct working]

5.4 The line of action of the pulling force passes through the turning point of the wheel / it will not produce a moment *[1 mark]*.

5.5 E.g. He could push the end of the bar downwards to create a larger moment on the wheel than when he applied force directly to the wheel (by increasing the distance between the line of action of the force and the pivot) *[1 mark]*.

6.1 A single point that you can consider the whole weight of the object to act from *[1 mark]*.

6.2 The centre of mass of a uniform cylinder is at its geometric centre *[1 mark]*. The weight of the cylinder acts from the centre of mass and, when tilted by 5°, the weight's line of action still passes through the cylinder's base *[1 mark]*. As a result, the weight produces a clockwise turning force about the cylinder's edge that is in contact with the floor, which pulls the cylinder back down onto its base *[1 mark]*.

6.3 The maximum angle occurs when the centre of mass is directly above the edge of cylinder.

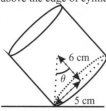

θ on this diagram will always be equal to the angle between the cylinder's base and the ground (due to angles in a triangle always adding to 180°).

$\tan \theta = 5 \div 6$

$\theta = \tan^{-1} (0.8333...) = 39.805...°$

So maximum angle is **40° (to 1 s.f.)**

[2 marks for correct answer, otherwise 1 mark for correctly determining that the centre of mass must be above the edge of the cylinder in contact with the floor]

Pages 37-40: Basics of Mechanics — 2

1.1 Distance from ship to island = x

$x^2 = 1.5^2 + 3.2^2 = 12.49$

$x = \sqrt{(12.49)} = 3.53...$ km

So distance = **3.5 km (to 2 s.f.)**

[2 marks for correct answer, otherwise 1 mark for correct working if answer incorrect]

1.2 The angle through which the man has turned = θ

$\tan \theta = 3.2 \div 1.5 = 2.133...$

$\theta = \tan^{-1}(2.133...) = 64.885...° = $ **65° (to 2 s.f.)**

[2 marks for correct answer, otherwise 1 mark for correct working if answer incorrect]

1.3 E.g.

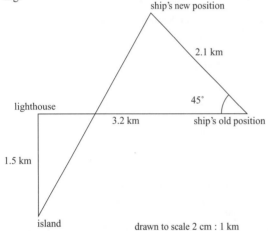

ship's new position

2.1 km

45°

lighthouse

3.2 km   ship's old position

1.5 km

island   drawn to scale 2 cm : 1 km

New distance from island to ship on the diagram = 6.9 cm, so the actual distance between the island and the ship is

$6.9 \div 2 = 3.45$ km = **3.5 km (to 2 s.f.)**

(accept between 3.4 km - 3.6 km)

[2 marks for correct answer, otherwise 1 mark for correctly drawing a scale diagram]

Give yourself the marks for value in between 3.4 km and 3.6 km obtained from a correctly drawn scale diagram.

2.1 Horizontal component = $5 \cos 53° = 3.00... = 3$ N (to 1 s.f.) *[1 mark]*

Vertical component = $5 \sin 53° = 3.99... = 4$ N (to 1 s.f.) *[1 mark]*

The horizontal components of the forces cancel out, but the vertical components combine to cause a resultant downward force *[1 mark]*.

2.2 Horizontal component of 5 N force = $5 \times \cos 60° = 2.5$ N

Vertical component of 5 N force = $5 \times \sin 60° = 4.33...$ N

Combining with 6 N force,

total horizontal force = 2.5 N to the right

total vertical force = $6 - 4.33... = 1.66...$ N down

Therefore, to be in equilibrium, the horizontal component of F must be 2.5 N left, and the vertical component of F must be 1.66... N up.

Magnitude of $F = \sqrt{(1.66...^2 + 2.5^2)}$

$= 3.00... $ N = **3.0 N (to 2 s.f.)**

Angle of F above horizontal = $\tan^{-1} (1.66... \div 2.5)$

$= 33.74... = $ **34° (to 2 s.f.)**

[4 marks for correct answers, otherwise 1 mark for each correct component of 5 N force, 1 mark for correctly calculating magnitude of the new force and 1 mark for correctly calculating the angle it makes with the horizontal]

3.1 E.g.

[1 mark for drawing an arrow parallel to the slope, directed up the incline]

3.2 $W \sin \theta$ *[1 mark]*

3.3 Friction is equal to the component of weight parallel to the slope: $F_{max} = W \sin \theta$ *[1 mark]*.

Reaction force is equal to the component of weight perpendicular to the slope: $R = W \cos \theta$ *[1 mark]*.

$F_{max} = \mu \times R$

$W \sin \theta = \mu \times W \cos \theta$, so $\mu = \sin \theta \div \cos \theta$ *[1 mark]*

3.4 If the coefficient of static friction is very large, then the critical angle at which the crate slides will be large *[1 mark]*. The crate may topple over before sliding *[1 mark]*.

Pages 41-43: Forces and Motion — 1

1 C *[1 mark]*

Impulse = change in momentum = $mv - mu$, so $v = \frac{5.5}{0.5} + (-7) = 4$ ms^{-1}

Remember to convert the mass from 500 g to 0.5 kg. Also, the initial velocity is given a minus sign since it's in the opposite direction to the impulse and the final velocity.

2 D *[1 mark]*

3 A *[1 mark]*

Acceleration is constant ($a = -g$), so $v = u + at$, giving $t = \frac{v - u}{a}$.

At time t, $v = \frac{u}{2}$, so $t = -\frac{u}{2a}$

At time t', $v = \frac{u}{4}$, so $t' = -\frac{3u}{4a} = \frac{3}{2}(-\frac{u}{2a}) = \frac{3}{2}t$

4 B *[1 mark]*

From the equations $F = ma$ and $a = \frac{\Delta v}{\Delta t}$, $F = m\frac{\Delta v}{\Delta t}$

Since the object comes to rest, $\Delta v = v - u = 0 - (-u) = u$

$F = m\frac{u}{\Delta t}$, so $\Delta t = \frac{mu}{F}$

5.1 Between 0 and 3 s the car accelerates from rest at a constant rate of 4 ms^{-2} *[1 mark]*. Between 3 and 6 s the car travels at a constant velocity of 12 ms^{-1} *[1 mark]*. Between 6 and 10 s the car experiences decreasing deceleration until it comes to rest. *[1 mark]*

5.2 distance travelled = area under v-t graph

distance travelled between 0 and 3 s = $½ \times 3 \times 12 = 18$ m

distance travelled between 3 and 6 s = $3 \times 12 = 36$ m

distance travelled between 6 and 10 s

= area under graph ≈ 6 big squares

1 big square (5 x 5 small squares) = 1 s $\times 2$ ms^{-1} = 2 m,

so 6 big squares = 12 m

total distance travelled = $18 + 36 + 12 = $ **66 m**

(allow values between 65 and 66 m)

[2 marks for correct answer, otherwise 1 mark for attempting to calculate the area under the graph]

5.3 E.g.

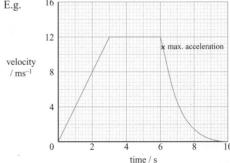

[1 mark for indicating any point between 6 and 6.8 s]

5.4 $a = \frac{\Delta v}{\Delta t} = (-12) \div 4 = -3 \text{ ms}^{-2}$ *[1 mark]*

6.1   change in momentum = impulse = area under *F-t* graph
= (½ × 0.010 × 120) + (0.005 × 120) + (½ × 0.005 × 120)
= 1.5 Ns
change in momentum = $\Delta(mv) = m\Delta v$
Δv = change in momentum ÷ m = 1.5 ÷ 0.05 = **30 ms⁻¹**
[2 marks for correct answer, otherwise 1 mark for correctly calculating change in momentum from the area under the graph]

6.2   Following through increases the time that the ball is in contact with the racket *[1 mark]*. Impulse is force × time, so for a given force a greater contact time causes a larger impulse and so the ball receives a greater increase in momentum and so a greater increase in speed *[1 mark]*.

6.3   Inelastic *[1 mark]*. The speed is lower after the collision because energy has been lost/transferred to other energy types (e.g. heat/ sound) *[1 mark]*.

Pages 44-46: Forces and Motion — 2

1.1   Lower air pressure leads to reduced air resistance, allowing the vehicle to achieve greater speeds for a given driving force / to reach a greater terminal velocity. *[1 mark]*

1.2   total distance travelled = 2 × 1.10 = 2.20 km = 2200 m

$s = \left(\frac{u+v}{2}\right)t$, so $t = \frac{2s}{(u+v)} = (2 \times 2200) \div (16.0 + 289)$
                 = 14.426... s = **14.4 s (to 3 s.f.)**
[2 marks for correct answer, otherwise 1 mark for correctly calculating total distance travelled]

1.3   Calculate acceleration experienced by the vehicle:
$v = u + at$
$a = \frac{v-u}{t} = (289 - 16.0) \div (14.426...) = 18.923... \text{ ms}^{-2}$
Calculate the resultant force required:
$F = ma = 1250 \times 18.923... = 23\,654.8... \text{ N} = \textbf{23\,700 N (to 3 s.f.)}$
[2 marks for correct answer, otherwise 1 mark for correctly calculating the vehicle's acceleration]

You could have also used $v^2 = u^2 + 2as$ to find the vehicle's acceleration.
If you got 1.2 wrong, but carried out the calculations in 1.3 correctly with the incorrect value from 1.2, give yourself the marks.

1.4   Since the speed of the vehicle through the tunnel is constant, the sum of the driving forces must be equal and opposite to the sum of the resistive forces *[1 mark]*.

2.1   B *[1 mark]*

2.2   At C (the peak height of the rocket's flight), the rocket starts to fall, accelerating downwards due to gravity *[1 mark]*. As its speed increases, so does air resistance, leading to a gradual decrease in the rocket's acceleration between C and D *[1 mark]*. By point D the rocket has reached its terminal velocity since the force of gravity is balanced by air resistance *[1 mark]*.

2.3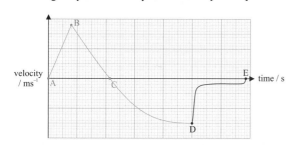

[1 mark for correctly sketching the shape of the curve including a sudden decrease in the magnitude of the velocity after point D]

2.4   Draw the tangent to the graph at the point where the displacement equals 40 m, e.g.

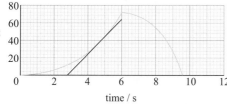

instantaneous velocity = gradient = $\Delta y \div \Delta x = 64 \div 3.2 = \textbf{20 ms}^{-1}$
[2 marks for a velocity in the range 18 - 22 ms⁻¹, otherwise 1 mark for drawing a tangent at the correct point]

3.1   240 g = 0.24 kg
impulse = change in momentum = $m(v - u)$
The ball's initial velocity $u = 0$.
v = impulse ÷ m = 0.84 ÷ 0.24 = **3.5 ms⁻¹** *[1 mark]*

3.2   A collision in which kinetic energy is not conserved *[1 mark]*.

3.3   momentum before collision = $m_1v_1 + m_2v_2$
                           = (0.24 × 3.5) + (0.24 × (−0.75))
                           = 0.66 kg m s⁻¹
momentum after collision = $m_1v_1 + m_2v_2$
                        = $(0.24 \times \frac{v}{2}) + (0.24 \times v) = 0.36v$
momentum is conserved, so:
momentum before collision = momentum after collision
0.66 = 0.36v
v = 0.66 ÷ 0.36 = 1.83... ms⁻¹ = **1.8 ms⁻¹ (to 2 s.f.)**
[2 marks for correct answer, otherwise 1 mark for correctly calculating total momentum before the collision]

3.4   84 cm = 0.84 m
If a ball just reaches the pocket, its final speed $v = 0$ ms⁻¹.
$v^2 = u^2 + 2as$
$a = (v^2 - u^2) \div (2s) = (0^2 - 1.83...^2) \div (2 \times 0.84) = -2.00... \text{ ms}^{-2}$
Calculate the size of the force causing this deceleration:
$F = ma = 0.24 \times 2.00... = 0.48... \text{ N} = \textbf{0.48 N (to 2 s.f.)}$
[2 marks for correct answer, otherwise 1 mark for correctly calculating the ball's deceleration]

If you got 3.3 wrong, but carried out the calculations in 3.4 correctly with the incorrect value from 3.3, give yourself the marks. You could also have calculated this using energy calculations, where at a maximum frictional force, the work done by the friction will equal the kinetic energy of the ball.

Pages 47-50: Forces and Motion — 3

1.1   Calculate change in displacement:
Δs = final displacement – initial displacement
     = −6 − 36 = −42 m
Calculate average velocity:
$v = \frac{\Delta s}{\Delta t} = -42 \div 60 = \textbf{−0.7 ms}^{-1}$ *[1 mark]*

1.2   Total distance travelled = 36 + 12 + 12 + 15 + 15 + 6 = 96 m
Average speed = total distance travelled ÷ time taken
                     = 96 ÷ 60 = **1.6 ms⁻¹** *[1 mark]*

1.3 $v = \frac{\Delta s}{\Delta t}$
From 8 - 20 s: $v = (-12 - 36) \div 12 = -4 \text{ ms}^{-1}$
From 32 - 38 s: $v = (15 - -12) \div 6 = 4.5 \text{ ms}^{-1}$
From 46 - 53 s: $v = (-6 - 15) \div 7 = -3 \text{ ms}^{-1}$

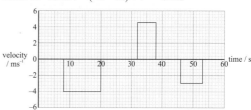

[2 marks for a complete and correct graph, otherwise 1 mark for at least 2 correctly calculated velocities]

2.1   The engine exerts a force on the probe equal and opposite to the force that the probe exerts on the engine *[1 mark]*.
This causes the probe to accelerate forwards as the engine is ejected *[1 mark]*.

You could also have explained this in terms of conservation of momentum.

2.2 $F = ma$, so $a = F \div m = 510 \div 60 = \textbf{8.5 ms}^{-2}$ *[1 mark]*

2.3 $a = \Delta v \div \Delta t$, so $\Delta v = a\Delta t = 8.5 \times 18$
                        = 153 ms⁻¹ = **150 ms⁻¹ (to 2 s.f.)** *[1 mark]*

2.4   Side B is less streamlined than side A, so when side B is facing the direction of travel, atmospheric resistance will be greater for a given speed *[1 mark]*. This will reduce the probe's acceleration and its terminal velocity *[1 mark]*.

2.5 The airbags increase the length of time over which the probe's momentum changes during the impact *[1 mark]*. Change in momentum = Ft, so this reduces the maximum force experienced by the probe during the impact *[1 mark]*.

3.1

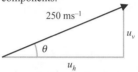

[1 mark for correctly labelled and appropriately scaled axes, 1 mark for six correctly plotted data points and 1 mark for a straight line of best fit passing through the data points]

3.2 $s = ut + \frac{1}{2}at^2$. The ball's initial velocity $u = 0$, since it is released from rest. Assuming gravity is the only force acting on the ball, $a = g$. $s = \frac{1}{2}gt^2$
So, the gradient of the graph of release height (s) against mean drop time squared (t^2) will give a value for $\frac{1}{2}g$.
$\frac{1}{2}g$ = gradient = $\Delta y \div \Delta x = (2.55 - 1.65) \div (0.87 - 0.625)$
        $= 3.67...$
$g = 2 \times 3.67... = 7.34... \text{ ms}^{-2}$
    $= \textbf{7.3 ms}^{-2}$ **(to 2 s.f., accept ± 0.4 ms⁻²)**
[2 marks for correct answer, otherwise 1 mark for correctly calculating gradient]

3.3 Horizontal and vertical motion of a projectile are independent, so restricting the ball to a vertical path will not improve the measurement's accuracy *[1 mark]*. Friction between the ball and tube may slow the ball, reducing the measurement's accuracy *[1 mark]*.

3.4 How to grade your answer:
Level 0: There is no relevant information. *[No marks]*
Level 1: A brief description and explanation of at least one reason for the difference in the actual value and the student's result is given. There are several errors with grammar, spelling, punctuation and there are some problems with legibility. Answer has no clear structure. *[1 to 2 marks]*
Level 2: A description and explanation of several reasons for the difference in the actual value and the student's result, with brief suggestions of how to reduce the effect for some of them. There may be a few errors with grammar, spelling, punctuation. There are few problems with legibility. Answer has some structure. *[3 to 4 marks]*
Level 3: A clear and well structured description and explanation of several reasons for the difference in the actual value and the student's result, and suggestions of how to reduce the effect of them. Grammar, spelling and punctuation are used accurately and there is no problem with legibility. Answer has a clear and logical structure. *[5 to 6 marks]*
Here are some points your answer may include:
There is a source of random error due to the student's reaction time when pressing the stopwatch. This is likely to be the largest source of error. This error could be reduced by using light gates to accurately record the time the ball is dropped and when it hits the floor, or by dropping the ball from a greater height.
Air resistance acting on the ball will prevent the student from measuring the true value of g. This effect could be reduced by using a ball that is more dense or by using a different object that is more streamlined, such as a pen.
The height measurement is a source of random error. This could be reduced by using a ruler or measuring tape with a higher resolution.
There could be a systematic error on the height measurement due to the student not positioning the tape measure vertically. This could be reduced by using a rigid ruler to measure the height and/or a spirit level to ensure the ruler is vertical.
There is a systematic error on the height measurement due to the student measuring the height from the top of the ball instead

of the bottom. This could be removed by measuring the height from the bottom of the ball.

Pages 51-53: Forces and Motion — 4

1.1 $0.60 \text{ g} = 0.00060 \text{ kg}$
impulse = change in momentum = $\Delta(mv) = m\Delta v = m(v - u)$
pellet is initially stationary inside the gun, $u = 0$
v = impulse $\div m = 0.15 \div 0.00060 = \textbf{250 ms}^{-1}$ *[1 mark]*

1.2 Calculate the time taken for the pellet to reach the target by considering the horizontal motion of the pellet:
$v = \Delta s \div \Delta t$, so $\Delta t = \Delta s \div v = 100 \div 250 = 0.4 \text{ s}$
Calculate the distance fallen by the pellet in that interval by considering its vertical motion:
$s = ut + \frac{1}{2}at^2 = (0 \times 0.4) + (\frac{1}{2} \times (9.81) \times 0.4^2) = 0.7848 \text{ m}$
Since the target's diameter is 1.2 m, the bottom of the target is 0.6 m below its centre. Since the pellet has fallen more than 0.6 m it cannot hit the target.
[3 marks for correct answer, otherwise 1 mark for correctly calculating time taken to reach the target and 1 mark for correctly calculating the distance fallen by the pellet]

1.3 Resolve the pellet's initial velocity into its vertical and horizontal components:

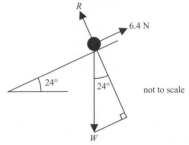

$u_v = 250 \sin \theta$, $u_h = 250 \cos \theta$
Find an expression for time taken to reach the target by considering the pellet's horizontal motion:
$u_h = \Delta s \div \Delta t$, so $\Delta t = \Delta s \div u_h = 100 \div (250 \cos \theta) = 0.4 \div \cos \theta$
Consider the pellet's vertical motion:
If the pellet is to hit the centre of the target, the change in its vertical displacement between being fired and hitting the target must be 0.
$s = u_v t + \frac{1}{2}at^2$
$0 = 250 \sin \theta \times \dfrac{0.4}{\cos \theta} + \frac{1}{2} \times (-g) \times \left(\dfrac{0.4}{\cos \theta}\right)^2$
$0 = 100 \dfrac{\sin \theta}{\cos \theta} - \dfrac{0.08g}{(\cos \theta)^2}$
Multiply both side of the equation by $(\cos \theta)^2$.
$0 = 100 \sin \theta \cos \theta - 0.08g$
$\sin \theta \cos \theta = 0.0008g$
[4 marks for complete working, otherwise 1 mark for finding an expression for Δt, 1 mark for stating change in vertical displacement will be 0 and 1 mark for correct substitution into the equation $s = ut + \frac{1}{2}at^2$]

2.1 Draw a free-body diagram showing the forces acting on the car.

$750 \text{ g} = 0.75 \text{ kg}$. The car's weight, $W = mg = 0.75g$
From the free-body diagram, the component of the car's weight acting down the ramp = $W \sin 24° = 0.75g \sin 24° = 2.992... \text{ N}$
resultant force acting up the ramp =
driving force – component of weight acting down the ramp
= $6.4 - 2.992... = 3.407... \text{ N}$
Calculate the car's acceleration up the ramp:
$F = ma$
$a = F \div m = 3.407... \div 0.75 = 4.543... \text{ ms}^{-2} = \textbf{4.5 ms}^{-2}$ **(2 s.f.)**
[3 marks for correct answer, otherwise 1 mark for correctly calculating the component of the car's weight acting down the ramp and 1 mark for correctly calculating the resultant force acting on the car]

R, the reaction force of the ramp on the car, will cancel with the component of the car's weight that is perpendicular to the ramp.

2.2   E.g. there are no resistive forces acting on the car *[1 mark]*.

2.3   Calculate, s, the length of the ramp:

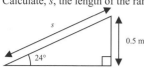

From the diagram, $s = 0.5 \div \sin 24° = 1.229...$ m
calculate the car's speed at the top of the ramp:
$v^2 = u^2 + 2as = 0^2 + 2 \times 4.543... \times 1.229... = 11.16...$
$v = \sqrt{11.16...} = 3.342...$ ms^{-1} = **3.3 ms^{-1} (to 2 s.f.)**
[2 marks for correct answer, otherwise 1 mark for correctly calculating the ramp's length]

2.4   Calculate the vertical component of the car's velocity as it leaves the ramp:

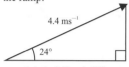

$u_v = 4.4 \sin 24° = 1.789...$ ms^{-1}
calculate the height the car rises after leaving the ramp:
initial vertical velocity = $1.789...$ ms^{-1}
vertical velocity at the peak of its trajectory = 0 ms^{-1}
$v_v^2 = u_v^2 + 2as$
$s = (v_v^2 - u_v^2) \div 2a = (0^2 - 1.789...^2) \div (2 \times (-9.81)) = 0.163...$ m
maximum height above the ground =
height of the ramp + height the car rises
$0.5. + 0.163... = 0.663...$ m = **0.66 m (to 2 s.f.)**
[3 marks for correct answer, otherwise 1 mark for correctly calculating the vertical component of the car's velocity as it leaves the ramp and 1 mark for correctly calculating the height risen by the car]

2.5   Calculate the time taken for the car to reach the ground after leaving the ramp by considering its vertical motion:
When the car reaches the ground it will be 0.5 m below its starting point, so $s = -0.5$ m.
$s = u_v t + \frac{1}{2}at^2$
$-0.5 = 1.789... \times t + \frac{1}{2} \times -9.81 \times t^2$
$4.905t^2 - 1.789... t - 0.5 = 0$
Use the quadratic formula to solve the quadratic for t:
$t = \dfrac{1.789... \pm \sqrt{(-1.789...)^2 - 4 \times 4.905 \times -0.5}}{2 \times 4.905}$
$= -0.185...$ s, $0.550...$ s

You can ignore the negative solution, so $t = 0.550...$ s.
Calculate the horizontal component of the car's velocity as it leaves the ramp:

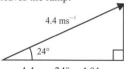

$u_h = 4.4 \cos 24° = 4.01...$ ms^{-1}
$u_h = \Delta s \div \Delta t$, where s is the horizontal distance travelled.
$\Delta s = u_h \Delta t = 4.01... \times 0.550... = 2.21...$ m = **2.2 m (to 2 s.f.)**
[4 marks for the correct answer, otherwise 1 mark for correctly substituting into s = ut + ½at², 1 mark for correctly calculating time taken for the car to reach the ground and 1 mark for correctly calculating the horizontal component of the car's velocity]

2.6   E.g. streamline the car to reduce air resistance / change the car's shape so lift is generated as it moves through the air *[1 mark]*.

Pages 54-56: Work and Energy

1   A *[1 mark]*
Nms^{-1} is a unit for power, e.g. power = force × velocity.
2   A *[1 mark]*
P = F × v, so v = P ÷ F = Y ÷ 0.5X = 2Y ÷ X.
3   B *[1 mark]*
Work done = F × d × cos θ = Hdcos15° + Fdcos180°. cos180° = −1, so W = Hdcos15° − Fd. This makes sense, because the work done by the horse is Hdcos15°, but some of this work (Fd) is used to overcome friction, so only (Hdcos15° − Fd) is used to do work on the carriage. Alternatively, you could have calculated the resultant force acting on the carriage in the direction of motion (Hcos15° − F) and then multiplied by distance, d.

4   D *[1 mark]*
The input energy into snowmobile 2 is 1.5 times more than that for snowmobile 1. The useful output energy is the kinetic energy gained by the snowmobiles. Snowmobile 1 has a kinetic energy (E_k) of ½mv², and snowmobile 2 has a kinetic energy of ½m(1.2v)² = 1.44E_k. Efficiency = useful output energy ÷ input energy, so the efficiency of snowmobile 2 is (1.44 ÷ 1.5) times that of snowmobile 1 = 0.96e.

5.1   Energy cannot be created or destroyed. Energy can be transferred from one form to another, but the total amount of energy in a closed system will not change *[1 mark]*.

5.2 $m = 0.25$ kg
Useful work done by motor = gravitational potential energy gained by the mass
$\qquad = m \times g \times \Delta h$
$\qquad = 0.25 \times 9.81 \times 0.5 = 1.22625$ J
Useful power output = work done by motor ÷ time
$\qquad = 1.22625 \div 1.28$
$\qquad = 0.958007...$ W = **0.96 W (to 2 s.f.)**
[2 marks for the correct answer to 2 significant figures, otherwise 1 mark for correctly calculating the work done by the motor]

5.3   Efficiency $= \dfrac{\text{useful output power}}{\text{input power}} \times 100$

$= \left(\dfrac{0.958007...}{1.3}\right) \times 100$

$= 73.6929...\% = $ **74% (to 2 s.f.)** *[1 mark]*

5.4   absolute uncertainty = 150 ms = 0.15 s
percentage uncertainty $= \dfrac{\text{absolute uncertainty}}{\text{measurement}} \times 100$

$= \dfrac{0.15}{1.28} \times 100$

$= 11.71875\% = $ **12% (to 2 s.f.)** *[1 mark]*

5.5   E.g. measure the time taken for the mass to travel a much larger vertical distance / use a greater mass / use light gates to measure the time taken for the mass to be raised *[1 mark]*.

6.1   The decrease in gravitational potential energy (E_P) of the bungee jumper is equal to the increase in kinetic energy (E_k).
$\Delta E_P = m \times g \times \Delta h = 65 \times 9.81 \times 20 = 12\,753$ J
$\Delta E_k = \frac{1}{2} \times m \times v^2 = \frac{1}{2} \times 65 \times v^2 = 12\,753$ J
$v^2 = 12\,753 \div (\frac{1}{2} \times 65) = 392.4$
$v = 19.809...$ ms^{-1} = **20 ms^{-1} (to 2 s.f.)**
[3 marks for the correct answer, otherwise 1 mark for correctly calculating ΔE_p and 1 mark for equating this to ΔE_k]

6.2   The gravitational potential energy and kinetic energy of the bungee jumper are transferred to the elastic potential energy / elastic strain energy of the bungee cord *[1 mark]*.

6.3   Work done by the bungee cord on the jumper is equal to the area under the force-distance graph / under AB.
Area of triangle = ½ × base × height
Base = 36 − 20 = 16 m
Height = 2.8 kN = 2800 N
Work done = ½ × 16 × 2800 = 22 400 J *[1 mark]*

Section Five — Materials

Pages 57-59: Materials — 1

1   D   *[1 mark]*
2   B   *[1 mark]*
3   A   *[1 mark]*
F = kΔL, so k = F ÷ ΔL = W ÷ 0.1 = 10W.
4   B   *[1 mark]*
Elastic strain energy = ½kΔL² (since F = kΔL). You know E = ½kx², so 2E = 2 × (½kx²). You also know that 2E = ½kΔL² (where ΔL is the new extension), so ½kΔL² = 2 × (½kx²). Cancelling the half and k on both sides gives ΔL² = 2x². Square root both sides to give ΔL = $\sqrt{2x^2} = \sqrt{2}x$.

5.1 $\Delta L = 11.5 − 10 = 1.5$ cm = 0.015 m
$F = k\Delta L = 0.50 \times 0.015 = $ **7.5 × 10^{-3} N** *[1 mark]*

5.2   E.g. by using a spring with a lower spring constant *[1 mark]*.
This would mean the force from the balloon would cause the spring to have a larger extension, and the percentage uncertainty in the extension measurement because the ruler's resolution would be lower *[1 mark]*.

5.3   Assume the balloon is a sphere with a radius of 9.5 cm.
Volume of a sphere $= \frac{4}{3}\pi r^3 = \frac{4}{3}\pi \times (0.095)^3 = 3.59... \times 10^{-3}$ m^3

Assume the balloon material is thin and so the volume of this sphere is approximately that of the helium inside the balloon.
Rearrange density = mass ÷ volume for mass:
mass = density × volume = $0.164 \times 3.59... \times 10^{-3}$
= $5.88... \times 10^{-4}$ kg = $\mathbf{5.9 \times 10^{-4}}$ **kg (to 2 s.f.)**
[2 marks for the correct answer, otherwise 1 mark for correctly estimating the volume of helium in the balloon]

6.1 The limit of proportionality is at approximately 300 N when the rope is extended by 0.4 m.
Energy stored = area under the force-extension graph
= ½ × 300 × 0.4 = **60 J**
[2 marks for the correct answer, otherwise 1 mark for correctly identifying the values of force and extension at the limit of proportionality]

6.2 The spring constant, k, is equal to the gradient of the linear part of the force-extension graph ($k = F \div \Delta L$).
Gradient = 300 ÷ 0.4 = **750 Nm⁻¹** *[1 mark]*

6.3 Work done to cause the deformation = area between the loading and unloading lines.
E.g. split the graph into two areas, A and B.

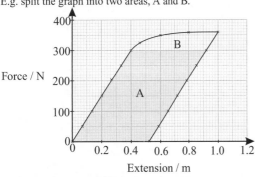

Area A = area of a parallelogram = 0.52 × 300 = 156 J
Count squares to find area B.
Each square is equal to 0.02 × 10 = 0.2 J.
There are approximately 132 squares in area B, so the work done represented by area B = 132 × 0.2 = 26.4 J.
Total work done = 182.4 J = **180 J (to 2 s.f.)**
[2 marks for calculating total work done, otherwise 1 mark for identifying that the work done is equal to the area between the loading and unloading lines]

If you get the area of B to be somewhere between 26 and 28 J you should get a good enough estimate of work done to get the marks.

Pages 60-63: Materials — 2

1.1 The Young modulus is equal to the gradient of the linear part of the graph.
E.g. gradient = $(6.0 \times 10^8) \div (1.5 \times 10^{-2}) = 4.0 \times 10^{10}$ Nm⁻²
The uncertainty in this value is equal to the uncertainty in the gradient of the linear part of the graph, i.e. the difference between the worst possible line that goes through all of the error bars and the line of best fit.
Draw worst lines that pass through all the error bars for the linear part of the graph. E.g.

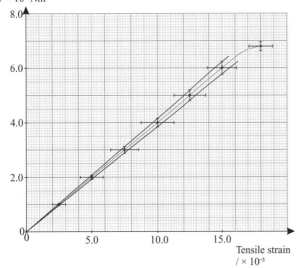

Gradient of highest possible line = $6.4 \times 10^8 \div 15.4 \times 10^{-3}$
= $4.15... \times 10^{10}$ Nm⁻²
Gradient of lowest possible line = $6.1 \times 10^8 \div 15.8 \times 10^{-3}$
= $3.86... \times 10^{10}$ Nm⁻²
The largest uncertainty in the gradient is between the highest possible line and the line of best fit.
Uncertainty in the gradient = $4.15... \times 10^{10} - 4.0 \times 10^{10}$
= $1.55... \times 10^9$ Nm⁻²
Percentage uncertainty = $\dfrac{(1.55... \times 10^9)}{(4.0 \times 10^{10})} \times 100$
= $3.89...$ % = 4% (to 1 s.f.)
So the Young modulus = $\mathbf{4.0 \times 10^{10}}$ **Nm⁻² ± 4% (to 1 s.f.)**
[4 marks for 4.0×10^{10} Nm⁻² with a percentage uncertainty between 2% and 5%. Otherwise 1 mark for correctly calculating the Young modulus from the graph, 1 mark for correctly calculating the gradient of a worst line that passes through the error bars of all the points in the linear part of the graph, 1 mark for correctly calculating the absolute uncertainty in the gradient]

1.2 E.g. Tensile stress = force ÷ area, so decreasing the uncertainty in the force measurement would decrease the uncertainty in the stress result *[1 mark]*. The student could use more accurate masses / measure the mass of each '100 g' mass to ensure the force applied to the wire was more accurately known *[1 mark]*. / Tensile stress = force ÷ area, so decreasing the uncertainty in the measurement of the cross-sectional area of the wire would decrease the uncertainty in the stress result *[1 mark]*. To do this, the student could measure the wire diameter used to calculate the area with a higher precision measuring instrument, e.g. a micrometer *[1 mark]*.

1.3 No, the Young modulus is a property of the material and doesn't depend on size or shape, so it will remain unchanged *[1 mark]*.

1.4 The area under a stress-strain graph for an object obeying Hooke's law will be a triangle, area = ½ × stress × strain.
Stress = force ÷ cross-sectional area of the material = $F \div A$
strain = $\Delta L \div L$ where L is the original length and ΔL is the extension.
So area = ½ × stress × strain
$= \frac{1}{2} \times \left(\dfrac{F}{A} \times \dfrac{\Delta L}{L} \right) = \left(\dfrac{\frac{1}{2}F\Delta L}{AL} \right)$
Volume = AL, and elastic strain energy = ½$F\Delta L$, so the area under a stress-strain graph is equal to the elastic strain energy stored per unit volume.
[2 marks, otherwise 1 mark for identifying the area of the graph to be equal to ½ × stress × strain]

1.5 From the graph, when strain = 15.0×10^{-3}, stress = 6.0×10^8 Nm⁻²
Energy per unit volume = ½ stress × strain
= ½ × $6.0 \times 10^8 \times 15.0 \times 10^{-3}$
= 4.5×10^6 J/m³
Volume of the wire = cross-sectional area × length
= $3.8 \times 10^{-7} \times 1.024 = 3.8912 \times 10^{-7}$ m³
Total energy stored = energy per unit volume × volume
= $4.5 \times 10^6 \times 3.8912 \times 10^{-7}$
= $1.751...$ J = **1.8 J (to 2 s.f.)**
[3 marks for correctly calculating the total energy, otherwise 1 mark for correctly calculating the energy per unit volume and 1 mark for calculating the volume of the wire]

1.6 Before both points on a force-extension graph, the deformation of a material is elastic. However, force and extension are only proportional up to the limit of proportionality; they may not be proportional at all points before the elastic limit *[1 mark]*.

2.1 E.g.

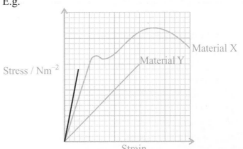

[1 mark for drawing a straight line that ends at a lower stress than material Y, 1 mark for the gradient of the straight line being greater than that of the linear part of the stress-strain graph for material X]

2.2 How to grade your answer:

Level 0: There is no relevant information. *[No marks]*

Level 1: There is a brief description of one property of at least two of the materials W, X and Y. There is some attempt at relating one of the properties to the useful properties of a car body in a collision. *[1 to 2 marks]*

Level 2: There is a brief description of one property of each of the materials. There is a brief discussion of whether this property would make each material useful for a car body in a collision. *[3 to 4 marks]*

Level 3: There is a clear and detailed explanation linking the properties of each material to the properties required to make a car body effective at absorbing energy and deforming plastically during a collision. *[5 to 6 marks]*

Here are some points your answer may include:

To minimise the energy transferred to passengers in a collision, the material of a car body needs to be able to deform without breaking under large stress in order to absorb a lot of energy. Material Y has the second largest ultimate tensile stress. However, it is brittle — if the breaking stress is reached, the material could break and transfer energy to the people involved in the collision.

Material Y also only deforms elastically. This means that although it will deform and store energy during a collision, once the force causing the deformation has been removed, the material will return to its original shape. This could in turn transfer, e.g. kinetic energy, to a person involved in the collision.

All of the above is also true for Material W. Material W is even less suitable than Material Y, as it has the lowest ultimate tensile strength and will therefore break at lower stresses, making it more likely it will break and transfer energy to the people in the collision.

Material W also deforms less for a given stress, so it stores less energy. This means that less energy can be absorbed by it in a collision, so more energy is transferred to the passengers instead.

Material X is the most suitable material to use. It has the highest ultimate tensile stress, meaning the material will be able to experience the most stress before breaking. The material also deforms plastically over a large range of strain. It permanently deforms and energy is used to break bonds and is dissipated as heat, meaning that it cannot be transferred to any people involved in the collision.

3.1 18 kJ = 18 000 J. Density, $\rho = m \div V$, so
$V = m \div \rho = 1.0 \div 8000 = 1.25 \times 10^{-4} \text{ m}^3$
At maximum compression, 45% of the kinetic energy is converted into the elastic strain energy of the rod.
$0.45 \times 18\,000 = 8100 \text{ J}$
Energy per unit volume = $8100 \div 1.25 \times 10^{-4} = 6.48 \times 10^7 \text{ Jm}^{-3}$
strain = 5% = 0.05
energy per unit volume = $\frac{1}{2} \times$ stress $\times$ strain
stress = (2 $\times$ energy per unit volume) $\div$ strain
$= (2 \times 6.48 \times 10^7) \div 0.05 = 2.592 \times 10^9 \text{ Nm}^{-2}$
Young modulus = stress $\div$ strain
$= 2.592 \times 10^9 \div 0.05$
$= 5.184 \times 10^{10} \text{ Nm}^{-2} = \mathbf{5.2 \times 10^{10} \text{ Nm}^{-2} \text{ (to 2 s.f.)}}$
[4 marks for correct answer, otherwise 1 mark for calculating the volume of the rod, 1 mark for calculating the stress of the rod, 1 mark for identifying strain = 0.05]

3.2 $\Delta l = \alpha \Delta T l$ and strain $= \Delta l \div l$, so strain $= \alpha \Delta T$.
Young modulus = stress $\div$ strain
$= \dfrac{\text{stress}}{\alpha \Delta T}$
Therefore stress = Young modulus $\times \alpha \Delta T$
Young modulus = 200 GPa = 2.00×10^{11} Pa
$\Delta T = 523 - 293 = 230$ K
So stress = $2.00 \times 10^{11} \times 1.3 \times 10^{-5} \times 230$
$= 5.98 \times 10^8 \text{ Pa} = \mathbf{6.0 \times 10^8 \text{ Pa} \text{ (to 2 s.f.)}}$
[3 marks for correct answer, otherwise 1 mark for correctly showing stress = Young modulus $\times \alpha \Delta T$ or correctly calculating strain, 1 mark for substituting into the equation for stress]

Section Six — Electricity

Pages 64-66: Electricity — 1

1 B *[1 mark]*
Total current into the junction is 1.1 A.
Total current out of the junction is 0.5 + X so X = 1.1 − 0.5 = 0.6 A

2 C *[1 mark]*
$P \propto I^2$ *so a graph of P against I will have a quadratic shape.*

3 B *[1 mark]*
$P = V^2 \div R = (230)^2 \div 57.5 = 920 \text{ W}$
$P = E \div t$ so $E = P \times t = 920 \times 50 = 46\,000 \text{ J}$

4 A *[1 mark]*
$\rho = \dfrac{RA}{L}$ so $R = \dfrac{rL}{A}$
$R_2 = \dfrac{r \times 1.25L}{0.80A} = 1.5625R = 1.5625 \times 60 = 93.75 = 93.8 \text{ n}\Omega \text{ (to 3 s.f.)}$

5.1 Copper *[1 mark]* because it has the lowest resistivity *[1 mark]*. This means that for identically sized wires made from each material, the copper wire would have the lowest resistance and so waste the least amount of energy due to heating *[1 mark]*.

5.2 $\rho = \dfrac{RA}{L}$ so $R = \dfrac{rL}{A}$, so the gradient of Figure 1 = $\rho \div A$.
E.g. gradient = $\dfrac{12.0 \times 10^{-3} - 6 \times 10^{-3}}{0.8 - 0.4} = 15 \times 10^{-3}$
gradient = $\rho \div A$ so ρ = gradient $\times A$
$= 15 \times 10^{-3} \times 1.4 \times 10^{-5} = 2.1 \times 10^{-7} \text{ } \Omega\text{m}$
Material = **lead**
[3 marks for correct answer with a supporting calculation, otherwise 1 mark for correctly calculating the gradient, 1 mark for multiplying the gradient by the cross-sectional area of the wire]

6.1 $P = IV = 2.50 \times 0.50 = 1.25 \text{ W}$
$P = E \div t$ so $E = P \times t = 1.25 \times 60.0 = \mathbf{75 \text{ J}}$
[2 marks in total, otherwise 1 mark for correctly calculating the power]

6.2 The potential difference used in the calculation is only the threshold potential difference, which is the minimum potential difference required for a current to flow through the diode and transfer energy *[1 mark]*.

6.3 The resistance of a diode in the reverse direction is very large *[1 mark]*. $P = V^2 \div R$, so a much larger resistance means the power will be much smaller *[1 mark]*.

6.4 $R = V \div I$ so $I = V \div R = 2.0 \div 0.5 = 4.0 \text{ A}$
$I = \Delta Q \div \Delta t$ so $Q = 4.0 \times 60 = 240 \text{ C}$
Number of charge carriers = total charge $\div$ charge of 1 electron = $240 \div 1.6 \times 10^{-19} = \mathbf{1.5 \times 10^{21}}$
[3 marks in total, otherwise 1 mark for a correct value of current, 1 mark for calculating a correct value of total charge]

Pages 67-70: Electricity — 2

1.1 $V = \varepsilon - Ir$ which corresponds to $y = mx + c$.
This means $-r$ is the gradient.
E.g. gradient = $\Delta y \div \Delta x = (8.0 - 8.9) \div (4.0 - 1.0) = -0.30 \text{ } \Omega$
So, $r = \mathbf{30 \text{ } \Omega}$
[2 marks in total, otherwise 1 mark for correct method of calculating the gradient]

1.2 Extend the graph to the y-axis:

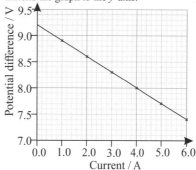

The point at which the line crosses the y-axis is the e.m.f.
= **9.2 V** *[1 mark]*

1.3 From the graph V at 5.0 A is 7.7 V. $9.2 - 7.7 = \mathbf{1.5 \text{ V}}$ *[1 mark]*

1.4 $I = Q \div t = 80.0 \div 20 = 4.0 \text{ A}$.
From the graph, at $I = 4.0$ A, $V = 8.0$ V
$V = W \div Q$ so $W = QV = 80 \times 8.0 = \mathbf{640 \text{ J}}$
[2 marks in total, otherwise 1 mark for correctly calculating the current]

1.5 The student's graph will have a steeper gradient than Figure 2 because the internal resistance is greater *[1 mark]*.

1.6 The resistance of the voltmeter must be very high so very little current will flow through it when it is connected to the cell *[1 mark]*. This means (the current flowing out of the cell will be very low, and so) the lost volts will be negligible, and the potential difference measured by the voltmeter will be approximately equal to the e.m.f. *[1 mark]*.

1.7 $\varepsilon = \dfrac{E}{Q} = \dfrac{5.0}{0.40} = 12.5\ V$

$\varepsilon = I(R + r)$ so $R = \left(\dfrac{\varepsilon}{I}\right) - r = \left(\dfrac{12.5}{0.80}\right) - 0.50$

$= 15.125\ \Omega = \mathbf{15\ \Omega}$ **(to 2 s.f.)**

[3 marks in total, otherwise 1 mark for correctly calculating ε, 1 mark for correct rearrangement and substitution into the equation for R]

2.1 Rate of energy transfer is power, $P = V^2 \div R$, so $V = \sqrt{P \times R_T}$.
$R_T = 9 + 6 = 15\ \Omega$ $V = \sqrt{2.4 \times 15} = 6\ V$
The variable resistor receives a share of $\dfrac{9}{9+6} = \dfrac{3}{5}$ of the source potential difference.
$6 \times \dfrac{3}{5} = \mathbf{3.6\ V}$

[3 marks for correct answer, otherwise 1 mark for calculating the total potential difference across the circuit, 1 mark for calculating the fraction or percentage share of the potential difference across the variable resistor]

2.2

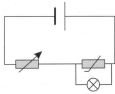

[1 mark for lamp drawn in parallel with the thermistor]
As the temperature decreases the resistance of the thermistor increases *[1 mark]*. This means that the thermistor has a larger share of the resistance in the circuit, and therefore the potential difference across the thermistor and lamp will increase, eventually leading to the lamp lighting up *[1 mark]*.

2.3 Adding another cell in series will increase the potential difference supplied by the cells *[1 mark]*. This means that for the same temperature, the potential difference across the thermistor will be larger and therefore the lamp will turn on at a higher temperature *[1 mark]*.

2.4 E.g. The lamp would be less bright, as less energy is supplied to the lamp due to some being wasted overcoming the internal resistance of the cells *[1 mark]*. / The lamp would be less bright because the terminal potential difference of the cells would be lower, so the potential difference across the lamp would be lower *[1 mark]*.

3.1 The resistor and component L are connected in series, so the current through the resistor is equal to the current through component L. Find the current through the resistor at 0.9 s by finding the gradient of the graph at 0.9 s using a tangent:
E.g.

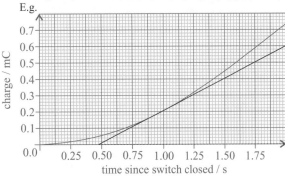

gradient $= \dfrac{0.6 \times 10^{-3} - 0}{2 - 0.475} = 3.934... \times 10^{-4}\ A$

$V = 0.40\ \mu V = 4.0 \times 10^{-7}\ V$
$R = V \div I = 4.0 \times 10^{-7} \div 3.934... \times 10^{-4}$
$= 1.0166... \times 10^{-3}\ \Omega = \mathbf{1.0 \times 10^{-3}\ \Omega}$ **(to 2 s.f.)**
(Allow between 0.9×10^{-3} and 1.1×10^{-3})
[3 marks for correct answer, otherwise 1 mark for tangent drawn at 0.9 s and 1 mark for calculation of the gradient of the tangent.]

3.2 The number of turns on a coil can be approximated from the length of the coil divided by the diameter of the wire.
Find diameter of the wire:
resistivity equation is $\rho = \dfrac{RA}{L}$ and cross-sectional area of wire in terms of diameter is $A = \dfrac{\pi d^2}{4}$ (since $r = d \div 2$)
so, $d = \sqrt{\dfrac{4\rho L}{\pi R}} = \sqrt{\dfrac{4 \times (1.7 \times 10^{-8}) \times 1.4}{\pi \times 0.12}} = 0.000502...\ m$
number of coils $= 0.02 \div 0.000502...$
$= 39.799... = \mathbf{40}$ (to the nearest whole number)
[3 marks for correct answer, otherwise 1 mark for correct use of resistivity equation and 1 mark for substitution to find diameter]

Pages 71-73: Electricity — 3

1.1 In order to calculate the total current, first the total resistance must be calculated:
$\dfrac{1}{R_{A+B}} = \dfrac{1}{R_A} + \dfrac{1}{R_B} = \dfrac{1}{6.0} + \dfrac{1}{2.0} = \dfrac{2}{3}$ so $R_{A+B} = 1 \div \dfrac{2}{3} = 1.5$
$\dfrac{1}{R_{C+D}} = \dfrac{1}{R_C} + \dfrac{1}{R_D} = \dfrac{1}{1.0} + \dfrac{1}{4.0} = \dfrac{5}{4}$ so $R_{C+D} = 1 \div \dfrac{5}{4} = 0.8$
$R_{A+B+C+D} = R_{A+B} + R_{C+D} = 1.5 + 0.8 = \mathbf{2.3\ \Omega}$
[3 marks in total, otherwise 1 mark for correct method of adding resistors in parallel, 1 mark for correct method of adding resistors in series]

1.2 $R = V \div I$ so $I = V \div R = 11.5 \div 2.3 = \mathbf{5.0\ A}$ *[1 mark]*

1.3 The potential difference of resistor B,
$R = V \div I$ so $V = IR = 5 \times 1.5 = 7.5\ V$
The current through resistor B,
$R = V \div I$ so $I = V \div R = 7.5 \div 2 = 3.75\ A$
$E = IVt = 3.75 \times 7.5 \times 64 = \mathbf{1800\ J}$
[3 marks in total, otherwise 1 mark for correctly calculating either the voltage, current or power and 1 mark for correctly using E = IVt or E = P × t to calculate the energy]
You could also answer this question by first calculating the power of resistor B, and then calculating the energy transferred using E = P × t.

1.4 As the resistance of the variable resistor increases, the combined resistance of C and D increases *[1 mark]*, tending towards the resistance of resistor C *[1 mark]* .

1.5 $P = I^2R$ so $I = \sqrt{P \div R} = \sqrt{25.0 \div 2.3} = 3.296...$
$\varepsilon = I(R + r)$ so $r = (\varepsilon \div I) - R = (8.0 \div 3.296...) - 2.3$
$= 0.1265... = \mathbf{0.13\ \Omega}$ **(to 2 s.f.)**
[2 marks in total, otherwise 1 mark for calculating the new current from total load resistance]

1.6 When the switch is closed, current flows through the cell, so there is a voltage drop (lost volts) caused by the internal resistance *[1 mark]*.

2.1 A *[1 mark]*
The resistivity is zero below a critical temperature *[1 mark]*

2.2 How to grade your answer:
Level 0: There is no relevant information. *[No marks]*
Level 1: A correct material for one application with a brief explanation is given. *[1 to 2 marks]*
Level 2: A correct material for each application is given, with a clear explanation for at least one material choice given. *[3 to 4 marks]*
Level 3: Correct materials for each application are given. Reasons are given for each application, including reasons why the other materials would be rejected for each application. The answer is clear and well structured. *[5 to 6 marks]*
Indicative content:
The electromagnet
Material A is most suitable for this application.
A is a superconducting material.
Below the critical temperature, the resistivity of A drops to zero.
A low resistivity allows a very large current to flow through the wire.
A high current used in an electromagnet can create very strong magnetic fields.
Materials B and C do not reach low enough resistivities to produce very strong magnetic fields if used in an electromagnet.
Lighting circuit
Material C is the most suitable for this application.

Answers

The wires in the circuit need to be good conductors of electricity. The wires in the circuit will be running at room temperature. Room temperature is about 300 K. At 300 K material C has the lowest resistivity. This means C will be the best conductor at this temperature. C will have the smallest energy losses due to thermal energy loss. At room temperature, A and B have higher resistivities and so would be less suitable for this application.

2.3 $r = d \div 2 = 0.5 \times 10^{-3} \div 2 = 0.25 \times 10^{-3}$ m
$A = \pi r^2 = \pi \times (0.25 \times 10^{-3})^2 = 1.963... \times 10^{-7}$ m^2
$\rho = \dfrac{RA}{L}$ so $L = \dfrac{RA}{r}$
$L = \dfrac{0.05 \times 1.963... \times 10^{-7}}{2.3 \times 10^{-8}} = 0.426... = $ **0.43 m (to 2 s.f.)**
[3 marks in total, otherwise 1 mark for calculating the cross-sectional area of the wire, 1 mark for rearranging and substituting into the equation for resistivity]

2.4   The resistance of a superconductor is zero. This means no energy is transferred and wasted as heat energy *[1 mark]*.

Section Seven — Further Mechanics

Pages 74-77: Further Mechanics — 1

1   **B** *[1 mark]*
A would increase the amplitude of the forced vibrations of the glass. C could make the glass resonate if the sound frequency approached the resonant frequency of the glass. D could allow the amplitude of vibrations of the glass to increase as it gains more and more energy from the sound. Each of these could make the glass more likely to smash due to the high amplitude forced vibrations. However, increasing the degree of damping reduces the amplitude of the forced vibrations of the glass at its resonant frequency, which would make it less likely to smash due to resonance.

2   **D** *[1 mark]*
$v = \omega\sqrt{A^2 - x^2}$. Amplitude is 20% of 2.5 = 0.50 cm = 5.0×10^{-3} m.
$\omega = 2\pi f = 2\pi \times 4.0 = 8.0\pi$ rad s^{-1}.
$v = 8.0\pi\sqrt{(5.0 \times 10^{-3})^2 - (2.0 \times 10^{-3})^2} = 0.1151...\, ms^{-1} = $ *0.12 ms^{-1} (to 2 s.f.)*

3   **C** *[1 mark]*
$F = \dfrac{mv^2}{r}$, where centripetal force (F) is constant, radius (r) is constant (e.g. hands are fixed at the end of the rope), m decreases with time, so v must increase.

4   **D** *[1 mark]*
$T = 2\pi\sqrt{\dfrac{l}{g}}$ — if l is doubled, T increases by a factor of $\sqrt{2}$. As $f = \dfrac{1}{T}$, f changes by a factor of $\dfrac{1}{\sqrt{2}}$.

5.1   The acceleration of the object is proportional to its displacement from the midpoint and is directed towards the midpoint / $a \propto -x$ *[1 mark]*.

5.2

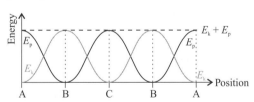

[3 marks in total — 1 mark for each correct line drawn]

5.3

x / v / a versus t graphs

[4 marks in total — 1 mark for each correct line drawn, 1 mark for correct maximum and minimum velocity, 1 mark for correct maximum and minimum acceleration]

5.4 $T = 2\pi\sqrt{\dfrac{l}{g}}$
Rearrange to make l the subject:
$T^2 = \dfrac{4\pi^2 l}{g} \Rightarrow l = \dfrac{T^2 g}{4\pi^2}$
For clock to correctly tell the time, each complete oscillation of the pendulum must take 2 seconds. Substitute in $T = 2$ s:
$l = \dfrac{2^2 \times 9.81}{4\pi^2} = 0.99396...$ m = **0.994 m (to 3 s.f.)** *[1 mark]*

5.5   E.g. friction at the pendulum's pivot / air resistance will cause energy to be lost from the system as heat *[1 mark]*.

5.6   The period/frequency of a simple harmonic oscillator/simple pendulum is independent of the amplitude of the oscillation *[1 mark]*, so a reduction in the oscillation's amplitude due to damping won't cause the period of oscillation to change from 2 seconds *[1 mark]*.

5.7 $T = 2\pi\sqrt{\dfrac{l}{g}}$
$l = 0.99396...$ m, $g = 9.78$ ms^{-2}
$T = 2\pi\sqrt{\dfrac{0.99396...}{9.78}} = 2.00306...$ s
For every 2.00306... s that passes, the clock moves forward 2 s, so for every 1 s that passes, the clock moves forward $\left(\dfrac{2}{2.00306...}\right)$ s.
One week = $(60 \times 60 \times 24 \times 7)$ s = 604 800 s.
In this time, clock moves forward $\dfrac{2 \times 604\,800}{2.00306...}$ s = 603 874.52... s.
603 874.52... − 604 800 = −925.478... s, so the clock is 925 s (to 3 s.f.)/15 minutes and 25 s slow after 1 week.
Time shown on clock after 1 week is **17:44:35**.
[3 marks for correct answer, otherwise 1 mark for calculating the period of the oscillation, 1 mark for calculating how far the clock has moved forward in 1 week]

6.1 v_{max} occurs when drum is spinning at 1250 rpm.
frequency = 1250 ÷ 60 = 20.8333... rps = 20.8333... Hz
$\omega = 2\pi f = 2\pi \times 20.8333... = 130.8996...$ rad s^{-1}
radius = diameter ÷ 2 = 0.35 ÷ 2 = 0.175 m
$v = \omega r = 130.8996... \times 0.175 = 22.9074...$ ms^{-1} = **23 ms^{-1} (to 2 s.f.)**
[2 marks for correct answer, otherwise 1 mark for calculating correct angular speed]

6.2   The rotation of the drum forces the washing machine to vibrate at the same frequency *[1 mark]*. As this driving frequency approaches the resonant frequency of the washing machine (750 rpm), the washing machine resonates/gains more and more energy from the driving force, causing the vibrations to increase in amplitude *[1 mark]*.

6.3   The profile would be flatter/less sharp/have a much smaller amplitude peak at the resonant frequency than the undamped model *[1 mark]*.

6.4   Critical damping *[1 mark]*, because the amplitude of the variation in weight measurements would be reduced in the shortest possible time *[1 mark]*.

Pages 78-80: Further Mechanics — 2

1.1 $m = 0.200$ kg:
$T^2 = 0.24^2 = 0.0576 = $ **0.06 s^2 (to 2 d.p.)**
% uncertainty in T^2 = % uncertainty in $T \times 2$
$\qquad\qquad = \left(\dfrac{0.06}{0.24} \times 100\right) \times 2 = 50\%$
Absolute uncertainty in $T^2 = 0.0576 \times 0.5$
$\qquad\qquad = 0.0288 = $ **0.03 s^2 (to 2 d.p.)**

$m = 1.200$ kg:
$T^2 = 0.59^2 = 0.3481 = $ **0.35 s^2 (to 2 d.p.)**
% uncertainty in T^2 = % uncertainty in $T \times 2$
$\qquad\qquad = \left(\dfrac{0.06}{0.59} \times 100\right) \times 2 = 20.338...\%$
Absolute uncertainty in $T^2 = 0.3481 \times 0.20338...$
$\qquad\qquad = 0.0708 = $ **0.07 s^2 (to 2 d.p.)**
[3 marks in total — 1 mark for correctly calculating both values of T^2, 1 mark for correctly calculating each percentage uncertainty]

1.2 E.g.

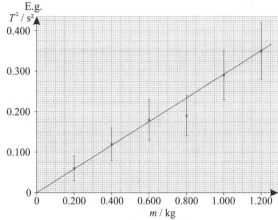

[4 marks in total — 1 mark for use of a sensible scale for y-axis (taking up more than half of available space and with sensible divisions), 1 mark for points plotted correctly, 1 mark for linear line of best fit (with similar numbers of points both above and below the line, ignoring the anomaly at 0.800 kg), 1 mark for error bars drawn correctly]

1.3 Squaring both sides of the equation, $T^2 = \frac{4\pi^2}{k}m$. As the spring constant, k, is controlled in the experiment, $\frac{4\pi^2}{k}$ is constant, so T^2 is directly proportional to m *[1 mark]*. The graph of T^2 against m is a linear graph through the origin. This shows that T^2 is directly proportional to m, so the graph supports the equation $T = 2\pi\sqrt{\frac{m}{k}}$ *[1 mark]*.

1.4 The spring constant, k, can be calculated from the gradient. Determine gradient of the line of best fit:
Passes through (1.110, 0.325) and (0, 0).
Gradient $= \frac{\Delta y}{\Delta x} = \frac{0.325}{1.110} = 0.29279...\text{s}^2\,\text{kg}^{-1}$
Gradient $= \frac{4\pi^2}{k}$, so $k = \frac{4\pi^2}{0.29279...} = 134.833...\text{Nm}^{-1}$
$= \textbf{135 Nm}^{-1}$ **(to 3 s.f.)**
Draw worst lines (ignoring the anomaly at 0.800 kg).

E.g.

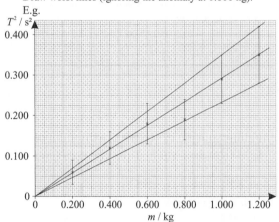

Highest possible line passes through (1.100, 0.385) and (0, 0), so gradient $= 0.385 \div 1.100 = 0.35\,\text{s}^2\,\text{kg}^{-1}$.

Lowest possible line passes through (0.750, 0.175) and (0, 0), so gradient $= 0.175 \div 0.750 = 0.23333...\,\text{s}^2\,\text{kg}^{-1}$.

Worst gradient is that of the lowest possible line.
Determining a value for the spring constant from this line:
$k = \frac{4\pi^2}{0.23333...} = 169.193...\text{Nm}^{-1}$.
Absolute uncertainty in $k = 169.193... - 134.833...$
$= 34.359...\text{Nm}^{-1}$
% uncertainty in $k = \frac{34.359...}{134.833...} \times 100 = 25.48...\%$
$= \textbf{25.5\% (to 3 s.f.)}$

[5 marks for 132-138 Nm⁻¹ with a percentage uncertainty of 23-27%, otherwise 1 mark for correctly calculating the gradient of the line of best fit, 1 mark for correctly calculating the spring constant from the gradient, 1 mark for correctly calculating the gradient of a worst line that passes through the error bars of all the points (ignoring the anomaly at 0.800 kg), 1 mark for correctly calculating the absolute uncertainty in the gradient. Full marks may be awarded if correct method is used on a graph that has been plotted incorrectly.]

1.5 E.g. measure the time taken for a larger number of complete oscillations to occur. This would reduce the percentage uncertainty for the period of the oscillation, and therefore the uncertainty in the spring constant. / Use a position sensor connected to a computer to record the displacement of the spring against time, and use that to find the period of the oscillation. This would reduce the absolute uncertainty in the timing measurements as it would eliminate reaction time errors/ human error. *[1 mark for valid improvement, 1 mark for correct explanation]*

2 Two forces acting on bobsleigh are its weight (W) and the reaction force from the track (R), e.g.

Resolve forces vertically:
$W = mg = R\cos(\phi)$ — equation 1
Resolve forces horizontally:
$R\sin(\phi) = $ resultant force — provides centripetal force that allows the bobsleigh to move round the corner.
Centripetal force, $F = \frac{mv^2}{r}$,
so $R\sin(\phi) = \frac{mv^2}{r}$ — equation 2.
Equation 2 ÷ equation 1: $\frac{R\sin(\phi)}{R\cos(\phi)} = \frac{mv^2}{rmg}$
Using $\tan(\phi) = \frac{\sin(\phi)}{\cos(\phi)}$, $\tan(\phi) = \frac{v^2}{rg}$
$v^2 = rg\tan(\phi)$
Use Figure 2 to calculate radius of circle, r:
144° in radians is $\frac{144 \times \pi}{180} = 0.8\pi$
$r = \frac{105}{0.8\pi} = 41.778...$ m
v_{max} occurs when $\tan(\phi)$ is at its maximum value. This occurs when ϕ is closest to 90°, so v_{max} occurs when $\phi = 71°$.
$v_{max}^2 = rg\tan(71°)$
$= 41.788... \times 9.81 \times \tan(71°) = 1190.273...$ m²s⁻²
$v_{max} = 34.500...$ ms⁻¹
So bobsleigh can theoretically go $\left(\frac{34.500... - 31}{31} \times 100\right)$
$= 11.2913...\% = \textbf{11\% (to 2 s.f.)}$ faster around the corner.
[6 marks for correct answer, otherwise 1 mark for correctly resolving forces vertically, 1 mark for correctly resolving forces horizontally, 1 mark for deriving an equation for v using centripetal force, 1 mark for calculating r, and 1 mark for calculating v_{max}]

Section Eight — Thermal Physics

Pages 81-83: Thermal Physics — 1

1 C *[1 mark]*
Particles suspended in a gas can also show Brownian motion, e.g. smoke particles in air.

2 B *[1 mark]*
A simplifying assumption of kinetic theory is that the time between a particle's collisions must be much greater than the duration of the collisions.

3 D *[1 mark]*
Temperature is proportional to the particles' average kinetic energy and, for an ideal gas, internal energy is equal to the total kinetic energy of the particles.

4 A *[1 mark]*
Charles's law gives: $\frac{V_1}{T_1} = \frac{V_2}{T_2}$. So, $V_2 = \frac{T_2 V_1}{T_1} = \frac{275 \times 1.8}{300} = 1.65\ m^3$.
$\Delta V = 1.8 - 1.65 = 0.15\ m^3$. $W = p\Delta V = 1.0 \times 10^5 \times 0.15 = 15\ 000\ J$.

5.1 Work is done on the gas to compress it, so energy is transferred to the gas *[1 mark]*. In order to maintain a constant temperature, the gas must transfer an equal amount of energy to its surroundings in the form of heat *[1 mark]*.

5.2

length / cm	pressure / kPa	$\dfrac{1}{pressure}$ / kPa^{-1}
20	100	0.010
18	111	0.0090
16	125	0.0080
14	143	0.0070
12	167	0.0060
10	200	0.0050

[1 mark if all values are correct and given to 2 significant figures]

5.3

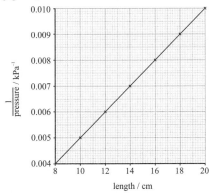

[1 mark for a sensibly scaled y-axis, 1 mark for correctly plotting data points and 1 mark for a line of best fit passing through all the data points]

5.4 The volume of the gas column: $V = \pi r^2 l$ where l is the length of the air column, and $pV = nRT$

Substitute in the expression for V, $p\pi r^2 l = nRT$ and rearrange to give: $\dfrac{1}{p} = \dfrac{\pi r^2 l}{nRT}$

The gradient of the graph of $\dfrac{1}{p}$ against l is given by $\dfrac{\pi r^2}{nRT}$

Calculate the graph's gradient, e.g.

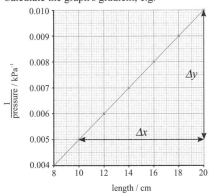

convert kPa^{-1} to Pa^{-1}: 0.010 kPa^{-1} = 1.0×10^{-5} Pa^{-1}
$\qquad\qquad\qquad\qquad\quad$ 0.005 kPa^{-1} = 0.5×10^{-5} Pa^{-1}

gradient = $\dfrac{\Delta y}{\Delta x} = \dfrac{1.0 \times 10^{-5} - 0.5 \times 10^{-5}}{0.20 - 0.10} = 5 \times 10^{-5}$

$n = \dfrac{\pi r^2}{\text{gradient} \times RT} = \dfrac{\pi \times 0.012^2}{5 \times 10^{-5} \times 8.31 \times 293}$
$= 3.71... \times 10^{-3}$ moles = **3.7×10^{-3} moles (to 2 s.f.)**

[3 marks for the correct answer, otherwise 1 mark for correctly calculating gradient and 1 mark for correctly expressing $\dfrac{1}{p}$ in terms of l]

5.5

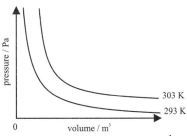

[1 mark for two lines shaped like $y = \dfrac{1}{x}$, 1 mark for indicating that the 303 K line will be located further from the origin]

5.6 Since the replacement vessel has a smaller radius, the smallest measurable increment in the air column's length will now correspond to a smaller increment in its volume. So, resolution is increased *[1 mark]*.

Pages 84-87: Thermal Physics — 2

1.1 If the 400 K chamber has volume V, the 350 K chamber will have volume $10.0 - V$. If the piston is stationary, there is no resultant force on the piston so pressure must be constant throughout the container. Charles's law states that at constant pressure, volume is proportional temperature. So, the ratio of the chambers' volumes will be equal to the ratio of their temperatures: $\dfrac{V}{10.0 - V} = \dfrac{400}{350}$
$350V = 4000 - 400V$
$750V = 4000$, so $V = \dfrac{4000}{750} = 5.33...$ m^3 = **5.3 m^3 (to 2 s.f.)**
[3 marks for correct answer, otherwise 1 mark for stating that pressure is constant and 1 mark for correctly using Charles's law]

Alternatively, you could have used the ideal gas law on both chambers and then solved the resulting simultaneous equations for V.

1.2 The 350 K chamber. In order to exert the same pressure as the 400 K chamber, the slower moving atoms in the 350 K must be colliding with the walls more frequently *[1 mark]*.

1.3 E.g. Total internal energy of an ideal gas = $N \times \dfrac{1}{2} m (c_{rms})^2$
$\qquad\qquad\qquad\qquad\qquad\qquad\qquad\qquad = \dfrac{3}{2} nRT$
Total internal energy before =
sum of the internal energies of the chambers
$= \dfrac{3}{2} nRT_1 + \dfrac{3}{2} nRT_2$
$= \left(\dfrac{3}{2} \times 3.5 \times 8.31 \times 350 \right) + \left(\dfrac{3}{2} \times 3.5 \times 8.31 \times 400 \right) = 32\,720.625$ J
Total internal energy after = $\dfrac{3}{2} nRT_{final}$
$\qquad\qquad\qquad\qquad\qquad = \dfrac{3}{2} \times 7 \times 8.31 \times T_{final} = 87.255 \times T_{final}$
Total internal energy after = Total internal energy before
$87.255 \times T_{final} = 32\,720.625$
$T_{final} = 32\,720.625 \div 87.255 = 375$ K
Average of the starting temperatures = $\dfrac{350 + 400}{2} = 375$ K
[1 mark for calculating the total internal energy from the initial conditions and 1 mark for calculating T_{final} and showing that it is the average of the initial temperatures]

Alternatively, you could have used the ideal gas equation to find expressions for the gas's temperature before and after mixing.

1.4 When the piston is removed, the more energetic particles from the 400 K chamber will undergo elastic collisions with the less energetic particles from the 350 K chamber and transfer energy to them *[1 mark]*.

2.1 The horizontal section of graph corresponding to the latent heat of vaporisation ($T = 100$ °C) is 42 little squares long.
Each little square corresponds to an energy of:
$(2.3 \times 10^6) \div 42 = 5.47... \times 10^4$ J
The horizontal section of graph corresponding to the latent heat of fusion ($T = 0$ °C) is 6 little squares long.
This corresponds to an energy of:
$(5.47... \times 10^4) \times 6 = 3.28... \times 10^5$ J
Since the graph is for 1.0 kg of water, this is equal to the specific latent heat of fusion, so:
specific latent heat of fusion = $3.28... \times 10^5$ Jkg^{-1}
$\qquad\qquad\qquad\qquad\qquad\qquad = $ **3.3×10^5 Jkg^{-1} (to 2 s.f.)**
[2 marks for correct answer, otherwise 1 mark for correctly identifying graph sections corresponding to fusion and vaporisation]

2.2 Overall the particles' potential energy has increased by the greater amount *[1 mark]*. During this interval, changes in state account for the majority of the increase in internal energy. (Internal energy = kinetic energy + potential energy). When matter changes state the potential energy of its particles increase, but the kinetic energy of its particles does not *[1 mark]*.

2.3 Liquid *[1 mark]*. The section of the graph corresponding to water's liquid phase shows the smallest increase in temperature for a unit increase in internal energy *[1 mark]*.

2.4 Increase in water's temperature $\Delta\theta_w = 22.0 - 20.0 = 2.0\ °C$
Decrease in brick's temperature $\Delta\theta_b = 50.0 - 22.0 = 28.0\ °C$
Since energy is conserved,
heat energy lost by the brick =
heat energy gained by the water
Energy gained by the water, $Q = m_w c_w \Delta\theta_w = 10 \times 4200 \times 2.0$
$= 84\ 000$ J
Find specific heat capacity of the brick:
$c_b = Q \div (m_b \Delta\theta_b) = 84\ 000 \div (3.5 \times 28.0)$
$= 857.142...\ \mathrm{Jkg^{-1}K^{-1}} = \textbf{0.86 kJkg}^{-1}\textbf{K}^{-1}$ **(to 2 s.f.)**
[2 marks for correct answer, otherwise 1 mark for calculating the energy transferred to the water]

3.1 Energy transferred to the heater in 1 second = 1100 J
useful energy transferred to air = efficiency × input energy
$= 0.76 \times 1100 = 836$ J
Calculate the mass of air that would be heated from 23.0 °C to 60.0 °C by this energy:
$Q = mc\Delta\theta$
$m = \dfrac{Q}{c\Delta\theta} = \dfrac{836}{1.0 \times 10^3 \times (60.0 - 23.0)} = 0.0225...$ kg
So, the hairdryer needs to expel air at a minimum rate of **0.023 kg s^{-1} (to 2 s.f.)**
[2 marks for correct answer, otherwise 1 mark for correctly calculating energy usefully transferred by the heater in 1 s]

3.2 $29.0\ \mathrm{gmol^{-1}} = 0.029\ \mathrm{kgmol^{-1}}$, 60.0 °C = 60.0 + 273 = 333 K,
Calculate the number of moles of air expelled by the hairdryer each second:
number of moles $= \dfrac{\text{mass}}{\text{molar mass}}$
$= \dfrac{0.0225...}{0.029} = 0.779...$ moles
Calculate the volume of air expelled by the hairdryer each second using the ideal gas equation:
$pV = nRT$
$V = \dfrac{nRT}{p} = \dfrac{0.779... \times 8.31 \times 333}{1.00 \times 10^5}$
$= 0.021560...\ \mathrm{m^3} = \textbf{0.0216 m}^3$ **(to 3 s.f.)**
[2 marks for correct answer, otherwise 1 mark for correctly calculating the numbers of moles of air expelled per second]

3.3 29.0 relative mass units = 29.0×1 atomic mass unit
$= 29.0 \times 1.661 \times 10^{-27}$
$= 4.81... \times 10^{-26}$ kg
$\frac{1}{2}m(c_{rms})^2 = \frac{3}{2}kT$
$c_{rms} = \sqrt{\dfrac{3kT}{m}} = \sqrt{\dfrac{3 \times 1.38 \times 10^{-23} \times 333}{4.81... \times 10^{-26}}}$
$= 534.9...\ \mathrm{ms^{-1}} = \textbf{535 ms}^{-1}$ **(to 3 s.f.)**
[2 marks for the correct answer, otherwise 1 mark for correct rearrangement and substitution]
You could also have calculated this using $\frac{1}{2}m(c_{rms})^2 = \frac{3}{2}\frac{RT}{N_A}$, and the fact that mN_A is equal to the molar mass.

4.1 E.g. kinetic theory is theoretical and so was based on assumptions and previous theories, whereas the ideal gas law is empirical and so was based on experimental observations *[1 mark]*.

4.2 Consider a single particle moving in one dimension with a velocity = u.
The particle collides elastically with the container's wall.
initial momentum = mu, final momentum = $-mu$
change in momentum = $(-mu) - mu = -2mu$
The force on the particle is equal to the rate of change of its momentum (Newton's 2nd law). The particle will exert an equal and opposite force on the wall (due to Newton's 3rd law) *[1 mark]*.
The time between consecutive collisions with the same wall of the container $t = \dfrac{2l}{u}$, therefore rate of collision $\dfrac{1}{t} = \dfrac{u}{2l}$.
Average force exerted on the container wall = change in momentum × rate of collision $= 2mu \times \dfrac{u}{2l} = \dfrac{mu^2}{l}$ *[1 mark]*
So, the total average force exerted by N particles is given by:
$F = \dfrac{m(u_1^2 + u_2^2 + ... + u_N^2)}{l}$

The mean square speed is defined as: $\overline{u^2} = \dfrac{(u_1^2 + u_2^2 + ... + u_N^2)}{N}$
Rearranging, $(u_1^2 + u_2^2 + ... + u_N^2) = N\overline{u^2}$
Substitute into expression for F: $F = \dfrac{Nm\overline{u^2}}{l}$ *[1 mark]*
Pressure $= \dfrac{F}{A}$. The area of one of the box's sides is $A = l^2$, so:
$p = \dfrac{\left(\dfrac{Nm\overline{u^2}}{l}\right)}{l^2} = \dfrac{Nm\overline{u^2}}{l^3}$
The volume of the box is $V = l^3$, so: $p = \dfrac{Nm\overline{u^2}}{V}$ *[1 mark]*
Let $\overline{c^2}$ be the mean square speed when particles are free to move in three dimensions.
By Pythagoras' theorem $\overline{c^2} = \overline{u^2} + \overline{v^2} + \overline{w^2}$, where u, v and w are the components of the velocity c in each of the three dimensions. Assuming that velocities are random, they will be evenly distributed between the three dimensions, so $\overline{u^2} = \overline{v^2} = \overline{w^2}$,
so $\overline{c^2} = 3\overline{u^2}$. Rearrange to give $\overline{u^2} = \frac{1}{3}\overline{c^2}$. Substitute this into
$p = \dfrac{Nm\overline{u^2}}{V}$ and rearrange to give: $pV = \frac{1}{3}Nm\overline{c^2}$ *[1 mark]*
The root mean square speed is defined as $c_{rms} = \sqrt{\overline{c^2}}$
Substituting this into the pressure equation gives
$pV = \frac{1}{3}Nm(c_{rms})^2$ *[1 mark]*

Section Nine — Gravitational and Electric Fields

Pages 88-90: Gravitational and Electric Fields — 1

1 **C** *[1 mark]*
$V = -\dfrac{GM}{r}$. *The drone remains at the same distance from the Earth's surface/ the centre of the Earth, so r is constant. G (gravitational constant) and M (mass of Earth) are constant, so the drone's gravitational potential, V, is constant. This means it must be travelling along an equipotential. Since the line AB is an equipotential, the gravitational field strength is constant along it. This means that the gravitational force acting on the drone is constant as it moves along AB.*

2 **B** *[1 mark]*
$T^2 \propto r^3$, *so* $T \propto r^{\frac{3}{2}}$ — *r has increased by a factor of 1.40, so T increases by a factor of* $1.40^{\frac{3}{2}} = 1.66$ *(to 3 s.f.).*

3 **D** *[1 mark]*
The escape velocity equation, $v = \sqrt{\dfrac{2GM}{r}}$, *rearranges to give the equation in option D. You could also have obtained the right answer by remembering that escape velocity is defined as the velocity of an object when its kinetic energy is equal to the negative of its gravitational potential energy, so* $\frac{1}{2}mv^2 = \dfrac{GMm}{r}$. *Then you can rearrange for v.*

4 **C** *[1 mark]*
For there to be zero net electrostatic force on the test charge, the forces exerted by Q_1 and by Q_2 must be equal and opposite. $F \propto \dfrac{Q}{r^2}$, *so when F = 0,* $\dfrac{9Q}{r_1^2} = \dfrac{Q}{r_2^2}$. *This rearranges to give $r_1 = 3r_2$, so the test charge needs to be 3 times further away from Q_1 than it is from Q_2.*

5.1 Rearrange $V = \dfrac{1}{4\pi\varepsilon_0}\dfrac{Q}{r}$ for Q:
$Q = 4\pi\varepsilon_0 rV = 4\pi \times 8.85 \times 10^{-12} \times 5.00 \times 10^{-14} \times 2650 \times 10^3$
$= 1.473... \times 10^{-17} = \textbf{1.47} \times \textbf{10}^{-17}$ **C (to 3 s.f.)** *[1 mark]*

5.2 $Q_B = Q - Q_A = (1.473... \times 10^{-17}) - (5.76 \times 10^{-18})$
$= 8.97... \times 10^{-18}$ C
Rearrange $F = \dfrac{1}{4\pi\varepsilon_0}\dfrac{Q_A Q_B}{r^2}$ for r:
$r = \sqrt{\dfrac{Q_A Q_B}{4\pi\varepsilon_0 F}} = \sqrt{\dfrac{5.76 \times 10^{-18} \times 8.97... \times 10^{-18}}{4\pi \times 8.85 \times 10^{-12} \times 181}} = 5.06... \times 10^{-14}$ m
Subtract the radius of nucleus A and the distance between the edges from this to find the radius of nucleus B:
$(5.06... \times 10^{-14}) - (3.71 \times 10^{-14}) - (6.32 \times 10^{-15})$
$= 7.259... \times 10^{-15} = \textbf{7.26} \times \textbf{10}^{-15}$ **m (to 3 s.f.)**
[2 marks for correct answer, otherwise 1 mark for correctly calculating the distance between the centres of the nuclei, r]
If you got 5.1 wrong, but carried out the calculations in 5.2 correctly with the incorrect value from 5.1, give yourself the marks.

6.1 An alpha particle is positively charged, so in the uniform electric field it would experience a constant electric force towards the negatively charged plates ($F = EQ$) *[1 mark]*. This is the only force acting on the alpha particle, so it accelerates towards the negatively charged plate, while the component of its velocity that is parallel to the plates remains constant *[1 mark]*. This causes the alpha particle to follow a parabolic path towards the negatively charged plates *[1 mark]*.

6.2   How to grade your answer:

Level 0:   There is no relevant information. *[No marks]*

Level 1:   A brief explanation is given of why at least one factor (particle mass or charge) makes it impossible to distinguish between the particles. Several errors with grammar, spelling, punctuation and legibility. The answer is poorly structured. *[1 to 2 marks]*

Level 2:   A brief explanation of why both the particles' mass and charge make it impossible to distinguish between the particles is given. There may be a few errors with grammar, spelling, punctuation and legibility. *[3 to 4 marks]*

Level 3:   A detailed explanation of why both particle mass and charge make it impossible to distinguish between the particles. The answer is well structured. Grammar, spelling and punctuation are used accurately and there is no problem with legibility. *[5 to 6 marks]*

Indicative content:

Electrons and positrons have equal and opposite charges, so will experience equal and opposite forces as they pass through the uniform electric field (as $F = EQ$).

Both particles have the same mass, so they will have equal and opposite accelerations towards their respective plates (as $F = ma$). Since the particles have the same constant horizontal speed and they accelerate towards the plates at the same rate, they will both travel the same distance through the detector and hit the same set of plates.

As a result, the paths of electrons and positrons will be identical, except electrons will move upwards to the positively-charged plate and positrons will move downwards to the negatively-charged plate.

As both particles are attracted to an oppositely-charged plate, the charge on the plate is always reduced when an electron/positron collides with it.

The size of charge is the same for both particles, so the charge on the plate is reduced or increased by the same amount in each case. As electric potential across the plates is proportional to the charge on the plates, both particles reduce or increase the overall potential difference of the same pair of plates by the same amount.

The observed fluctuation in the voltmeter reading will therefore be identical for either a positron or an electron, so they cannot be distinguished from one another in the particle detector.

6.3   Rearrange $g = \dfrac{F_{grav}}{m}$ for F_{grav}:

$F_{grav} = mg = 9.11 \times 10^{-31} \times 9.81 = 8.93691 \times 10^{-30}$ N

For the positron to pass through the detector without deflecting, the resultant force acting on the positron must be zero.

$F_{grav} - F_{elec} = 0$, so $F_{elec} = 8.93691 \times 10^{-30}$ N

$E = \dfrac{F_{elec}}{Q} = \dfrac{8.93691 \times 10^{-30}}{1.60 \times 10^{-19}} = 5.5855... \times 10^{-11}$ NC^{-1}

Rearrange $E = \dfrac{V}{d}$ for V:

$V = Ed = (5.5855... \times 10^{-11}) \times (5.0 \times 10^{-3})$

$= 2.7927... \times 10^{-13} = \mathbf{2.8 \times 10^{-13}}$ **V (to 2 s.f.)**

[3 marks for correct answer, otherwise 1 mark for correctly calculating electric force required, 1 mark for correctly calculating the electric field strength required]

Pages 91-93: Gravitational and Electric Fields — 2

1.1   E.g. they can be used to send TV/telephone signals *[1 mark]*. A satellite in a synchronous orbit remains above the same point on Earth, so the receiver/transmitter on Earth doesn't have to change its angle to remain pointing at the satellite *[1 mark]*.

1.2   E.g. the total energy of the satellite is constant once it is in orbit, so it would only need to use fuel for additional movement or functions, such as rotation *[1 mark]*.

1.3   The force acting on an object in circular motion is $F = \dfrac{mv^2}{r}$. The force causing this is the gravitational attraction towards Earth, $F = \dfrac{GMm}{r^2}$.

Equating the two forces: $\dfrac{mv^2}{r} = \dfrac{GMm}{r^2}$, $v^2 = \dfrac{GM}{r}$

$v = \sqrt{\dfrac{GM}{r}} = \sqrt{\dfrac{(6.67 \times 10^{-11}) \times (5.97 \times 10^{24})}{42\,200 \times 10^3}}$

$= 3071.80...$ ms^{-1} = **3070 ms^{-1} (to 3 s.f.)**

[2 marks for correct answer, otherwise 1 mark for equating centripetal force and gravitational force and rearranging for v]

You could have also calculated this answer by finding the distance travelled in one day, which is equal to the circumference of a circle with a radius equal to the orbital radius. You'd then use speed = distance ÷ time to get the answer.

1.4   Change in gravitational potential energy (ΔGPE) = $m\Delta V$

$= 2200 \times 5.3 \times 10^7 = 1.166 \times 10^{11}$ J

Kinetic energy (KE) = $\dfrac{1}{2}mv^2$

KE (final) = $\dfrac{1}{2} \times 2200 \times (3071.80...)^2 = 1.037... \times 10^{10}$ J

No frictional forces, so (GPE + KE) is constant.

KE (initial) = KE (final) + ΔGPE

$= (1.037... \times 10^{10}) + (1.166 \times 10^{11}) = 1.269... \times 10^{11}$ J

$v = \sqrt{\dfrac{2KE}{m}} = \sqrt{\dfrac{2 \times (1.269... \times 10^{11})}{2200}} = 10\,744.11...$ ms^{-1}

$= \mathbf{11\,000}$ **ms^{-1} (to 2 s.f.)**

[4 marks for correct answer, otherwise 1 mark for correctly calculating ΔGPE, 1 mark for correctly calculating the final KE, and 1 mark for correctly calculating the initial KE]

1.5   Change in gravitational potential (ΔV) can be calculated from the area under the g-r graph between 42.2×10^6 m and 42.5×10^6 m:

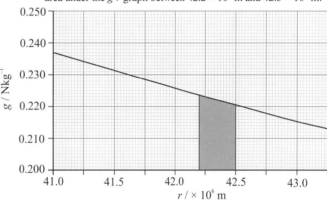

g / Nkg^{-1} (y-axis), *r / × 10^6 m* (x-axis)

Note the y-axis doesn't end at zero. However the area under the graph needs to include the area not shown by this graph between 0 and 0.200 Nkg^{-1} between the two values of r.

Total area of trapezium

$= 0.5 \times (0.2236 + 0.2205) \times ((42.5 - 42.2) \times 10^6)$

$= 66\,615 = \mathbf{66\,600}$ **Jkg^{-1} (to 3 s.f.)**

[2 marks for a final answer between 66 400 – 66 800 Jkg^{-1}, otherwise 1 mark for attempting to calculate the area under the graph between 42.2×10^6 m and 42.5×10^6 m]

Make sure you always check the values graph axes start at, it might not be zero.

2.1 $E = 20.0$ kNC^{-1} = 20.0×10^3 NC^{-1}, $d = 1.66$ km = 1660 m

Rearrange $E = \dfrac{V}{d}$: $V = Ed = 20.0 \times 10^3 \times 1660 = 3.32 \times 10^7$ V

Rearrange $\Delta W = Q\Delta V$ for Q: $Q = \dfrac{\Delta W}{\Delta V}$

Earth = 0 V, so $\Delta V = V$.

$Q = \dfrac{5.0 \times 10^8}{3.32 \times 10^7} = 15.0602...$ C = **15 C (to 2 s.f.)**

[2 marks for correct answer, otherwise 1 mark for correctly calculating the potential difference between the cloud and ground]

2.2   The bottom of the cloud is closer to the top of the tower than the ground. Electric field strength is inversely proportional to the distance between two charged plates, so the electric field strength between the cloud and the tower is stronger than the electric field strength between the cloud and the ground *[1 mark]*.

2.3   Close to Earth's surface, so can assume uniform gravitational field where $g = 9.81$ N/kg.

$g = \dfrac{F_g}{m}$ so $F_g = mg$

$= 1.04 \times 10^{-4} \times 9.81 = 1.02024 \times 10^{-3}$ N *[1 mark]*

Rearrange $E = \frac{F_e}{Q}$ for F_e:

$F_e = EQ = 20\,000 \times 1.7 \times 10^{-12} = 3.4 \times 10^{-8}$ N *[1 mark]*

The electrostatic force is approximately 10^5 times smaller than the force due to gravity, so the charge on the storm cloud will have no noticeable effect on graupel falling from the storm cloud *[1 mark]*.

Pages 94-96: Gravitational and Electric Fields — 3

1.1 Centripetal force keeping Dysnomia orbiting around Eris is

$F = \frac{mv^2}{r}$. This is caused by the gravitational attraction of Eris,

$F = \frac{GMm}{r^2}$.

Equating the two forces: $\frac{mv^2}{r} = \frac{GMm}{r^2}$ *[1 mark]*

$v^2 = \frac{GMmr}{mr^2} = \frac{GM}{r}$

$v = \sqrt{\frac{GM}{r}}$ — as $\sqrt{GM}$ is constant, $v \propto \frac{1}{\sqrt{r}}$ *[1 mark]*

1.2 distance = speed × time

During one complete orbit, Dysnomia travels a distance of $2\pi r$ in time T, so $T = \frac{2\pi r}{v}$.

Substituting $v = \sqrt{\frac{GM}{r}}$ into $T = \frac{2\pi r}{v}$:

$T = \frac{2\pi r}{\left(\sqrt{\frac{GM}{r}}\right)} \Rightarrow T = \frac{2\pi r \sqrt{r}}{\sqrt{GM}} \Rightarrow T^2 = \frac{4\pi^2 r^3}{GM} \Rightarrow M = \frac{4\pi^2 r^3}{GT^2}$

$T = 15.77 \times 24 \times 60 \times 60 = 1.362528 \times 10^6$ s

$M = \frac{4\pi^2 \times (3.735 \times 10^7)^3}{(6.67 \times 10^{-11}) \times (1.362528 \times 10^6)^2} = \frac{2.05698... \times 10^{24}}{123.827...}$

$= 1.661... \times 10^{22}$ kg $= \mathbf{1.66 \times 10^{22}}$ **kg (to 3 s.f.)**

[3 marks for correct answer, otherwise 1 mark for substitution to eliminate v and 1 mark for showing that $T^2 = \frac{4\pi^2 r^3}{GM}$]

1.3 E.g. Because the distance and period of an object's orbit is independent of its mass / because the mass of Dysnomia cancels out in any calculation where centripetal force and gravitational force are equated *[1 mark]*.

1.4 $V = -\frac{GM}{r}$

$V_A = -\frac{(6.67 \times 10^{-11}) \times (1.99 \times 10^{30})}{1.46 \times 10^{13}} = -9.091... \times 10^6$ Jkg^{-1}

$V_A - V_B = 1.38 \times 10^7$ Jkg^{-1}

$V_B = (-9.091... \times 10^6) - (1.38 \times 10^7) = -2.289...\times 10^7$ Jkg^{-1}

$r_B = -\frac{GM}{V_B} = -\frac{(6.67 \times 10^{-11}) \times (1.99 \times 10^{30})}{-2.289... \times 10^7}$

$r_B = 5.798... \times 10^{12}$ m $= \mathbf{5.80 \times 10^{12}}$ **m (to 3 s.f.)**

[3 marks for correct answer, otherwise 1 mark for correctly calculating V_A, 1 mark for correctly calculating V_B]

Make sure you get V_B and V_A the right way round in this calculation. Point B is closer to the Sun than A, so you should find that the gravitational potential at B is more negative than at A.

2.1 E.g.

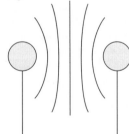

[1 mark]

If you're not sure what equipotentials will look like, try sketching field lines first. Then the equipotentials are perpendicular to these.

2.2 First, rearrange $\Delta W = Q\Delta V$ to calculate the change in potential of the left-hand sphere as it is moved:

$\Delta V = \frac{\Delta W}{Q} = \frac{0.34 \times 10^{-3}}{0.11 \times 10^{-6}} = 3090.90...$ V

Let the initial distance between the spheres be r_1 and the new distance between the spheres be r_2.

Since $V = \frac{1}{4\pi\varepsilon_0}\frac{Q}{r}$, the change in potential is:

$\Delta V = \frac{Q}{4\pi\varepsilon_0}\left(\frac{1}{r_2} - \frac{1}{r_1}\right)$

Rearrange for r_2:

$\frac{1}{r_2} - \frac{1}{r_1} = \frac{4\pi\varepsilon_0 \Delta V}{Q}$

$r_2 = 1 \div \left(\frac{4\pi\varepsilon_0 \Delta V}{Q} + \frac{1}{r_1}\right)$

$= 1 \div \left(\frac{4\pi \times 8.85 \times 10^{-12} \times 3090.90...}{-0.11 \times 10^{-6}} + \frac{1}{7.0 \times 10^{-2}}\right) = 0.0895...$ m

$F = \frac{1}{4\pi\varepsilon_0}\frac{Q_1 Q_2}{r_2^2}$

$= \frac{1}{4\pi \times 8.85 \times 10^{-12}} \times \frac{0.11 \times 10^{-6} \times -0.11 \times 10^{-6}}{(0.0895...)^2} = -0.0135...$ N

So the magnitude of the force = **0.014 N (to 2 s.f.)**

[3 marks for correct answer, otherwise 1 mark for calculating the change in potential of the left-hand sphere and 1 mark for calculating the new distance between the spheres]

2.3 E.g. The total downwards force acting on the balance is equal to the measured mass multiplied by the gravitational field strength. The downward force is equal to the sum of the sphere's weight, W, and the electrostatic force acting on the ball, F:

$F + W = mg$

Rearrange for m: $m = \frac{F + W}{g} = \frac{F}{g} + m_{sphere}$

Rearrange $E = \frac{F}{Q}$ for F and substitute into the equation:

$F = EQ \Rightarrow m = \frac{EQ}{g} + m_{sphere}$

$E = \frac{V}{d}$ so: $\Rightarrow m = \frac{QV}{dg} + m_{sphere}$

The equation of the graph is $y = mx + c$, so: gradient $= \frac{Q}{dg}$

Rearrange for Q: $Q = $ gradient $\times dg$

gradient $= \frac{\text{change in } y}{\text{change in } x}$

The mass is in grams but needs to be in kilograms to be able to be substituted into the equation, so:

gradient $= \frac{0.20136 - 0.20120}{37.0 - 0.0} = 4.32... \times 10^{-6}$

$Q = 4.32... \times 10^{-6} \times 0.20 \times 9.81 = 8.48... \times 10^{-6}$

$= \mathbf{8.5 \times 10^{-6}}$ **C (to 2 s.f.)**

[3 marks for correct answer, otherwise 1 mark for obtaining $m = \frac{QV}{dg} + m_{ball}$ and 1 mark for correctly calculating the gradient]

Section Ten — Capacitors

Pages 97-99: Capacitors — 1

1 C *[1 mark]*

Q and V are directly proportional for a capacitor. The area under a Q-V graph is equal to the area of a triangle with a height Q and a base V, area $= \frac{1}{2}QV$. This is equal to the energy stored by the capacitor $E = \frac{1}{2}QV$.

2 A *[1 mark]*

$C = Q \div V$, where Q is the size of the charge on one of the plates.

$144\ \mu C = 1.44 \times 10^{-4}$ C

$C = Q \div V = 1.44 \times 10^{-4} \div 12 = 1.2 \times 10^{-5}$ F $= 12\ \mu F$

3 B *[1 mark]*

4 C *[1 mark]*

$V_0 = 8.0$ V, $R = 60.0\ k\Omega = 60\,000\ \Omega$,

$C = 20.0\ \mu F = 2.00 \times 10^{-5}$ F, $t = 1.2$ s.

$V = V_0 e^{\frac{-t}{RC}} = 8.0e^{\left(\frac{-1.2}{60\,000 \times 2.00 \times 10^{-5}}\right)} = 8.0e^{-1} = 2.94...$ V $= 2.9$ V (to 2 s.f.)

5.1 $C = \frac{A\varepsilon_0 \varepsilon_r}{d}$, $\varepsilon_0 = 8.85 \times 10^{-12}$ Fm^{-1}, $\varepsilon_r = 1.0$ for air,

$A = 0.40$ m^2, $d = 5.0$ cm $= 0.050$ m.

So $C = \frac{0.40 \times 8.85 \times 10^{-12} \times 1.0}{0.050} = 7.08 \times 10^{-11}$ F

$= \mathbf{7.1 \times 10^{-11}}$ **F (to 2 s.f.)** *[1 mark]*

5.2 $E = \frac{1}{2}CV^2 = \frac{1}{2} \times 7.08 \times 10^{-11} \times 20.0^2$

$= 1.416 \times 10^{-8}$ J $= \mathbf{1.4 \times 10^{-8}}$ **J (to 2 s.f.)** *[1 mark]*

If you calculated the wrong value in 5.1 but used your answer to calculate the energy stored correctly in 5.2, you'd get the mark for this part.

5.3 Originally $C = \frac{A\varepsilon_0 \varepsilon_r}{d}$.

The area is changed to $0.5A$ and the distance $= 2d$,

so the new capacitance $C_{new} = \frac{0.5A\varepsilon_0 \varepsilon_r}{2d} = \frac{A\varepsilon_0 \varepsilon_r}{4d} = \frac{C}{4}$.

So the capacitance will be a quarter of the original capacitance.

[1 mark for stating the maximum capacitance will be a quarter of the original capacitance, 1 mark for a correct supporting explanation]

6.1 $C = 100.0 \text{ nF} = 100.0 \times 10^{-9} \text{ F}$

$E = \dfrac{1}{2}\dfrac{Q^2}{C}$, which rearranges to give

$Q = \sqrt{2EC} = \sqrt{2 \times 7.2 \times 10^{-6} \times 100.0 \times 10^{-9}} = \mathbf{1.2 \times 10^{-6} \text{ C}}$

[2 marks for correct answer, otherwise 1 mark for correct rearrangement and substitution into the equation]

6.2 The time for the charge to halve = $T_{\frac{1}{2}} = 0.69RC$.

$R = T_{\frac{1}{2}} \div 0.69C = (8.0 \times 10^{-3}) \div (0.69 \times 100.0 \times 10^{-9})$

$= 115\,942.0... \ \Omega = \mathbf{120\,000 \ \Omega \text{ (to 2 s.f.)}}$

[2 marks for correct answer, otherwise 1 mark for stating $T_{\frac{1}{2}} = 0.69RC$]

You could have also answered this question by plugging the numbers into the equation for charge for a discharging capacitor and rearranging to find R.

6.3 $t = 4.0 \text{ ms} = 4.0 \times 10^{-3} \text{ s}$

$Q = Q_0 e^{\left(\frac{-t}{RC}\right)} = (1.2 \times 10^{-6})e^{\left(\frac{-4.0 \times 10^{-3}}{115\,942.0... \times 100.0 \times 10^{-9}}\right)}$

$= 8.49... \times 10^{-7} \text{ C} = \mathbf{8.5 \times 10^{-7} \text{ C} \text{ (to 2 s.f.)}}$

[2 marks for correct answer, otherwise 1 mark for correct substitution]

7.1 $400 \text{ cm}^2 = 0.04 \text{ m}^2$, $0.40 \text{ mm} = 0.00040 \text{ m}$

$C = \dfrac{A\varepsilon_0\varepsilon_r}{d}$, so:

$\varepsilon_r = \dfrac{Cd}{A\varepsilon_0} = (3.27 \times 10^{-9} \times 0.00040) \div (0.04 \times 8.85 \times 10^{-12})$

$= 3.69... = \mathbf{3.7 \text{ (to 2 s.f.)}}$

[2 marks for correct answer, otherwise 1 mark for correct rearrangement and substitution]

7.2 How to grade your answer:

Level 0:   There is no relevant information. *[No marks]*

Level 1:   There is an incomplete explanation of how a dielectric increases the capacitance of a capacitor. The answer is poorly structured and there are several errors with grammar, spelling, punctuation and legibility. *[1 to 2 marks]*

Level 2:   There is a brief explanation of how a dielectric increases the capacitance of a capacitor, with some reference to polarisation. There are only a few errors with grammar, spelling, punctuation and legibility. *[3 to 4 marks]*

Level 3:   There is a full explanation of how a dielectric increases the capacitance of a capacitor. The answer is well structured. Grammar, spelling and punctuation are used accurately and there is no problem with legibility. *[5 to 6 marks]*

Indicative content:

When a charge builds up on the plates of a capacitor, an electric field is created between the two plates.

The electrons inside a dielectric are not free to move.

When the dielectric material is in the presence of the electric field generated by the capacitor, molecules within the dielectric rotate and align themselves with the electric field. This is known as polarisation.

The molecules have their own electric fields, which oppose the applied electric field due to the charges on the capacitor plates.

This results in an overall reduction of the electric field strength between the two plates.

The electric field strength is related to the potential difference required to move charges between the plates of the capacitor.

The stronger the electric field, the larger the potential difference must be to move a set amount of charge.

So by reducing the electric field strength, the potential difference needed to move a charge Q is reduced.

Capacitance is defined as the ratio of charge stored to potential difference, $C = Q \div V$. So as V for a given Q has decreased, this causes an increase in the capacitance, C.

Pages 100-101: Capacitors — 2

1.1 $L = 10.0 \text{ cm} = 0.100 \text{ m}$,

$a = 5.0 \text{ cm} = 0.050 \text{ m}$, $b = 6.0 \text{ cm} = 0.060 \text{ m}$

$\dfrac{C}{L} = \dfrac{2\pi\varepsilon_0\varepsilon_r}{\ln\left(\frac{b}{a}\right)}$

$C = \dfrac{2\pi\varepsilon_0\varepsilon_r L}{\ln\left(\frac{b}{a}\right)} = \dfrac{2\pi \times 8.85 \times 10^{-12} \times 2.5 \times 0.100}{\ln\left(\frac{0.060}{0.050}\right)}$

$= 7.624... \times 10^{-11} \text{ F} = \mathbf{7.6 \times 10^{-11} \text{ F} \text{ (to 2 s.f.)}}$

[2 marks for correct answer, otherwise 1 mark for correct rearrangement and substitution]

1.2 $R = 1.2 \text{ M}\Omega = 1.2 \times 10^6 \ \Omega$, $C = 7.624... \times 10^{-11} \text{ F}$, $V_0 = 25 \text{ V}$

$V = V_0\left(1 - e^{\left(\frac{-t}{RC}\right)}\right)$

$e^{\left(\frac{-t}{RC}\right)} = 1 - \dfrac{V}{V_0}$

$\dfrac{-t}{RC} = \ln\left(1 - \dfrac{V}{V_0}\right)$

$t = -RC\ln\left(1 - \dfrac{V}{V_0}\right)$

$= -(1.2 \times 10^6 \times 7.624... \times 10^{-11}) \times \ln\left(1 - \dfrac{14}{25}\right)$

$= 0.00007511... \text{ s}$

$= \mathbf{7.5 \times 10^{-5} \text{ s} \text{ (to 2 s.f.)}}$

[3 marks for correct answer, otherwise 1 mark for correct rearrangement for t, 1 mark for correct substitution]

1.3 How to grade your answer:

Level 0:   There is no relevant information. *[No marks]*

Level 1:   There is an incomplete method describing how to investigate how capacitance varies with length. The answer is poorly structured and there are several errors with grammar, spelling, punctuation and legibility. *[1 to 2 marks]*

Level 2:   There is a brief method describing how to investigate how capacitance varies with length. There is at least one step in the method that will help minimise the error in the results. There are only a few errors with grammar, spelling, punctuation and legibility. *[3 to 4 marks]*

Level 3:   There is a full, clear method of how to investigate how capacitance varies with length, including ways of minimising errors in the results. The answer is well structured. Grammar, spelling and punctuation are used accurately and there is no problem with legibility. *[5 to 6 marks]*

Indicative content:

Measure the total length of the inner tube (and all subsequent length measurements) using, e.g. a millimetre ruler.

Find L (the overlap length) by measuring the length of the inner tube outside the larger tube and subtract this from the total length of the inner tube.

The capacitor should then be fully charged.

A multimeter could then be attached across the capacitor to measure its capacitance.

The circuit should then be disconnected and the capacitor discharged. The length of the capacitor, L, should then be altered by, e.g. 2 cm.

The capacitor could then be recharged and its capacitance measured.

This process of changing the length and measuring the capacitance should be repeated at least 5 times. The experiment should then be repeated and a mean capacitance calculated for each length L.

The equation given shows that capacitance and length are directly proportional.

Plot the mean values of capacitance against length and draw a line of best fit to show whether the results show these variables are directly proportional or not.

You could also calculate the gradient and confirm it is equal to $\dfrac{2\pi\varepsilon_0\varepsilon_r}{\ln\left(\frac{b}{a}\right)}$.

To minimise the uncertainty in the results, you would use high precision measuring equipment to minimise the uncertainty in individual length and capacitance measurements.

Taking multiple measurements and taking the mean of those values can increase the accuracy and decrease the overall uncertainty in those measurements.

Having multiple measurements can also make it easier to identify anomalous results which will also help to minimise the uncertainty in the results.

2.1 $Q = Q_0 e^{\left(\frac{-t}{RC}\right)}$ for a discharging capacitor.

The graph is linear and so has an equation of the form $y = mx + c$. Rearrange the equation for Q to be in the form $y = mx + c$, where $y = \ln Q$ and $x = t$.

Taking ln of both sides gives: $\ln Q = \ln Q_0 - \dfrac{t}{RC}$.

The gradient, m, of the graph is equal to $-\dfrac{1}{RC}$, and the

y-intercept of the graph is equal to $\ln Q_0$.

Gradient of the graph $= \dfrac{\text{change in } y}{\text{change in } x} = \dfrac{(6.5 - 6.9)}{20.0 - 0} = -0.02$

$-\dfrac{1}{RC} = -0.02$, so time constant $= RC = \textbf{50 s}$

[3 marks for correct answer, otherwise 1 mark for showing gradient = -(1 ÷ RC), 1 mark for correct calculation of gradient]

2.2 $I = I_0 e^{\left(\frac{-t}{RC}\right)} = 1.2 \times 10^{-3} \times e^{(-8.0 \div 50)}$

        $= 0.0010225... \text{ A} = \textbf{0.0010 A (to 2 s.f.)}$

[2 marks for correct answer, otherwise 1 mark for correct substitution]

2.3   Time taken for $Q = 0.4Q_0$

For a discharging capacitor:

$Q = Q_0 e^{\left(\frac{-t}{RC}\right)} = 0.4Q_0 \Rightarrow e^{\left(\frac{-t}{RC}\right)} = 0.4 \Rightarrow \dfrac{-t}{RC} = \ln 0.4$

$t = -RC \ln 0.4 = -50 \ln 0.4 = 45.8... \text{ s} = \textbf{46 s (to 2 s.f.)}$

[3 marks for correct answer, otherwise 1 mark for correct rearrangement for t, 1 mark for correct substitution]

Section Eleven — Magnetic Fields

Pages 102-105: Magnetic Fields — 1

1   B *[1 mark]*

2   C *[1 mark]*

input power = 184 210 000 = $I_p V_p$

efficiency = $\dfrac{I_s V_s}{I_p V_p} = \dfrac{1400 \times 125\,000}{184\,210\,000} = 0.9500... = 95\%$ (to 2 s.f.)

3   D *[1 mark]*

The peak current shown in the trace, $I_0 = 2.1$ A.

$I_{rms} = I_0 \div \sqrt{2} = 2.1 \div \sqrt{2} = 1.484...$ A

$V_{rms} = P_{rms} \div I_{rms} = 9.00 \div 1.484... = 6.060...$ V $= 6.1$ V (to 2 s.f.)

4   B *[1 mark]*

$N\phi = BAN\cos\theta$, so $B = \phi \div A\cos\theta$

Current through the side of the coil is perpendicular to field, so the force on it is given by $F = BIl$. Using expression for B above:

$F = \dfrac{\phi \times l \times l}{A \times \cos\theta} = \dfrac{(8.66 \times 10^{-3}) \times 2.0 \times 0.060}{(0.060^2) \times \cos 30°} = 0.3333...$ N

$= 0.33$ N (to 2 s.f.)

5.1   From Table 1, the mass recorded for the 5.88 A current is 7.1 g = 0.0071 kg. The error in the mass = 0.1 g = 0.0001 kg

The force on the wire using these results,

$F = mg = 0.0071 \times 9.81 = 0.069651 \text{ N} = 0.070$ N (to 2 s.f.)

Error in this force $= 0.0001 \times 9.81$

                $= 0.000981 = 0.001$ N (to 3 d.p.)

So experimental force $= 0.070 \pm 0.001$ N

Theoretical force, $F = BIl = (80 \times 10^{-3}) \times 5.88 \times 0.15$

                       $= 0.07056$ N

This lies within the uncertainty range of the experimental result, so the student's result agrees with the result predicted by the theory.

[3 marks for correct conclusion with supporting calculations, otherwise 1 mark for correct calculation of experimental force using F = mg and 1 mark for correct calculation of theoretical force from F = BIl]

5.2   Any two from: e.g. the student could alter the experimental set-up such that only the length of wire between the magnets is perpendicular to the magnetic field, and the rest of the wire is parallel to the field. This would reduce the systematic error on the mass reading caused by the force on the wire outside the length being considered. / The student could switch off the power supply between readings, which would allow the wire to cool down/would stop the wire from overheating. This would improve the accuracy of the student's results by reducing the random error caused by the resistance of the wire increasing with the temperature of the wire, which may cause the current through the wire to change during measurement. / The student could use a set square to make sure that the test wire is perfectly parallel to the faces of the magnets/perpendicular to the magnetic field. This would improve the accuracy of the student's results by reducing the systematic error in the results, as the force on the wire will be lower than stated by the theory if the wire is not perpendicular to the field. *[2 marks — 1 mark for each correct answer]*

5.3

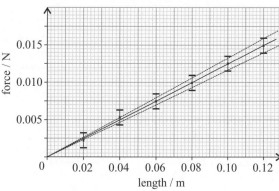

The gradient of the graph is equal to $\dfrac{F}{l}$.

Gradient $= \dfrac{0.015 - 0}{0.12 - 0} = 0.125$

$F = BIl$, so $B = \dfrac{F}{Il} = \text{gradient} \div I = 0.125 \div 2.5 = 0.050$ T

To find the uncertainty, draw a line of worst fit (shown by dotted lines) and find the gradient. In this instance, you can tell by eye that the difference in gradient between each worst line and the best fit line is the same (as both lines start at the origin and end an equal distance from the line of best fit). Either line can be used to calculate the uncertainty in the gradient.

Using the bottom line: gradient $= \dfrac{0.014 - 0}{0.12 - 0} = 0.116...$

Worst value of B = gradient of worst line $\div I$

                $= 0.116... \div 2.5 = 0.0466...$ T

Uncertainty in $B = 0.050 - 0.04666...$

                $= 0.00333... = 0.003$ T (to 3 d.p.)

So $B = \textbf{0.050} \pm \textbf{0.003 T}$

[4 marks for correct answer, otherwise 1 mark for correct calculation of gradient, 1 mark for correct rearrangement and substitution for B, and 1 mark for correct calculation of worst gradient]

6.1   E.g. a cyclotron consists of two semicircular electrodes, placed inside a uniform magnetic field *[1 mark]*. Charged particles are fired into the centre of the cyclotron, where they are deflected by the magnetic field into a circular path *[1 mark]*. When they reach the edge of one semicircular electrode, they are accelerated by a potential difference between the electrodes until they reach the second semicircular electrode *[1 mark]*. The magnetic field again deflects the particle so it still follows a circular path in the second electrode, but the radius of the particle's path is larger as its speed has increased. It returns to the first electrode and this process continues until the particle has been accelerated to a high speed and is then released from the cyclotron *[1 mark]*.

6.2

Force

⊗   ⊗   ⊗

   ↑ v →

⊗   P⊗   ⊗*[1 mark]*

$F = BQv = 0.38 \times 1.6 \times 10^{-19} \times 1.2 \times 10^7 = 7.296 \times 10^{-13}$ N

$F = ma$, so $a = \dfrac{F}{m}$

$a = \dfrac{7.296 \times 10^{-13}}{1.67 \times 10^{-27}} = 4.3688... \times 10^{14} \text{ ms}^{-2}$

           $= \textbf{4.4} \times \textbf{10}^{14} \textbf{ ms}^{-2}$ **(to 2 s.f.)** *[1 mark]*

6.3 $F = BQv$ and $F = \dfrac{mv^2}{r}$, so $BQv = \dfrac{mv^2}{r}$

Rearrange for v: $v = \dfrac{BQr}{m}$

$E_k = \frac{1}{2}mv^2$, so: $E_k = \frac{1}{2} \times m \times \left(\dfrac{BQr}{m}\right)^2 = \dfrac{B^2 Q^2 r^2}{2m}$

$E_k = \dfrac{0.38^2 \times (1.6 \times 10^{-19})^2 \times 1.5^2}{2 \times 1.67 \times 10^{-27}} = 2.490... \times 10^{-12}$

                         $= \textbf{2.5} \times \textbf{10}^{-12}$ **J (to 2 s.f.)**

[3 marks for correct answer, otherwise 1 mark for correct expression for velocity of the proton and 1 mark for correct substitution]

Pages 106-109: Magnetic Fields — 2

1.1   When the test coil is switched on, a magnetic field is generated causing a large rate of change in magnetic flux through the search coil, causing the first emf peak in the trace *[1 mark]*. The magnetic flux then remains constant, so no emf is induced until the test coil is switched off. At that point, another change in magnetic flux occurs as the field strength decreases, generating the second emf peak in the opposite direction *[1 mark]*.

1.2 The size of the induced emf depends on the rate of change of flux linkage, which is directly proportional to the magnetic flux density (as flux linkage = $BAN\cos\theta$) *[1 mark]*. The larger the radius of the test coil, the lower the induced emf is in the search coil, and therefore the weaker the magnetic field near the centre of the test coil *[1 mark]*.

1.3 The induced emf is equal to the rate of change of flux linkage *[1 mark]*. In position A, there is a large amount of flux linkage (many field lines pass through the coil). If the coil undergoes rotation by a small angle, the flux linkage (and the number of field lines through the coil) will not change significantly, meaning little to no emf would be induced *[1 mark]*. In position B, the flux linkage is zero (no field lines pass through the coil). If the coil undergoes rotation by a small angle, the flux linkage will increase significantly (as the number of field lines passing through the coil will increase significantly), causing a large emf to be induced *[1 mark]*.

1.4 Position A in Figure 4 will produce the maximum magnitude of emf, and Position B will produce the minimum magnitude of emf *[1 mark]*. In position A, a maximum number of field lines are passing through the search coil, so its flux linkage is at a maximum. When the current alternates, the field will change direction, and so it will experience its largest change in flux linkage, and produce a maximum magnitude of emf *[1 mark]*. In position B, no field lines pass through the search coil, and so the coil has a flux linkage of 0. When the current alternates and the field changes direction, the coil still has no field lines passing through it, so there is no change in flux linkage and no emf is induced *[1 mark]*.

2.1 Design B would be more efficient than design A. Eddy currents will be induced in the core of the transformer in design A *[1 mark]*. They will create a magnetic field that opposes the magnetic field that induced them, reducing the field strength. They will also dissipate energy as heat *[1 mark]*. The lamination of the core in design B helps to reduce eddy currents, and so less energy will be wasted by them in this transformer compared to design A *[1 mark]*.

2.2 efficiency = $\dfrac{I_s V_s}{I_p V_p}$

Input power is the same for both transformers, so can find input power from transformer X:

Input power = $I_p V_p = \dfrac{I_{sX} V_{sX}}{(\text{efficiency})_X} = \dfrac{1200.0 \times 275\,000}{0.9867}$
$= 3.344... \times 10^8$ W

For transformer Y:
efficiency = $\dfrac{I_{sY} V_{sY}}{I_p V_p} = \dfrac{830.0 \times 400\,000}{3.344... \times 10^8}$
$= 0.99268 = 99.268\% = $ **99.27% (to 4 s.f.)**

[3 marks for correct answer, otherwise 1 mark for correct calculation of input power and 1 mark for correct substitution]

2.3 Force on the second cable is equal to $F = BI_2l$, where B is the magnetic flux density of the field generated by the first cable, and I_2 is the current through the second cable.

$B = \dfrac{\mu_0 I_1}{2\pi r} = \dfrac{4\pi \times 10^{-7} \times 1200}{2 \times \pi \times 5.2} = 4.615... \times 10^{-5}$ T

Force per unit length on second wire,
$\dfrac{F}{l} = BI_2 = 4.615... \times 10^{-5} \times 1200$
$= 0.05538...$ Nm^{-1} = **5.5 $\times 10^{-2}$ Nm^{-1} (to 2 s.f.)**

[3 marks for correct answer, otherwise 1 mark for correct calculation of magnetic flux density and 1 mark for correct rearrangement and substitution]

3.1 flux linkage = $N\phi = BAN\cos\theta$, so $B = \dfrac{N\phi}{AN\cos\theta}$.

$A = (\text{side length})^2 = 0.022^2 = 0.000484$ m^2

$B = \dfrac{7.0 \times 10^{-3}}{0.000484 \times 25 \times \cos 45°} = 0.818...$ T = **0.82 T (to 2 s.f.)**

Percentage uncertainty in A
$= 2 \times$ percentage uncertainty in length
$= 2 \times (0.001 \div 0.022) = 0.0909... = 9.09...\%$

Percentage uncertainty in $N\phi$
$= (((0.1 \times 10^{-3}) \div (7.0 \times 10^{-3})) \times 100) = 1.428...\%$

Percentage uncertainty in B is equal to percentage uncertainty in $N\phi$ + percentage uncertainty in A

Percentage uncertainty in $B = 1.428... + 9.09...$
$= 10.5...\% = 11\%$ (to 2 s.f.)

$B =$ **0.82 T ± 11% (to 2 s.f.)**

[3 marks for correct answer, otherwise 1 mark for correct working to find B and 1 mark for correct calculation of uncertainties]

3.2 $V_{rms} = V_{peak} \div \sqrt{2}$

V_{peak} is equal to the maximum emf induced by the rotating coil.
$V_{peak} = \sqrt{2}\, V_{rms} = \sqrt{2} \times 0.11 = 0.1555...$ V *[1 mark]*
V_{peak} and peak emf occur when $\varepsilon = BAN\omega\sin(\omega t)$ is at a maximum. This occurs when $\sin(\omega t) = 1$. *[1 mark]*
So $\varepsilon = BAN\omega$
$\omega = \varepsilon \div BAN = 0.1555... \div (0.818... \times 0.022^2 \times 25)$
$= 15.71$ rad s^{-1} = **16 rad s^{-1} (to 2 s.f.)** *[1 mark]*
Percentage uncertainty in ε = percentage uncertainty in V_{rms} (since $\sqrt{2}$ is constant) = $((0.01 \div 0.11) \times 100) = 9.09...\%$
Percentage uncertainty in $B = 10.5...\%$
Percentage uncertainty in $A = 9.09...\%$
So, percentage uncertainty in ω
$= 10.5... + 9.09... + 9.09... = 28.70... =$ **29 % (to 2 s.f.)** *[1 mark]*
E.g. The result is very inaccurate, as the percentage uncertainty is very large. The measurement for side length has a large percentage uncertainty, so a piece of equipment with a higher resolution, e.g. a calliper, could be used to make these length measurements. / The magnetic flux density of the field could be measured directly to reduce the uncertainty introduced from calculating it *[1 mark for commenting that the accuracy is poor and for suggesting one way to improve it]*.

Section Twelve — Nuclear Physics

Pages 110-113: Nuclear Decay and Half-Life — 1

1   D *[1 mark]*
Nuclear density is roughly constant for all nuclei.
2   C *[1 mark]*
3   C *[1 mark]*
$\Delta N \div \Delta t = -\lambda N$ so $\Delta N = -\Delta t \lambda N = -20 \times 2.5 \times 10^{-4} \times 10\,000 = -50$
4   D *[1 mark]*
The intensity and the distance from the source are related by an inverse square law. The same detector is used both times, so the area radiation is detected over is constant. This means the count rate detected is also related to the distance by an inverse square law. The distance has halved, so the intensity will have increased by a factor of $(1 \div (0.5)^2) = 4$. 4×144 cps $= 576$ cps.
5   B *[1 mark]*
$A = A_0 e^{-\lambda t}$ so $\ln(A) = -\lambda t + \ln(A_0)$ which corresponds to $y = mx + c$
so the gradient, $m = -\lambda$.
E.g. $m = \Delta y \div \Delta x = (9.6 - 11.4) \div (6.0 - 0.0) = -0.3$ so $\lambda = 0.3$ s^{-1}

6.1 The student could measure the counts per second when there is no radioactive source present, and subtract this from their results for the counts per second of the radioactive sources to remove the background radiation count rate from their readings *[1 mark]*. This would reduce the systematic error in their results *[1 mark]*.

6.2 Any two from: e.g. radon (gas) / rocks / cosmic rays / radioactive isotopes in living things / nuclear waste / medical sources *[2 marks — 1 mark for each correct answer]*.

6.3 Any two from: e.g. store the radioactive source in a lead-lined container when they are not using it, as the lead will absorb all of the radiation / use tongs when handling the radioactive sources to reduce the risk of contamination / minimise the exposure to radiation by staying as far away from the radioactive sources as possible (as intensity of radiation is inversely proportional to the square of the distance from the source), e.g. using tongs to hold the radioactive source as far away from the body as possible *[2 marks — 1 mark for each correct answer]*.

6.4 Beta radiation is produced because the count rate falls substantially (but not to zero) when a 2 cm sheet of aluminium is used, but does not when paper is used *[1 mark]*. Gamma radiation is produced because the count rate falls to a lower value than with aluminium when a 2 cm sheet of lead is used *[1 mark]*.

6.5 E.g. controlling aluminium foil thickness as strontium-90 produces beta radiation, which would be only partially absorbed by thin aluminium, but is totally absorbed past a certain thickness, so changes in the absorption can be used to monitor thickness *[1 mark for a correct use and 1 mark for a supporting explanation]*.

6.6 The initial count rate is 40 cps, it takes 34 s for this to drop to 20 cps.
$T_{1/2} = \ln 2 \div \lambda$ so $\lambda = \ln 2 \div T_{1/2} = \ln 2 \div 34$
$\qquad\qquad = 0.0203... \text{ s}^{-1} = \textbf{0.020 s}^{-1} \textbf{ (to 2 s.f.)}$
[2 marks for correct answer, otherwise 1 mark for correctly determining the half-life]

6.7 Find the number of nuclei from the mass of the sample:
number of nuclei = (mass × N_A) ÷ mass number
$\qquad\qquad = (2.0 \times 6.02 \times 10^{23}) \div 262 = 4.595... \times 10^{21}$
$N = N_0 e^{-\lambda t} = 4.595... \times 10^{21} \times e^{-0.0203... \times 210}$
$\qquad\qquad = 6.3536... \times 10^{19} = \textbf{6.4} \times \textbf{10}^{19} \textbf{ (to 2 s.f.)}$
[2 marks for correct answer, otherwise 1 mark for correctly calculating the number of nuclei in the sample]

7.1 Find the number of nuclei from the mass of the sample:
number of nuclei = (mass × N_A) ÷ mass number
$\qquad\qquad = (5.0 \times 6.02 \times 10^{23}) \div 236 = 1.275... \times 10^{22}$
Convert the half-life to seconds:
$1.5 \times 10^5 \times 365 \times 24 \times 60 \times 60 = 4.7304 \times 10^{12}$ s
$T_{1/2} = \ln 2 \div \lambda$
so $\lambda = \ln 2 \div T_{1/2} = \ln 2 \div 4.7304 \times 10^{12} = 1.465... \times 10^{-13} \text{ s}^{-1}$
$A = \lambda N = 1.465... \times 10^{-13} \times 1.275... \times 10^{22}$
$\qquad\qquad = 1.868... \times 10^9 \text{ Bq} = \textbf{1.9} \times \textbf{10}^9 \textbf{ Bq (to 2 s.f.)}$
[3 marks for correct answer, otherwise 1 mark correctly calculating the initial number of atoms, 1 mark for correctly calculating the decay constant]

7.2 A nucleus captures one of its own orbiting electrons *[1 mark]* causing a proton in the nucleus to change into a neutron, releasing a gamma ray (and a neutrino) *[1 mark]*.

7.3 Find the number of nuclei in 2.5 g of uranium-236:
number of nuclei = (mass × N_A) ÷ mass number
$\qquad\qquad = (2.5 \times 6.02 \times 10^{23}) \div 236 = 6.377... \times 10^{21}$
The total number of neptunium-236 nuclei that have decayed to create this number of uranium-236 nuclei is:
$6.377... \times 10^{21} \div 0.873 = 7.304... \times 10^{21}$
$N = N_0$ − number of decayed nuclei
$\qquad = 1.275... \times 10^{22} - 7.304... \times 10^{21} = 5.449... \times 10^{21}$
Rearrange $N = N_0 e^{-\lambda t}$ to find t:
$\dfrac{N}{N_0} = e^{-\lambda t} \Rightarrow \ln\left(\dfrac{N}{N_0}\right) = -\lambda t \Rightarrow$
$t = -\dfrac{\ln\left(\frac{N}{N_0}\right)}{l} = -\dfrac{\ln\left(\frac{5.449...\times 10^{21}}{1.275...\times 10^{22}}\right)}{1.465...\times 10^{-13}}$
$\qquad = 5.803... \times 10^{12} \text{ s} = \textbf{5.8} \times \textbf{10}^{12} \textbf{ s (to 2 s.f.)}$
[4 marks for the correct answer, otherwise 1 mark for correctly calculating the number of nuclei in 2.5 g of uranium, 1 mark for correctly determining the number of neptunium nuclei that have decayed, 1 mark for correct rearrangement and substitution to find the time]

Pages 114-116: Nuclear Decay and Half-Life — 2

1.1 $T_{1/2} = \ln 2 \div \lambda$, where the decay constant, λ, is the probability that a nucleus will decay per second. *[1 mark]*.

1.2 A nuclear excited state is where a nucleus has excess energy (due to a proton or neutron being excited to a higher energy level) *[1 mark]*.

1.3 $\gamma_1 = B - C = 2.50 - 1.33 = \textbf{1.17 MeV}$ *[1 mark]*
$\beta_1 = A - \gamma_1 = 1.48 - 1.17 = \textbf{0.31 MeV}$ *[1 mark]*

1.4 E.g. external treatment of cancer, as its decay produces gamma radiation. Gamma radiation is ionising radiation, so it damages and kills cells when it is absorbed. It can penetrate through materials, so it can travel through the patient's body to the tumour *[1 mark for a correct use and 1 mark for a supporting explanation]*.

2.1 Activity is 12 Ci = $12 \times 3.7 \times 10^{10} = 4.44 \times 10^{11}$ Bq
$A = \lambda N$, so $\lambda = A \div N = 4.44 \times 10^{11} \div 3.2 \times 10^{22}$
$\qquad\qquad = 1.3875 \times 10^{-11} = \textbf{1.4} \times \textbf{10}^{-11} \textbf{ s}^{-1} \textbf{ (to 2 s.f.)}$
[2 marks for correct answer, otherwise 1 mark for correct rearrangement and substitution into equation for the decay constant]

2.2 Any three from: e.g. both radium-226 and radon-222 emit alpha particles which are highly ionising and can damage and kill cells in the body. / Radon-222 is a gas meaning that the contamination risk is higher than for radium-226, as it can be easily breathed in. / Radon-222 is colourless and odourless so it is hard to detect, increasing the contamination risk. / Radon-222 has a much shorter half-life than radium-226, meaning that over a given

time, more alpha particles will be released by radon than radium, so if it gets inside the body, radon delivers a higher dose to the person and has a greater risk of damaging the body. *[3 marks — 1 mark for each correct answer]*
Contamination is a term for when radioactive material gets into or onto a body or object. If you've talked generally about this rather than using that specific word, you'll still get the marks.

2.3 Equilibrium happens when the number of radon nuclei produced per second is equal to the number of radon nuclei decaying per second. Therefore, the activity of radium must be equal to the activity of radon. So:
N_{radon} = activity of radium ÷ λ_{radon}
$\lambda_{radon} = \ln 2 \div T_{1/2}$ and $T_{1/2} = 3.8 \times 24 \times 60 \times 60 = 328\,320$ s
So $\lambda_{radon} = \ln 2 \div 328\,320 = 2.11... \times 10^{-6} \text{ s}^{-1}$
$N_{radon} = 4.44 \times 10^{11} \div 2.11... \times 10^{-6}$
$\qquad\qquad = 2.103... \times 10^{17} = \textbf{2.1} \times \textbf{10}^{17} \textbf{ (to 2 s.f.)}$
[3 marks for correct answer, otherwise 1 mark for correct rearrangement for N_{radon} and 1 mark for correct determination of λ_{radon}]

3.1 $A = \lambda N$, so $N = A \div \lambda = 980 \div (4.9 \times 10^{-18})$
$\qquad\qquad = \textbf{2.0} \times \textbf{10}^{20}$ *[1 mark]*

3.2 $T_{1/2} = \ln 2 \div \lambda = \ln 2 \div 4.9 \times 10^{-18} = 1.414... \times 10^{17}$ s
Convert to years: $1.414... \times 10^{17} \div (365 \times 24 \times 60 \times 60)$
$= 4.485... \times 10^9 = \textbf{4.5} \times \textbf{10}^9 \textbf{ years (to 2 s.f.)}$ *[1 mark]*
The half-life is too long so the activity of the plate will not have decreased enough for it to be dated *[1 mark]*.

3.3 Convert the half-life to seconds:
$T_{1/2} = 1.25 \times 10^9 \times 365 \times 24 \times 60 \times 60 = 3.942 \times 10^{16}$ s
No. of nuclei = no. of moles × Avogadro's constant,
Avogadro's constant = 6.02×10^{23} mol^{-1}
$K = 5.0 \times 10^{-2} \times 6.02 \times 10^{23} = 3.01 \times 10^{22}$
$Ar = 4.6 \times 10^{-6} \times 6.02 \times 10^{23} = 2.7692 \times 10^{18}$
$t = \dfrac{3.942 \times 10^{16}}{\ln 2} \ln\left(\dfrac{3.01 \times 10^{22} + \frac{2.7692 \times 10^{18}}{0.109}}{3.01 \times 10^{22}}\right)$
$\qquad = 4.798... \times 10^{13} \text{ s} = \textbf{4.8} \times \textbf{10}^{13} \textbf{ s (to 2 s.f.)}$
[3 marks for correct answer, otherwise 1 mark for correctly calculating the number of potassium and argon nuclei in the sample, 1 mark for correct substitution into the equation for t]

3.4 E.g. $N = N_0 e^{-\lambda t}$, so $K = K_0 e^{-\lambda t}$
$-\lambda t = \ln\left(\dfrac{K}{K_0}\right) \Rightarrow \lambda t = \ln\left(\dfrac{K_0}{K}\right) \Rightarrow t = \dfrac{1}{\lambda} \ln\left(\dfrac{K_0}{K}\right)$ *[1 mark]*
K_0 is the initial number of K-40 atoms present. This is equal to the current number of K-40 atoms plus the calcium and argon atoms produced. As argon is produced by 10.9% of the decays, the total number of decayed K-40 atoms is equal to number of argon atoms ÷ 0.109 *[1 mark]*.
$T_{1/2} = \ln 2 \div \lambda$ so $\lambda = \ln 2 \div T_{1/2}$
$t = \dfrac{T_{1/2}}{\ln 2} \ln\left(\dfrac{K + \frac{Ar}{0.109}}{K}\right)$ *[1 mark]*

Pages 117-119: Scattering and Gamma Rays

1.1 Rest energy of an electron = 0.510999 MeV
Total rest energy of electron-positron pair = 2 × 0.510999
$\qquad\qquad\qquad\qquad\qquad = 1.021998$ MeV
1.1 MeV > 1.021998 MeV, so yes, the gamma ray could produce an electron-positron pair. *[1 mark]*
You could also have done this by calculating the electron and positron rest energies using $E = mc^2$, and converting from J to MeV.

1.2 The total rest energy of the particle and antiparticle is equal to the gamma ray's kinetic energy minus the kinetic energies of particle and antiparticle:
rest energy = $3.6 \times 10^{-11} - (2 \times 1.0 \times 10^{-12}) = 3.4 \times 10^{-11}$ J
$E = mc^2$, so $m = E \div c^2 = (3.4 \times 10^{-11}) \div (3.00 \times 10^8)^2$
$\qquad\qquad = 3.777... \times 10^{-28}$ kg
This is for the pair, so the mass of the particle is
$(3.777... \times 10^{-28}) \div 2 = 1.888... \times 10^{-28}$ kg
$\qquad\qquad = \textbf{1.9} \times \textbf{10}^{-28} \textbf{ kg (to 2 s.f.)}$
[2 marks for correct answer, otherwise 1 mark for correct calculation of the total particle and antiparticle rest energy]

2 How to grade your answer:
Level 0: There is no relevant information. *[No marks]*
Level 1: A basic diagram of the apparatus used has been

drawn and a brief method given. The expected results may not be stated. *[1 to 2 marks]*

Level 2: A clear, labelled diagram of the apparatus has been drawn. A clear, logical method is given and at least one safety measure has been included. The expected results of the experiment are stated. *[3 to 4 marks]*

Level 3: A clear, well labelled diagram of the apparatus has been drawn. A detailed and logical method is given, including several safety measures that need to be taken throughout the experiment. The expected results are stated. *[5 to 6 marks]*

Indicative content:

Diagram

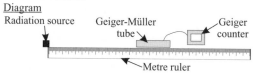
Radiation source — Geiger-Müller tube — Geiger counter — Metre ruler

Method

1. Measure the average count rate due to background radiation. To do this, use the Geiger-Müller tube and counter to measure the count rate three times without the radiation source being present and calculate the mean count rate.

2. Place the radiation source in line with the 0 cm marker on the ruler. Use the ruler to place the end of the Geiger-Müller tube at e.g. 10 cm from the source.

3. Use the Geiger-Müller tube and counter to measure the count rate at this distance three times and calculate the mean count rate detected. Subtract the average background radiation count rate from this mean value to correct for background radiation.

4. Repeat step 3 for a range of distances, e.g. 20 cm, 30 cm, 40 cm, 50 cm.

5. Plot a graph of distance from the source against mean count rate.

The graph/results should show that the mean count rate is proportional to $1 \div \text{distance}^2$.

A graph of $1 \div \text{distance}^2$ against mean count rate should be a straight line through the origin.

Safety measures

The student should try and minimise their exposure to ionising radiation by keeping the radiation stored in a lead-lined container when it is not being used.

The student should also try and keep as far from the radiation source as possible during the experiment. E.g. using tongs to handle the source and keeping the source at arms length when moving it.

The student should also wear a lab coat and gloves during the experiment to reduce the risk of being contaminated by the source.

3.1 E.g. alpha particles were fired at a thin sheet of gold foil and a detector was used to trace their deflected paths *[1 mark]*. Most alpha particles went straight through the foil, which showed that most of the atom was empty space *[1 mark]*. However, some were deflected by large angles, which was evidence that there is a mass with a large positive charge in the centre of the atom *[1 mark]*.

3.2 $E_k = \dfrac{Q_{gold} Q_{alpha}}{4\pi\varepsilon_0 r}$ so $r = \dfrac{Q_{gold} Q_{alpha}}{4\pi\varepsilon_0 E_k}$

$= \dfrac{(79 \times 1.60 \times 10^{-19}) \times (2 \times 1.60 \times 10^{-19})}{4\pi \times 8.85 \times 10^{-12} \times 7.7 \times 10^6 \times 1.60 \times 10^{-19}}$

$= 2.952... \times 10^{-14} = \textbf{3.0} \times \textbf{10}^{-14}$ **m (to 2 s.f.)**

[2 marks for correct answer, otherwise 1 mark for correct rearrangement and substitution]

3.3 $R = R_0 A^{1/3} = 1.4 \times 10^{-15} \times 197^{1/3} = 8.146... \times 10^{-15}$
$= \textbf{8.1} \times \textbf{10}^{-15}$ **m (to 2 s.f.)** *[1 mark]*

3.4 $\rho = m \div V$

The nucleus can be modelled as a sphere of radius R. The mass is equal to the to the number of nucleons, A, multiplied by the average mass of a nucleon (i.e. 1 u).

$\rho = (A \times m_{\text{nucleon}}) \div \left(\dfrac{4}{3}\pi R^3\right)$

Substituting $R = R_0 A^{1/3}$ into this equation gives:

$\rho = (A \times m_{\text{nucleon}}) \div \left(\dfrac{4}{3}\pi \times (R_0 A^{1/3})^3\right)$

$= m_{\text{nucleon}} \div \left(\dfrac{4}{3}\pi \times R_0^3\right) = \text{constant}$

[2 marks for correct, otherwise 1 mark for showing
$\rho = (A \times m_{\text{nucleon}}) \div \left(\dfrac{4}{3}\pi R^3\right)$ *]*

3.5 From the graph, the angle of the first minimum is 15.5°.
$\sin\theta = 1.22\lambda \div 2R$
so $R = 1.22\lambda \div 2\sin\theta = (1.22 \times 1.28 \times 10^{-15}) \div 2\sin(15.5°)$
$= 2.92... \times 10^{-15}$ m $= \textbf{2.9} \times \textbf{10}^{-15}$ **m (to 2 s.f.)**

[3 marks for correct answer, otherwise 1 mark for correct determination of angle of the first minima, and 1 mark for correct substitution into the equation for radius]

3.6 $\rho = m \div V$
$m = 9 \times m_{\text{nucleon}} = 9.0$ u $= 9.0 \times 1.661 \times 10^{-27} = 1.4949 \times 10^{-26}$ kg
$V = \dfrac{4}{3}\pi R^3 = \dfrac{4}{3}\pi \times (2.922 \times 10^{-15})^3 = 1.0450... \times 10^{-43}$ m^3
$\rho = (1.4949 \times 10^{-26}) \div (1.0450... \times 10^{-43})$
$= 1.4304 \times 10^{17} = \textbf{1.4} \times \textbf{10}^{17}$ **kgm**$^{-3}$ **(to 2 s.f.)**

[2 marks for correct answer, otherwise 1 mark for correct working]

Pages 120-122: Nuclear Fission and Fusion

1.1 The mass of nuclear fuel needed for a chain reaction to continue on its own at a steady rate, where one fission follows another *[1 mark]*.

1.2 The coolant transfers heat energy away from the reactor *[1 mark]*. The control rods absorb neutrons to limit the rate of nuclear fission *[1 mark]*.

1.3 E.g. boron *[1 mark]*

1.4 Any three from: e.g. emergency shut-down measures are in place in nuclear power plants to stop the fission of uranium in the event of an emergency. / The core of the reactor, where fission occurs, is shielded with a thick concrete casing which absorbs most of the ionising radiation. / Employees handle fuel and waste remotely, increasing their distance from it which reduces their exposure, whilst also reducing their risk of being contaminated with any radioactive substances. / Air in nuclear power plants is filtered to remove radioactive isotopes from the air, reducing the risk of contamination.

[3 marks — 1 mark for each correct answer]

1.5 E.g. on balance, the risks are seen by many as being small compared to the advantages of generating electricity using nuclear power, because e.g. it is very reliable / doesn't produce greenhouse gases / can produce a large amount of electricity *[1 mark]*.

2.1 The neutrons would not be slow enough to cause further fission *[1 mark]*, so the fission reaction would slow down/stop *[1 mark]*.

2.2 The neutrons produced by fission undergo elastic collisions with atoms in the moderator. The neutron loses some kinetic energy to the moderator atoms during the collision and therefore slows down *[1 mark]*.

2.3 E.g. the size of the material's particles — a moderator with particles of a similar mass to a neutron mass is most efficient *[1 mark]*.

2.4 Due to conservation of energy, the total energy before the reaction equals the total energy after the reaction.
Energy before = rest energy of uranium-235 and neutron
Rest energy of U-235 = 2.196×10^5 MeV
Rest energy of a neutron = 939.551 MeV
Energy after = rest energy of nuclei and neutrons + kinetic energy of nuclei + kinetic energy of neutrons + energy emitted as EM radiation
So, kinetic energy of neutrons = rest energy of uranium-235 and neutron – (rest energy of nuclei and neutrons + kinetic energy of nuclei + energy emitted as EM radiation)
kinetic energy of neutrons equals:
$(2.196 \times 10^5 + 939.551) - ((1.3165 \times 10^5 + 8.5888 \times 10^4 + (3 \times 939.551)) + 152.00 + 25.000) = 5.8980...$ MeV
Three neutrons are produced, so kinetic energy of 1 neutron
$= 5.8980... \div 3 = 1.9660...$ MeV $= \textbf{1.966 MeV (to 4 s.f.)}$

[2 marks for correct answer, otherwise 1 mark for correct application of conservation of energy to find total kinetic energy of neutrons]

3.1 The binding energy is the energy needed to separate all the nucleons in the nucleus / the energy equivalent to the mass difference between the nucleus and its separate parts *[1 mark]*.

3.2   A, combining small nuclei like A will increases the average binding energy per nucleon dramatically, which means a lot of energy would released during nuclear fusion. *[1 mark]*.

3.3 $\Delta m = (5m_p + 5m_n) - m_{boron} = 5(1.00728 + 1.00867) - 10.01294$
$= 0.06681$ u $= 0.06681 \times 1.661 \times 10^{-27} = 1.109... \times 10^{-28}$ kg
$E = mc^2 = 1.109... \times 10^{-28} \times (3.00 \times 10^8)^2 = 9.987... \times 10^{-12}$ J
This is the total binding energy of the nucleus. To convert this to the binding energy per nucleon, divide by the number of nucleons: $(9.987... \times 10^{-12}) \div 10 = 9.987... \times 10^{-13}$ J
Convert to eV: $= (9.987... \times 10^{-13}) \div (1.60 \times 10^{-19})$
$= 6.242... \times 10^6 = \mathbf{6.24 \times 10^6}$ **eV (to 3 s.f.)**
[3 marks for correct answer, otherwise 1 mark for correctly calculating the mass defect and 1 mark for calculating the energy of the mass defect]

You could also do this by multiplying the mass defect of 0.06681 u by 931.5 MeV and dividing by the number of nucleons.

3.4   Mass difference between carbon-10 and boron-10:
$10.01685 - 10.01294 = 0.00391$ u
Mass difference between beryllium-10 and boron-10:
$10.01353 - 10.01294 = 0.00059$ u
The mass difference between carbon-10 and boron-10 is larger than the mass difference between beryllium-10 and boron-10. This means that more energy is released when carbon-10 decays into boron-10 *[1 mark]*. This means the beta-plus particle from this decay would have more kinetic energy and travel at a higher velocity *[1 mark]*, as the kinetic energy of the particle = total energy released – beta particle rest energy (and the rest energy of both beta particles is the same) *[1 mark]*.

3.5 $\Delta m = (2m_{He3}) - (2m_{H1} + m_{He4})$
$= (2 \times 3.01603) - (2 \times 1.00783 + 4.0026)$
$= 0.0138$ u $= 0.0138 \times 1.661 \times 10^{-27}$ kg $= 2.292... \times 10^{-29}$ kg
$E = mc^2 = 2.292... \times 10^{-29} \times (3.00 \times 10^8)^2$
$= 2.0629... \times 10^{-12} = \mathbf{2.06 \times 10^{-12}}$ **J (to 3 s.f.)**
[2 marks for correct answer, otherwise 1 mark for calculating the mass defect]

Section Thirteen: Option A — Astrophysics

Pages 123-125: Astrophysics — 1

1.1   hydrogen *[1 mark]*

1.2 $m - M = 5\log\left(\dfrac{d}{10}\right)$,
Rearrange for absolute magnitude, M:
$M = m - 5 \log\left(\dfrac{d}{10}\right) = 1.16 - \left(5 \times \log\left(\dfrac{7.7}{10}\right)\right)$
$= 1.72754... = \mathbf{1.7}$ **(to 2 s.f.)**
[2 marks for correct answer, otherwise 1 mark for correct rearrangement and substitution]

1.3
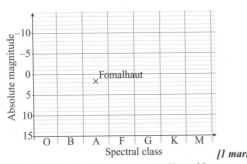
[1 mark]
(Fomalhaut is a) main sequence star *[1 mark]*.

1.4   E.g. tiny red shifts and blue shifts in the absorption spectrum of the star *[1 mark]*. The orbit of an exoplanet around the star would cause tiny variations in the star's motion which would cause these red shifts and blue shifts *[1 mark]*. / Variations in the apparent magnitude of the star *[1 mark]*. The presence of an exoplanet would cause a dip in apparent magnitude at regular time intervals as it passes in front of the star *[1 mark]*.

2.1
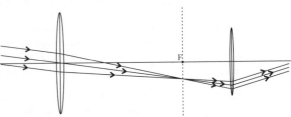
[1 mark for a straight ray drawn from each point of incidence on objective lens to the eyepiece lens through the same point on the focal line, 1 mark for a straight ray drawn from each point of incidence on the eyepiece lens, parallel to each other and pointing towards the principle axis]

The ray passing through the centre of the lens doesn't refract. The rays parallel to the ray passing through the centre of the lens will come to a focus at the point where this ray crosses the dashed line. Remember, when rays emerge from the eyepiece lens, they should be refracted so they are all parallel to each other again.

2.2   E.g. refracting telescopes can experience chromatic aberration / the large glass lenses used can become distorted / telescopes have to be very long to have suitable magnification which makes them expensive to build and house / it is expensive to make lenses with the required purity/quality *[1 mark]*.

2.3 $M = \dfrac{f_o}{f_e} = \dfrac{1.65}{0.15} = \mathbf{11}$ *[1 mark]*

2.4   Find angular separation of the two stars:

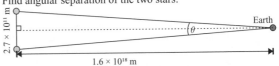

Since the distance to the stars is so much bigger than the distance between the stars, the small angle approximation can be used to find half of the angular separation, using the right angled triangle shown by the dotted line:
$\dfrac{\theta}{2} \approx \dfrac{\frac{1}{2} \times \text{distance between stars}}{\text{distance to stars from Earth}} \approx \dfrac{0.5 \times 2.7 \times 10^{11}}{1.6 \times 10^{18}}$
$\approx 8.4375 \times 10^{-8}$ rad
So, $\theta \approx 2 \times 8.4375 \times 10^{-8} \approx 1.6875 \times 10^{-7}$ rad
Angular resolution of telescope:
$\theta \approx \dfrac{\lambda}{D} \approx \dfrac{570 \times 10^{-9}}{0.2} \approx 2.85 \times 10^{-6}$ rad
The angular separation of the stars is less than the angular resolution, so the telescope won't be able to resolve the two stars.
[3 marks for correct answer with supporting calculation, otherwise 1 mark for calculation of angle subtended by the two stars and 1 mark for calculation of the angular resolution of the telescope]

You could also have used $\tan\theta$ to find the angular separation of the stars rather than using the small angle approximation.

3.1   Red shift is the effect by which the electromagnetic radiation from an astronomical object is observed to have a longer wavelength/lower frequency than it was emitted at due to the object moving away from the observer *[1 mark]*. The primary cause of red shift of distant astronomical objects is the expansion of the Universe *[1 mark]*.

3.2   Convert Gpc to Mpc: $d = 3.68 \times 10^3 = 3680$ Mpc.
$v = Hd = 72.0 \times 3680 = 264\,960$ kms$^{-1} = \mathbf{2.65 \times 10^8}$ **ms^{-1} (to 3 s.f.)**
[2 marks for correct answer, otherwise 1 mark for correct unit conversions]

3.3   Because $z = -\dfrac{v}{c}$ is only true when $v \ll c$, and 2.65×10^8 ms^{-1} is very close to c (3.00×10^8 ms^{-1}) *[1 mark]*.

3.4 $z = \dfrac{\Delta\lambda}{\lambda}$ so: $\Delta\lambda = z\lambda = 3.91 \times (1.5 \times 10^{-5}) = 5.865 \times 10^{-5}$
Wavelength on Earth $= \lambda + \Delta\lambda = (1.5 \times 10^{-5}) + (5.865 \times 10^{-5})$
$= 7.365 \times 10^{-5} = \mathbf{7.4 \times 10^{-5}}$ **m (to 2 s.f)**
[2 marks for correct answer, otherwise 1 mark for correct calculation of $\Delta\lambda$]

3.5 $P \propto Id^2$, so: $\dfrac{P_L}{P_X} = \dfrac{I_L}{I_X}\left(\dfrac{d_L}{d_X}\right)^2$
Rearrange for distance to quasar X:
$d_X = \sqrt{\dfrac{P_X}{P_L}\dfrac{I_L}{I_X}} \times d_L$, $I_L = 2.3I_X$, so $\dfrac{I_L}{I_X} = 2.3$
$d_X = \left(\sqrt{\dfrac{1.5 \times 10^{39}}{3.8 \times 10^{40}} \times 2.3}\right) \times 3.68 \times 10^9$
$= 1.108... \times 10^9$ pc $= \mathbf{1.1 \times 10^9}$ **pc (to 2 s.f.)**
[2 marks for correct answer, otherwise 1 mark for showing correct proportionality relation]

Pages 126-129: Astrophysics — 2

1.1 E.g.

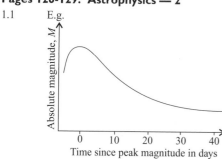

Absolute magnitude, M (y-axis)
Time since peak magnitude in days (x-axis): 0, 10, 20, 30, 40

[1 mark for curve drawn starting before time = 0 with peak at 0 days, that then decreases with decreasing gradient with time]

1.2 Type 1a supernovae serve as standard candles because their absolute magnitude is predictable/has a known value *[1 mark]*. The apparent magnitude of an object, m, is related to its absolute magnitude, M, and its distance from Earth, d, by the equation $m - M = 5 \log(d/10)$ *[1 mark]*. So, by measuring its apparent magnitude (a measure of brightness), the distance of a type 1a supernova from Earth can be directly calculated using this equation *[1 mark]*.

1.3 $f = 880 \times 10^{12}$ Hz,
$c = f\lambda$, so $\lambda = \dfrac{c}{f} = \dfrac{3.00 \times 10^8}{880 \times 10^{12}} = 3.4090... \times 10^{-7}$ m
$\lambda_{max}T = 2.9 \times 10^{-3}$ m K
so $T = \dfrac{2.9 \times 10^{-3}}{3.4090... \times 10^{-7}} = 8506.6...$ K = **8500 K (to 2 s.f.)**
[2 marks for correct answer, otherwise 1 mark for correct calculation of wavelength]

2.1 Intensity, I, is inversely proportional to distance, x, squared:
$I = \dfrac{k}{x^2}$, so $\dfrac{I_{Earth}}{I} = \left(\dfrac{x}{x_{Earth}}\right)^2$
$I_{Earth} = \left(\dfrac{10.0}{2750}\right)^2 \times I = 1.322... \times 10^{-5} I = \mathbf{1.32 \times 10^{-5}} I$ **(to 3 s.f.)**
[2 marks for correct answer, otherwise 1 mark for showing correct proportionality relation]

2.2 Convert light years to m:
$(1.3 \times 10^{-6}) \times (9.46 \times 10^{15}) = 1.2298 \times 10^{10}$ m
$R_s \approx \dfrac{2GM}{c^2}$, so
$M \approx \dfrac{R_s c^2}{2G} = \dfrac{(1.2298 \times 10^{10}) \times (3.00 \times 10^8)^2}{2 \times 6.67 \times 10^{-11}}$
$= 8.29700... \times 10^{36}$ kg = **8.3 × 10³⁶ kg (to 2 s.f.)**
[2 marks for correct answer, otherwise 1 mark for correct rearrangement and substitution]

2.3 Quasars are made up of a supermassive black hole that is taking in matter from a surrounding mass of whirling gas *[1 mark]*. The gas emits bright light as it is accelerated towards the black hole *[1 mark]*. This light undergoes a large red shift as it travels from the quasar to Earth, and so appears to observers on Earth as radio waves *[1 mark]*.

2.4 Quasars have very high power outputs compared to other astronomical objects *[1 mark]*. Since intensity is proportional to power, and inversely proportional to distance-squared, they are some of the only objects powerful enough to have detectable intensities at very large distances *[1 mark]*.

3.1 E.g.

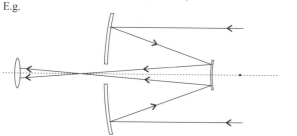

[1 mark for each ray correctly drawn reflected from each mirror, and 1 mark for the rays intersecting between the eyepiece and the primary mirror]
When the rays reflect from the primary mirror, they should reflect as if they are going to pass through the principle focus of the primary mirror.

3.2 How to grade your answer:
Level 0: There is no relevant information. *[No marks]*
Level 1: Some properties of telescopes designed to detect visible light and radio waves are listed, but with little detail. There are several errors with grammar, spelling, punctuation and legibility. Answer lacks structure. *[1 to 2 marks]*
Level 2: There is a comparison of some similarities and differences between telescopes designed to detect visible light and radio waves, including at least two of position, basic structure, resolving power and collecting power, with some explanation. There are only a few errors with grammar, spelling, punctuation and legibility. Answer has a fairly logical structure. *[3 to 4 marks]*
Level 3: There is a clear comparison and explanation of the similarities and differences in the properties of telescopes designed to detect visible light and radio waves, including their positioning, structure and relative resolving and collecting powers. Grammar, spelling and punctuation are used accurately and there is no problem with legibility. Answer follows an appropriate and logical structure. *[5 to 6 marks]*

Indicative content:
Similarities:
Both types of telescope can be placed on Earth, as both visible light and radio waves can pass through the Earth's atmosphere.
Both types of telescope use a parabolic reflector in order to bring waves to a focus.
Both types of telescope can usually be manoeuvred to point at different parts of the sky and track the motion of moving astronomical objects.
Differences:
Radio wave telescopes need to be much larger than visible light telescopes.
This is because radio waves have much larger wavelengths than visible light, so the parabolic reflectors need to have a very large diameter to have a high enough resolving power to form a useful image.
This is due to the Rayleigh criterion, which states that for a given resolving power, the diameter of a telescope is proportional to the wavelength it is detecting, $\theta \approx \lambda \div D$.
As a result of this, radio telescopes often have a lower resolution than visible light telescopes.
Radio telescopes can be linked together to improve their resolution.
Multiple radio telescopes are needed to produce a similar resolving power to a single visible light telescope.
The large size of the primary reflectors in radio telescopes gives them much larger collecting powers than visible light telescopes, since the collecting power of a telescope is proportional to its diameter squared.
This allows radio telescopes to detect dimmer objects.
The parabolic reflector in a radio telescope can be made of wire mesh, but in a visible light telescope the reflector must be made from a complete solid surface.
This is because waves will reflect off surfaces that have gaps that are notably smaller than their wavelength.
The shape of the dish must be significantly different from a parabola before spherical aberration becomes noticeable in a radio telescope, due to the large wavelengths involved.
So radio telescopes can use parabolic reflectors that are less precise / have some imperfections, while only small imperfections in reflectors will have a large negative effect on the image quality of visible light telescopes.

4.1 In a red giant star, there is an outwards pressure in the core due to the energy released in nuclear fusion which balances the gravitational attraction of the matter in the core *[1 mark]*. A white dwarf is produced when nuclear fusion ceases, so this outwards pressure disappears, and the core contracts under gravitational attraction, so the white dwarf is smaller than the core that created it *[1 mark]*.

4.2 Evaluate the temperature of the star at 0.8 Gyrs:
Temperature, $T = 0.75 \times 10^4$ K,
$P = \sigma A T^4$, and area of a sphere = $4\pi r^2$, so
$P = \sigma(4\pi r^2)T^4 = 5.67 \times 10^{-8} \times 4\pi \times (6.4 \times 10^6)^2 \times (0.75 \times 10^4)^4$
$= 9.23417... \times 10^{22}$ W = **9.2 × 10²² W (to 2 s.f.)**
[3 marks for correct answer, otherwise 1 mark for correct reading from the graph and 1 mark for correct substitution]

4.3 The age of the universe can be estimated from the inverse of the Hubble constant:
$$t = \frac{1}{H_0} = \frac{1}{2.1 \times 10^{-18}} = 4.761... \times 10^{17} \text{ s}$$
Convert to years: $t = 4.761... \times 10^{17} \div (60 \times 60 \times 24 \times 365)$
$$= 1.5099... \times 10^{10} \text{ years}$$
$10^{15} > 1.5099... \times 10^{10}$, so no black dwarves should exist because it is predicted to take longer than the current age of the universe for a white dwarf to become a black dwarf.
[2 marks for correct answer with supporting calculation, otherwise 1 mark for attempt to estimate the age of the universe from the Hubble constant]

Section Thirteen: Option B — Medical Physics

Pages 130-132: Medical Physics — 1

1.1 Rays of light are sent into the optical fibres at an angle of incidence greater than the critical angle *[1 mark]*. This leads to total internal reflection of the light at the boundary between the core of the fibres and the cladding around the fibre. This causes the light to be reflected multiple times and travel down the fibre until it reaches the end and illuminates the body *[1 mark]*.

1.2 In a coherent bundle, the relative positions of fibres in the bundle are the same at each end *[1 mark]*. This ensures that a clear image can be transmitted from one end to the other, so in this case it will transmit a clear image to the surgeon *[1 mark]*.

1.3 E.g. endoscopes allow surgeons to see inside the body without making large incisions, allowing them to perform keyhole surgery. Performing keyhole surgery instead of traditional surgery means that the risk of infection is reduced / patients tend to recover quicker / patients have less scarring *[1 mark]*.

2.1 Hypermetropic (long-sighted) people are unable to focus clearly on near objects. (This happens if their near point is further away than normal (25 cm or more).) *[1 mark]* The focusing system is too weak and images of near objects are brought into focus behind the retina *[1 mark]*. This condition occurs either because the cornea and lens are too weak *[1 mark]* or the eyeball is too short *[1 mark]*.

2.2 $P = 1 \div f$ so $f = 1 \div P = 1 \div 2.5 = \textbf{0.40 m}$ *[1 mark]*

2.3
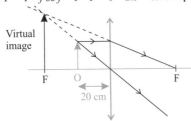
[1 mark for parallel ray, 1 mark for centre ray and virtual image drawn]

3.1
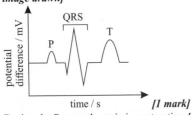
[1 mark]
During the P wave the atria is contracting *[1 mark]*.
During the QRS wave the ventricles are contracting *[1 mark]*.
During the T wave the ventricles are relaxing *[1 mark]*.

3.2 Speed of sound through heart wall,
$$v = \Delta s \div \Delta t = 0.010 \div (6.4 \times 10^{-6}) = 1562.5 \text{ ms}^{-1}$$
$1.05 \text{ g cm}^{-3} = 1.05 \times 10^6 \text{ g m}^{-3} = 1.05 \times 10^3 \text{ kg m}^{-3}$
$Z = \rho c = 1.05 \times 10^3 \times 1562.5$
$$= 1.64... \times 10^6 = \textbf{1.6} \times \textbf{10}^6 \textbf{ kgm}^{-2}\textbf{s}^{-1} \textbf{ (to 2 s.f.)}$$
[2 marks in total, otherwise 1 mark for correct value for the speed of sound through cardiac tissue]

3.3 $\frac{I_r}{I_i} = \left(\frac{Z_2 - Z_1}{Z_2 + Z_1}\right)^2 = \left(\frac{1.64... \times 10^6 - 1.4 \times 10^6}{1.64... \times 10^6 + 1.4 \times 10^6}\right)^2 = 6.26... \times 10^{-3}$
So I_r is $6.26... \times 10^{-3}$ times the size of I_i.
As a percentage, this $= 6.26... \times 10^{-3} \times 100$
$$= 0.626...\% = \textbf{0.63\% (to 2 s.f.)}$$
[2 marks for correct answer, otherwise 1 mark for correct value of $\frac{I_r}{I_i}$]

If you got the wrong answer to 3.2 but used the correct method for 3.3, you still get full marks.

4.1 Radio pulses excite hydrogen nuclei/protons in the body that have a precessional frequency that matches the radio wave frequency *[1 mark]*. When the radio waves are switched off, the protons de-excite and re-emit radio waves at their precessional frequency *[1 mark]*. The gradient of magnetic field strength means protons in different regions of the body will have different precessional frequencies, so each region will absorb and re-emit different frequencies of radio waves *[1 mark]*. These re-emitted radio waves are detected, and their frequencies and positions are recorded. A computer then converts them into an image *[1 mark]*.

4.2 How to grade your answer:
Level 0: There is no relevant information. *[No marks]*
Level 1: One aspect is covered well OR two aspects are covered but they are incomplete and not always accurate. The answer is not in a logical order and/or is one-sided and lacks comparison between the two imaging techniques. *[1 to 2 marks]*
Level 2: Two aspects are covered well OR all three aspects are covered but they are incomplete and not always accurate. The answer is mostly in a logical order and gives advantages and disadvantages of MR scans with some comparison to CT scans. *[3 to 4 marks]*
Level 3: All three aspects are covered comprehensively and accurately. The answer is coherent, is in a logical order, and gives advantages and disadvantages of MR scans with clear comparison to CT scans. *[5 to 6 marks]*

Indicative content:

Patient safety
MR scans don't use ionising radiation, whereas CT scans use X-rays, which are ionising. Ionising radiation can damage cells and increase the risk of developing cancer, so MR scans are less dangerous than CT scans.

Convenience
MR scans take longer to carry out than CT scans.
MR scans are noisy, which some patients may find unpleasant.
Some patients may find an MR scan claustrophobic.
MR imaging involves using a strong magnetic field, so cannot be performed on people with pacemakers or metal implants (as it would be very harmful). CT scans don't use a magnetic field, so they can be used to image people with pacemakers or metal implants.
Both MR and CT scans are expensive to run.
CT scans are becoming more portable, MR scanners are very large and so are currently not portable.

Quality of images produced
An MR image can be made for any slice in any orientation from a single scan.
The resolution of both MR scans and CT images is high.
MR scans produce higher resolution images of soft tissue than CT scans. This is because the contrast can be weighted to investigate different tissue types in an MR scan.
Bones are imaged at a much lower resolution in MR scans than in CT scans.
MR scans can provide real-time images.

Pages 133-136: Medical Physics — 2

1.1 The physical half-life of Tc-99m is too short for it to be practically transported to hospitals *[1 mark]*.

1.2 A = Lead shielding, B = (Sodium iodide) Crystal / scintillator, C = Lead collimator
[2 marks for all correct, 1 mark for two correct]

1.3 Each photomultiplier tube releases an electron (by the photoelectric effect) when hit by a photon emitted by the crystal, turning the flashes of light from the crystal into a clear electrical signal *[1 mark]*. Each electron is then multiplied into a cascade of electrons *[1 mark]*.

1.4 The physical half-life of Tc-99m is 6.0 hours *[1 mark]*.
$\frac{1}{T_E} = \frac{1}{T_B} + \frac{1}{T_P}$ so $T_B = 1 \div \left(\frac{1}{T_E} - \frac{1}{T_P}\right)$
$T_B = 1 \div \left(\frac{1}{4.8} - \frac{1}{6.0}\right) = \textbf{24 hours}$ *[1 mark]*

1.5   The physical half-life of a tracer is a measure of the average time it takes for half the number of radioactive nuclei in the tracer to undergo radioactive decay. It depends on the type of radioactive isotope used in the tracer *[1 mark]*. The biological half-life of a tracer is a measure of how long it takes for the body to metabolise/use up half the tracer. It depends on the body's response to the tracer or the substance it is bound to *[1 mark]*. Both half-lives need to be considered as they both determine how long the body is exposed to radiation. This needs to be long enough for the structure and function of the area of interest to be observed, but as short as possible to minimise risk associated with radiation *[1 mark]*.

2.1   Exposure to excessive noise *[1 mark]*.

2.2   The dBA (adjusted decibel scale) takes into account the ear's response to different frequencies of sound, whereas the dB scale does not. As a result, the dBA scale allows hearing issues at particular frequencies to be identified *[1 mark]*.

2.3   Intensity level, $IL = 10\log\left(\frac{I}{I_0}\right)$ so $\frac{IL}{10} = \log\left(\frac{I}{I_0}\right)$

If $a = \log b$, then $b = 10^a$, so $\frac{I}{I_0} = 10^{\frac{IL}{10}}$

So $I = 10^{\frac{IL}{10}} \times I_0 = 10^{\frac{55}{10}} \times 1.0 \times 10^{-12} = 3.16227... \times 10^{-7}$ Wm^{-2}

The sound spreads out equally over the surface area of a sphere of radius 1.5 m.

Surface area of sphere $= 4\pi r^2 = 4\pi \times 1.5^2 = 9\pi$ m^2

$I = P \div A$, so $P = I \times A = 3.16227... \times 10^{-7} \times 9\pi$
$= 8.941... \times 10^{-6}$ W
$= \mathbf{8.9 \times 10^{-6}}$ **W (to 2 s.f.)**

[4 marks in total, otherwise 1 mark for making intensity the subject of the intensity level equation, 1 mark for correctly calculating the intensity of sound 1.5 m from the machine, 1 mark for correct surface area of sphere of sound]

3.1   An alternating potential difference (p.d.) is applied to the crystal, causing it to vibrate *[1 mark]*. The vibration of the crystal generates high frequency sound waves/ultrasound with the same frequency as the alternating p.d. *[1 mark]*. When ultrasound waves are incident on the crystal, it vibrates and produces an alternating p.d. that can be detected *[1 mark]*. In detectors, the crystal should have a thickness of half the wavelength of the ultrasound that is generated *[1 mark]*. This is because the reflected waves will cause the crystal to resonate when they are received, producing a large p.d. signal that can easily be detected *[1 mark]*.

3.2   An A-scan records the amplitude of the reflected ultrasound waves as vertical deflections on a cathode ray oscilloscope (CRO) screen *[1 mark]*. The horizontal axis represents the time between the transmission and detection of the wave, so is an indication of the depth of the boundary that the wave reflected off *[1 mark]*. An A-scan therefore only records information in one dimension of space *[1 mark]*. B-scans display amplitude as brightness — the larger the amplitude of the reflected wave, the brighter the spot appears *[1 mark]*. Depth is shown vertically, and a linear array of transducers can allow information to be recorded in two dimensions of space to form a 2D image *[1 mark]*.

4.1   How to grade your answer:

Level 0:   There is no relevant information. *[No marks]*

Level 1:   At least one mechanism of X-ray production is briefly described. Little reference is made to the diagram. The answer lacks a logical structure. *[1 to 2 marks]*

Level 2:   Both mechanisms of X-ray production are described with appropriate references to Figure 3. At least one feature that helps the X-ray tube produce X-rays efficiently is stated. The answer has a logical structure. *[3 to 4 marks]*

Level 3:   The mechanisms of X-ray production are described in detail with appropriate references to Figure 3. There is a clear explanation of how at least one feature of the X-ray tube helps it to efficiently produce X-rays. The answer has a clear and logical structure. *[5 to 6 marks]*

Indicative content:

The cathode in Figure 3 is heated, and electrons are released from the cathode by thermionic emission.

The high potential difference between the anode and cathode generates a strong electric field that is used to accelerate the electrons towards the tungsten anode.

When accelerated electrons hit the tungsten anode, X-rays are produced through two mechanisms.

Firstly, the electrons decelerate as they collide with the anode, and some of the electron's kinetic energy is converted into electromagnetic energy as X-ray photons.

With this mechanism, the anode emits a continuous spectrum of X-rays, called bremsstrahlung radiation.

The second mechanism of X-ray production occurs when the accelerated electrons collide with inner shell electrons in the tungsten atoms and eject them from the atoms.

Only specific photon energies are possible with this second mechanism. These energies are characteristic to tungsten, so the photons are called "characteristic X-rays".

The features shown in Figure 3 that help the X-ray tube efficiently produce X-rays are:

The glass casing — it allows the X-ray tube to be kept at a low pressure / a vacuum. This stops the accelerating electrons from bumping into other atoms and slowing down before hitting the anode, allowing for more efficient X-ray production.

Rotating the tungsten anode using a motor — the tungsten anode increases in temperature as the accelerated electrons transfer most of their kinetic energy to it. If it gets too hot, it may damage the X-ray tube and prevent further X-ray production. The motor rotates the tungsten anode to help cool it down, allowing for more efficient X-ray production.

4.2 $x_{\frac{1}{2}} = 0.25$ mm $= 0.25 \times 10^{-3}$ m
$x_{\frac{1}{2}} = (\ln 2) \div \mu$, so $\mu = (\ln 2) \div x_{\frac{1}{2}}$
      $= (\ln 2) \div (0.25 \times 10^{-3}) = 2772.58...$ m^{-1}
Thickness of lead shielding $= 3.0$ mm $= 3.0 \times 10^{-3}$ m
$I = I_0 \, e^{-\mu x} = (2.0 \times 10^5) \times e^{(-2772.58... \times 3.0 \times 10^{-3})}$
      $= 48.828... = \mathbf{49}$ **Wm^{-2} (to 2 s.f.)**

[2 marks for correct answer, otherwise 1 mark for correct value for μ]

4.3   The current through the filament has increased *[1 mark]*. The beam intensity has increased because more electrons are hitting the anode and therefore more X-rays are produced, but the maximum energy of the X-rays hasn't increased so the tube voltage has not been changed *[1 mark]*.

4.4   The features labelled X are line spectra due to characteristic radiation *[1 mark]*. When the beam of electrons from the cathode hit the anode, they can remove electrons from the inner energy levels of the tungsten atoms. Electrons in the tungsten atoms' outer shells move into the vacancies in the lower energy levels, and release energy in the form of (X-ray) photons *[1 mark]*. The energies of these photons are known for a given metal as they relate to the energy between electron shells in the metal. Because the same tungsten anode is present, the characteristic radiation photons released have the same energies and so show up at the same points on each energy curve *[1 mark]*.

Section Thirteen: Option C — Engineering Physics

Pages 137-140: Engineering Physics — 1

1.1 $\omega_2 = \omega_1 + \alpha t$
Rearrange for t:
$t = \frac{\omega_2 - \omega_1}{\alpha} = \frac{(32.3 - 0)}{2.9} = 11.137... = \mathbf{11}$ **s (to 2 s.f.)** *[1 mark]*

1.2 $I = mr^2 = 1.8 \times (0.31)^2 = 0.172...$ kg m^2
Rotational kinetic energy E_K
$= \frac{1}{2} I \omega^2 = \frac{1}{2} \times 0.172... \times (32.3)^2 = 90.2341... $ J $= \mathbf{90}$ **J (to 2 s.f.)**
[2 marks for correct answer, otherwise 1 mark for correct calculation of the moment of inertia]

1.3   Find angular displacement, $\theta = 52.4 \times 2\pi = 329.23...$ rad
$\omega_2^2 = \omega_1^2 + 2\alpha\theta$
Rearrange for α:
$\alpha = \frac{\omega_2^2 - \omega_1^2}{2\theta} = \frac{0^2 - 32.3^2}{2 \times 329.23...} = -1.584...$ rad s^{-2}
So the magnitude is $\alpha = \mathbf{1.58}$ **rad s^{-2} (to 3 s.f.)**
[2 marks for correct answer, otherwise 1 mark for calculation of total angular displacement]

1.4 $T = I\alpha = 0.172... \times 1.584...$
      $= 0.274...$ Nm $= \mathbf{0.274}$ **Nm (to 3 s.f.)** *[1 mark]*

You could also have calculated this using $W = T\theta$, where W is the rotational kinetic energy of the wheel and θ is the total angular displacement.

1.5 Since the mass of the solid wheel is uniformly distributed, the moment of inertia of the solid wheel will be smaller than that of the traditional wheel (which has all its mass concentrated at the centre) *[1 mark]*. For a given torque, angular acceleration is inversely proportional to moment of inertia ($\alpha = T \div I$), so the angular acceleration of the solid wheel is higher *[1 mark]*. This will allow it to reach a greater angular speed than a traditional wheel under the same torque, which would allow a bicycle fitted with it to travel faster *[1 mark]*

2.1 $T = I\alpha$, and $I = \frac{1}{2}mr^2$, so $T = \frac{1}{2}mr^2\alpha$
$m = 0.50$ kg, $r = 32$ cm $= 0.32$ m
Rearrange $T = \frac{1}{2}mr^2\alpha$ for α:
$$\alpha = \frac{2T}{mr^2} = \frac{2 \times 0.12}{0.5 \times 0.32^2} = 4.6875 \text{ rad s}^{-2} = \mathbf{4.7 \text{ rad s}^{-2} \text{ (to 2 s.f.)}}$$
[2 marks for correct answer, otherwise 1 mark for correct rearrangement and substitution]

2.2 E.g.

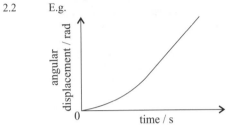

[1 mark for single line, with positive gradient that increases to a constant value]
There is initially a net torque causing an acceleration (since $\alpha = T \div I$), shown by the increasing gradient on the graph *[1 mark]*. Since frictional torque increases with angular velocity and the motor applies a constant torque, the magnitude of the frictional torque will eventually equal the magnitude of the torque applied by the motor *[1 mark]*. At this point, the net torque will be zero, resulting in no angular acceleration, so the turntable moves at a constant angular speed, shown by the constant gradient *[1 mark]*.

2.3 Angle turned through in ten minutes $= 33.3 \times 10 \times 2\pi$
$= 2092.30...$ rad
$W = T\theta = 5.0 \times 10^{-3} \times 2092.30... = 10.46... \text{ J} = \mathbf{10 \text{ J} \text{ (2 s.f.)}}$
[2 marks for correct answer, otherwise 1 mark for correct substitution]

2.4 The needle applies a constant force at a decreasing radius, so the torque due to the needle decreases as the record plays (since $T = Fr$) *[1 mark]*.

3 How to grade your answer:
Level 0: There is no relevant information. *[No marks]*
Level 1: A brief description of the processes is given, but there is little to no comparison of the validity of the methods or explanation of differing results. Several errors with grammar, spelling, punctuation and legibility. The answer is poorly structured. *[1 to 2 marks]*
Level 2: A description of the processes is given, and there is a comparison of their validity and description of differing results, but they may not be fully explained. Only a few errors with grammar, spelling, punctuation and legibility. Answer is logically structured. *[3 to 4 marks]*
Level 3: A detailed description of the processes is given, including a thorough comparison of their validity. The differences in the results of the processes are explained clearly. Grammar, spelling and punctuation are used accurately and there is no problem with legibility. The answer is well structured. *[5 to 6 marks]*

Indicative content:
In methods 1 and 2, the net output of work (per cycle) from a cylinder of the engine is the area within the closed loop on the indicator diagram.
Multiply this by 6 to get the total output work from the engine.
Divide this by the time taken to complete a full engine cycle / multiply this by the number of full engine cycles per second to get the power ($P = E \div t$).
In method 3, measuring the energy transformed by decelerating the car to rest is equivalent to measuring the amount of energy that was transferred to the wheels, i.e. the total amount of useful work from the engine.
Divide this energy by the time taken for the car to accelerate to its initial speed from rest to estimate the useful output power.
The discrepancy between the values determined from methods 1 and 2 (29 kW) is the amount of energy "lost" through non-ideal thermodynamic processes in the engine that are not taken into account in the theoretical p-V diagram.
For example, in a real engine there are no constant-volume processes / heat is conducted through the cylinder/piston / incomplete combustion of gas can occur / there is friction between piston and cylinder.
The discrepancy between the values determined from methods 2 and 3 (6.7 kW) is the power lost between the engine cylinders and the wheels, e.g. friction from crankshaft/bearings/axles etc.
While the real p-V diagram does give an accurate representation of the power generated in the engine, this is not the useful power delivered to the wheels.
Measuring the power at the brakes (i.e. method 3) is the most valid/accurate method.
Using a theoretical indicator diagram (i.e. method 1) is the least valid/accurate method

Pages 141-144: Engineering Physics — 2

1.1 An adiabatic process is one in which no heat is transferred between the system and its surroundings, but real engines always lose heat (through conduction) during the expansion stroke / generate heat through friction between moving parts *[1 mark]*.

1.2 For an adiabatic process, $p_1V_1^\gamma = p_2V_2^\gamma$
$$p_2 = p_1\left(\frac{V_1}{V_2}\right)^\gamma = 1.0 \times 10^5 \times (10.0)^{1.4} = 2.51188... \times 10^6$$
$$= \mathbf{2.5 \times 10^6 \text{ Pa} \text{ (to 2 s.f.)}}$$
[2 marks for correct answer, otherwise 1 mark for correct rearrangement and substitution]

1.3 E.g.

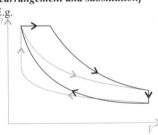

[1 mark for closed loop featuring two opposite curved lines with decreasing gradient, and a vertical line at the maximum value of V, each correctly labelled with an arrow, 1 mark for a horizontal line at the maximum value of P, labelled with a correct arrow, as part of a closed loop]

2.1 $pV = nRT$, and volume of gas and amount of gas in the refrigerator remains constant between the initial and final state, so:
$$\frac{p_i}{T_i} = \frac{nR}{V} = \frac{p_f}{T_f}, \text{ so: } p_f = \frac{p_i}{T_i} \times T_f$$
convert temperatures to K: $T_i = 0.0 + 273 = 273$ K,
$T_f = -40.0 + 273 = 233$ K
$$p_f = \frac{110\,000}{273} \times 233 = 93\,882.78... = \mathbf{94\,000 \text{ Pa} \text{ (to 2 s.f.)}}$$
[2 marks for correct answer, otherwise 1 mark for correct rearrangement and substitution]

2.2 E.g.

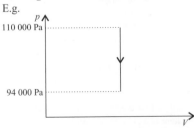

[1 mark for straight vertical line drawn between two points, 1 mark for the top point labelled 110 000 Pa and the bottom point labelled with your answer to 2.2]
No work is done on the gas during the process *[1 mark]*.

2.3 $COP_{ref} = \dfrac{Q_C}{Q_H - Q_C}$

The refrigerator is running at maximum efficiency, so

$COP_{ref} = \dfrac{T_C}{T_H - T_C}$

T_H is the temperature of the lab and T_C is the temperature of the fridge. Rearrange for T_H:

$T_H = \dfrac{T_C}{COP_{ref}} + T_c = \dfrac{233}{3.1} + 233 = 308.1612...$ K

Convert to °C: $T_H = 308.1612... - 273 = 35.1612...$°C

= **35 °C (to 2 s.f.)**

[2 marks for correct answer, otherwise 1 mark for correct rearrangement and substitution]

2.4 Reverse heat engines transfer energy from a cold reservoir to a hot reservoir, with the input of work *[1 mark]*. Leaving the door of a refrigerator open will effectively join the hot and cold reservoirs, so that there is no hot reservoir to transfer the heat to, so the entire system is no longer a reverse heat pump *[1 mark]*.

3.1 The peak power consumption of the reactor exceeds the maximum power output of the national grid *[1 mark]*. The flywheels store energy from the national grid as rotational kinetic energy, so can be 'charged' and then later decelerated to transfer energy rapidly to the reactor and help supply the required power during a pulse *[1 mark]*.

3.2 Find the angular speed of the flywheel:

Rearrange $E_K = \frac{1}{2} I\omega^2$ for ω:

$\omega = \sqrt{\dfrac{2E_K}{I}} = \sqrt{\dfrac{2 \times 3.40 \times 10^9}{1.30 \times 10^7}} = 22.870...$ rad s^{-1}

$P = 400.0$ MW $= 4.000 \times 10^8$ W

$P = T\omega$, rearrange for T:

$T = \dfrac{P}{\omega} = \dfrac{4.000 \times 10^8}{22.870...} = 1.74894... \times 10^7$ Nm

= **1.75 × 10⁷ Nm (to 3 s.f.)**

[2 marks for correct answer, otherwise 1 mark for correct calculation of angular speed]

3.3 Before connection:

angular momentum of wheel A = 0 (as it is at rest)

angular momentum of driving wheel:

$I_1\omega_i = 6.28 \times 10^{-4} \times 12.0 = 7.536 \times 10^{-3}$ kg m^{-2}

total momentum before connection = 7.536×10^{-3} kg m^{-2}

After connection:

angular momentum of wheel A = $I_2\omega_2$

angular momentum of driving wheel = $I_1\omega_1$

total angular momentum after connection = $I_1\omega_1 + I_2\omega_2$

total angular momentum before = total angular momentum before (conservation of momentum).

$7.536 \times 10^{-3} = I_1\omega_1 + I_2\omega_2$

Rearrange for ω_2:

$\omega_2 = \dfrac{(7.536 \times 10^{-3}) - (I_1\omega_1)}{I_2}$

$= \dfrac{(7.536 \times 10^{-3}) - (6.28 \times 10^{-4} \times 0.429)}{5.09 \times 10^{-2}}$

= $0.1427... $ rad s^{-1} = **0.143 rad s⁻¹ (to 3 s.f.)**

[3 marks for correct answer, otherwise 1 mark for correct calculation of angular momentum before connection and 1 mark for correct application of conservation of angular momentum]

4.1 Calculate the work done by the heat pump's engine:

input power = calorific value × fuel flow rate

fuel flow rate = 0.1 g s^{-1} = 0.0001 kg s^{-1}

input power = $5.0 \times 10^7 \times 0.0001 = 5000$ W

So energy transferred by fuel in 15 s = $5000 \times 15 = 75\,000$ J

Work done by engine = $0.60 \times 75\,000 = 45\,000$ J

$Q_H = \Delta U + W = \Delta U + p\Delta V$ for constant pressure

For processes at constant pressure, $\dfrac{V_1}{T_1} = \dfrac{V_2}{T_2}$

$V_1 = T_1 \times \dfrac{V_2}{T_2} = 293 \times \dfrac{1.2}{493} = 0.7131...$ m^3

$Q_H = \Delta U + p\Delta V = 54\,000 + (100\,000 \times (1.2 - 0.7131...))$

= 102 681.541... J

$COP_{HP} = \dfrac{Q_H}{W} = \dfrac{102\,681.541...}{45\,000} = 2.2818... = $ **2.3 (to 2 s.f.)**

[5 marks for correct answer, otherwise 1 mark for correct calculation of input power, 1 mark for correct calculation of work done by engine, 1 mark for correct calculation of initial volume and 1 mark for correct calculation of energy transferred to the system by heating]

4.2 For a heat engine to have an efficiency greater than 1, it would have to output more work than the energy taken in from the hot reservoir. This is not possible because energy must be conserved *[1 mark]*. A refrigerator can have a coefficient of performance greater than 1, because the energy transferred to the hot reservoir can exceed the work put in, as energy is taken from the cold reservoir and transferred to the hot reservoir *[1 mark]*.

Section Thirteen: Option D — Turning Points in Physics

Pages 145-147: Turning Points in Physics — 1

1.1 E.g. a probe with a very fine point is placed over the surface and a voltage is applied between the probe and the surface. Electrons from the probe "tunnel" to the surface, producing a weak current *[1 mark]*. The smaller the distance between the probe and the surface, the bigger the current *[1 mark]*. An image is produced by scanning the probe over the whole surface and measuring the current *[1 mark]*.

1.2 Thermionic emission *[1 mark]*

1.3 $\lambda = \dfrac{h}{\sqrt{2meV}}$ so $V = \dfrac{1}{2me} \times \left(\dfrac{h}{\lambda}\right)^2$

$V = \dfrac{1}{2 \times 9.11 \times 10^{-31} \times 1.60 \times 10^{-19}} \times \left(\dfrac{6.63 \times 10^{-34}}{0.002 \times 10^{-9}}\right)^2$

= 376 962.9... = **380 000 V (to 2 s.f.)**

[2 marks for correct answer, otherwise 1 mark for correct working]

1.4 Yes, because the de Broglie wavelength of electrons accelerated by it will be approximately equal to the atomic spacing the metal, so it would allow two adjacent atoms to be resolved and the organisation of the atoms to be seen *[1 mark]*.

1.5 E.g. If the accelerating potential difference is increased, the speed of the electrons would be higher when they reach the sample *[1 mark]*. Since the speed of the electrons is higher, the rings in the diffraction pattern produced will be smaller. This means the image produced would be less blurry/the resolution of the image would be higher *[1 mark]*.

2.1 Newton's theory said that light was made up of tiny particles, called corpuscles, which were affected by forces that caused reflection and refraction *[1 mark]*. Huygens' theory stated that light was a wave, where every point on a wavefront could be treated as a point source for secondary wavelets *[1 mark]*.

2.2 Young's double-slit experiment supported Huygens' theory *[1 mark]*. In this experiment, a beam of light was shone through two narrow slits, and a pattern of light and dark fringes was produced on a far screen *[1 mark]*. This showed that light could diffract and interfere, which are phenomena that could only be described if light behaved like a wave *[1 mark]*.

2.3 Wave theory indicated that when a beam of light was shone onto a metal, the energy from the light would be evenly distributed among the electrons on the surface of the metal *[1 mark]*. This didn't explain why electrons weren't emitted if the light was below a threshold frequency, since the theory indicated that even if light of a low frequency was used, eventually electrons would collect enough energy to escape *[1 mark]*.

2.4 Planck suggested that electromagnetic radiation was only released in discrete bursts (or wave-packets), called quanta *[1 mark]*.

2.5 $c = f\lambda$, rearrange for λ:

$\lambda = c \div f = (3.00 \times 10^8) \div (6.5 \times 10^5) = 461.53...$ m

$p = h \div \lambda = (6.63 \times 10^{-34}) \div 461.53...$

= $1.4365 \times 10^{-36} = $ **1.4 × 10⁻³⁶ kgms⁻² (to 2 s.f.)**

[2 marks for correct answer, otherwise 1 mark for calculating correct wavelength or for substituting $c = f\lambda$ into $p = h \div \lambda$]

3.1 How to grade your answer:

Level 0: There is no relevant information. *[No marks]*

Level 1: A brief description of the Michelson and Morley experiment is given. There is little or no mention of expected or actual results or the significance of these results. Several errors with grammar, spelling, punctuation and legibility. Answer lacks structure. *[1 to 2 marks]*

Level 2: A description of the Michelson and Morley experiment is given. There is some mention of expected and actual results, or of the significance of the results. Only a few errors with grammar, spelling, punctuation and legibility. Answer has some structure. *[3 to 4 marks]*

Level 3: A full description of the Michelson and Morley experiment is given. Their expected and actual results are stated and a full explanation is given as to the significance of these results. Grammar, spelling and punctuation are used accurately and there is no problem with legibility. Answer is well-structured. *[5 to 6 marks]*

Indicative content:

In the experiment, a beam of light was sent towards a semi-silvered glass block. This block acted as a partial reflector which split the light into two beams travelling perpendicular to each other.

The two beams were reflected by mirrors spaced an equal distance from the partial reflector (shown as L in Figure 1). The reflected beams met back at the partial reflector and caused an interference pattern that was recorded by an observer.

The apparatus was then rotated by 90° and the experiment was repeated.

Michelson and Morley expected to see a change in the interference pattern produced.

They theorised that this would be because one beam would be travelling in the same direction as the Earth's motion, and the other beam would be travelling perpendicular to the Earth's motion.

If the aether were present, then the speed of the beam travelling parallel to the Earth's motion would be equal to the sum of its speed at rest in the aether and the speed of the lab, and one beam would end up faster than the other.

After the apparatus is rotated, the beam travel times would be different, so the interference pattern produced would change. However, they found no difference between the patterns/they got a null result.

This led to the conclusion that the aether did not exist.

It showed that light did not need a medium in order to propagate.

3.2 Rearrange $t = \dfrac{t_0}{\sqrt{1 - \frac{v^2}{c^2}}}$ for v:

$\dfrac{t_0}{t} = \sqrt{1 - \dfrac{v^2}{c^2}} \Rightarrow 1 - \left(\dfrac{t_0}{t}\right)^2 = \dfrac{v^2}{c^2} \Rightarrow v = \sqrt{c^2\left(1 - \left(\dfrac{t_0}{t}\right)^2\right)}$

$t_0 = 0.8t$ so $v = \sqrt{(3.00 \times 10^8)^2 (1 - 0.8^2)} = \mathbf{1.8 \times 10^8\ ms^{-1}}$
[2 marks for correct answer, otherwise 1 mark for correct rearrangement and substitution]

Pages 148-150: Turning Points in Physics — 2

1.1 $E_k = eV = 1.6 \times 10^{-19} \times 0.50 = 0.80 \times 10^{-19}$ J

Rearrange $E_k = \frac{1}{2}mv^2$ for v:

$v = \sqrt{\dfrac{2E_k}{m}} = \sqrt{\dfrac{2 \times 0.80 \times 10^{-19}}{9.11 \times 10^{-31}}} = 4.19... \times 10^5\ ms^{-1}$

$= \mathbf{4.2 \times 10^5\ ms^{-1}}$ **(to 2 s.f.)**
[2 marks for correct answer, otherwise 1 mark for correctly calculating the kinetic energy of the electron]

1.2 The work done by the potential difference in an electron gun causes an increase in the kinetic energy of an electron, so assuming the electron starts at rest $QV = \frac{1}{2}mv^2$.

Rearrange for velocity: $v = \sqrt{\dfrac{2QV}{m}}$ *[1 mark]*

The electron travels in a circular path, centripetal force, $F = \dfrac{mv^2}{r}$. This is the same as the force acting on the electron due to the magnetic field, $F = BQv$. So $BQv = \dfrac{mv^2}{r}$ *[1 mark]*

$\dfrac{Q}{m} = \dfrac{v}{Br}$

Substitute in for v: $\dfrac{Q}{m} = \sqrt{\dfrac{2QV}{m}} \times \dfrac{1}{Br}$

Square both sides: $\dfrac{Q^2}{m^2} = \dfrac{2QV}{m} \times \dfrac{1}{B^2r^2}$

Divide by $\dfrac{Q}{m}$: $\dfrac{Q}{m} = 2V \times \dfrac{1}{B^2r^2} = \dfrac{2V}{B^2r^2}$ *[1 mark]*

1.3 Charged oil droplets were allowed to fall between two parallel metal plates *[1 mark]*. An eyepiece was used to view the paths of the droplets, allowing distances, and therefore the velocity of each droplet, to be measured. From this velocity, the drop's radius could be calculated (using Stokes' law) *[1 mark]*. A potential difference was applied across the plates, causing an electric field to be generated between them. The strength of the field was varied until the droplets became stationary *[1 mark]*. At this point, the force from the electric field acting on each droplet (plus the upthrust from the air) was equal to the weight of the droplet. Millikan used this to work out the charge on each droplet *[1 mark]*.

2.1 Based on Newtonian predictions, the graph should be a straight line (since they state that the kinetic energy of an object is proportional to the square of its velocity) *[1 mark]*. However, special relativity predicts a curved, asymptotic graph as shown in Figure 1. According to special relativity, the faster a particle travels, the more massive it becomes. This explains the large increases in kinetic energy for small increases in speed at large speeds shown in Figure 1 *[1 mark]*. Special relativity also states that nothing can travel faster than the speed of light. Bertozzi's results match this as the ratio of $\dfrac{v^2}{c^2}$ approaches but never reaches 1 *[1 mark]*.

2.2 In the muon's frame, the distance between the muon and the Earth's surface is contracted.

$l = l_0\sqrt{1 - \dfrac{v^2}{c^2}} = 8000 \times \sqrt{(1 - 0.98^2)}$

$= 1591.9... \text{ m} = \mathbf{1.6\ km}$ **(to 2 s.f.)** *[1 mark]*

2.3 The mean lifetime of muons is so short that we would expect only a small number of muons produced high in the atmosphere to reach the Earth's surface *[1 mark]*. However, as muons are moving close to the speed of light, their 'internal clocks' run slower than time on Earth *[1 mark]*. That means that fewer half-lives have passed within the muon's reference frame than on Earth, so fewer muons have decayed and more muons than classical mechanics predicts are detected at the Earth's surface *[1 mark]*.

3.1 The time taken for light to travel from one gap to the next is $t_g = \dfrac{T}{N}$ where T is the time taken for one rotation of the wheel *[1 mark]*.

The frequency of the wheel is equal to $\dfrac{1}{T}$, so: $t_g = \dfrac{1}{fN}$

The time for light to travel from one gap to the tooth next to it takes half this time: $t_{gt} = \dfrac{1}{2fN}$ *[1 mark]*

During this time the light has travelled a distance of $2D$. The speed of light is equal to the distance it travels over the time taken so: $v = \dfrac{d}{t_{gt}} = 2D \times 2fN = 4DNf$ *[1 mark]*

3.2 Fizeau's value for the speed of light is:

$v = 4DNf = 4 \times 8633 \times 720 \times 12.6 = \mathbf{313\ 274\ 304\ ms^{-1}}$
Maxwell's formula for the speed of an electromagnetic wave:

$c = \dfrac{1}{\sqrt{m_0 \times e_0}} = \dfrac{1}{\sqrt{(4 \times \pi \times 10^{-7}) \times (8.85 \times 10^{-12})}}$

$= 2.998... \times 10^8\ ms^{-1}$

5% of this is: $0.05 \times 2.998... \times 10^8 = 1.49... \times 10^7\ ms^{-1}$
So to be within 5% of Maxwell's value, Fizeau's value must be less than:
$(2.998... \times 10^8) + (0.149... \times 10^8) = 3.148... \times 10^8\ ms^{-1}$
It is, so Fizeau's value is within 5% of Maxwell's value.
[1 mark for calculating Fizeau's value for the speed of light correctly, 1 mark for calculating that it is within 5% of Maxwell's value]

Section Fourteen — Mixed Questions

Pages 151-153: Mixed Questions — 1

1 C *[1 mark]*
Strangeness is not conserved in weak interactions.

2 C *[1 mark]*
The electrical power, IV, is equal to the work done on the mass in one second. In one second the mass moves through a height of 0.35 m, so,

$I = \dfrac{mg\Delta h}{V} = \dfrac{9.0 \times 9.81 \times 0.35}{230} = 0.13\ A$ *(to 2 s.f.)*

3   B *[1 mark]*

The box is on the verge of toppling when the line of action of the cube's weight passes from its centre of mass, through the edge of its base, as shown:

This corresponds to an incline of 45°.

4   B *[1 mark]*

When the resistances are equal, voltage will be shared in the ratio 1:1, each receiving half the total. When the resistance of the variable resistor is double that of the fixed resistor, the voltage will be shared in the ratio 2:1, meaning the variable resistor receives two thirds of the total. So its voltage has increased by: $\frac{2}{3}V_{total} \div \frac{1}{2}V_{total} = \frac{4}{3}$

5.1   E.g. the laser light diffracts through each slit, such that each slit acts as a coherent wave source. The waves from each slit interfere with each other *[1 mark]*. At certain points on the screen, the path difference between light from the two sources is a whole multiple of a wavelength of the light *[1 mark]*. At this point, the waves from the two sources are in-phase, and so constructive interference occurs, producing a bright fringe on the screen *[1 mark]*. The gaps between the fringes are caused by destructive interference of the light at those points on the screen *[1 mark]*.

5.2

s / m	w / m	$\frac{1}{s}$ / m^{-1}
2.00×10^{-4}	0.0088	5000
3.00×10^{-4}	0.0058	3330
4.00×10^{-4}	0.0044	2500
5.00×10^{-4}	0.0035	2000
6.00×10^{-4}	0.0029	1670
7.00×10^{-4}	0.0025	1430

[2 marks for a fully and correctly completed table, otherwise 1 mark for at least four correctly calculated $\frac{1}{s}$ values]

5.3   E.g.

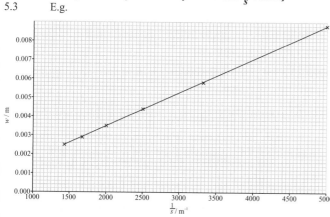

[1 mark for 6 correctly plotted data points, 1 mark for appropriately scaled and labelled axes and 1 mark for correct straight line of best fit]

5.4 $w = \frac{\lambda D}{s}$, so in a plot of w against $\frac{1}{s}$, the gradient is equal to λD.

E.g. gradient of line $= \frac{0.0080 - 0.0028}{4550 - 1600} = 1.7627... \times 10^{-6}$

(accept between 1.755×10^{-6} and 1.775×10^{-6})

Distance to screen, D = gradient ÷ λ

So to find maximum D, divide the gradient by the minimum value of λ.

Minimum λ of visible light = 4.00×10^{-7} m

Maximum $D = (1.7627... \times 10^{-6}) \div (4.00 \times 10^{-7})$

                $= 4.40677...$ m $= \textbf{4.4 m (to 2 s.f.) (accept 4.3-4.5 m)}$

[3 marks for correct answer, otherwise 1 mark for correct calculation of gradient and 1 mark for correct substitution to find maximum D]

If you've calculated an answer from a correctly calculated gradient of an incorrect plot, give yourself full marks.

5.5 $hf = \phi + E_{k(max)}$. Minimum energy threshold for electron emission is when kinetic energy, $E_{k(max)} = 0$, and $hf = \frac{hc}{\lambda}$.

So, maximum wavelength that could cause the photoelectric effect occurs when $\frac{hc}{\lambda} = \phi$, so:

$\lambda = \frac{hc}{\phi} = \frac{6.63 \times 10^{-34} \times 3.00 \times 10^8}{6.53 \times 10^{-19}} = 3.0459... \times 10^{-7}$

               $= \textbf{3.05} \times \textbf{10}^{-7}$ **m (to 3 s.f.)**

[2 marks for correct answer, otherwise 1 mark for correct rearrangement and substitution]

Pages 154-156: Mixed Questions — 2

1.1   Consider the ball's vertical motion as it falls to the hole in order to calculate the time it is in the air:

$s = -0.80$ m, $u = 0$ ms^{-1} and $a = -9.81$ ms^{-2}

$s = ut + \frac{1}{2}at^2$, becomes $s = \frac{1}{2}at^2$ since $u = 0$

$t = \sqrt{\frac{2s}{a}} = \sqrt{\frac{2 \times (-0.80)}{-9.81}} = 0.403...$ s

Consider the ball's horizontal motion in order to calculate v_f:

$v = \frac{\Delta s}{\Delta t}$

$v_f = 1.2 \div 0.403... = 2.97...$ ms^{-1} $= \textbf{3.0 ms}^{-1}$ **(to 2 s.f.)**

[2 marks for correct answer, otherwise 1 mark for correctly calculating the time the ball is in the air]

1.2   Use conservation on energy:

initial total energy = final total energy

initial kinetic energy = final kinetic energy + change in gravitational potential energy

$\frac{1}{2}mv_i^2 = \frac{1}{2}mv_f^2 + mg\Delta h$

$v_i = \sqrt{v_f^2 + 2g\Delta h}$

   $= \sqrt{(2.97...)^2 + (2 \times 9.81 \times 0.80)} = 4.95...$ ms^{-1}

                  $= \textbf{5.0 ms}^{-1}$ **(to 2 s.f.)**

[2 marks for the correct answer, otherwise 1 mark for equating correct expressions for initial and final total energies]

1.3   50.0 g = 0.050 kg

force = rate of change of momentum

      $= \frac{\Delta(mv)}{\Delta t}$

      $= \frac{m(v_f - v_i)}{t}$

      $= \frac{0.005 \times (2.97... - (-4.95...))}{0.37}$

      $= 1.07...$ N

      $= \textbf{1.1 N (to 2 s.f.) }$*[1 mark]*

2.1 $\bar{\nu}_e + u \longrightarrow d + e^+$ *[1 mark]*

    W$^+$ boson *[1 mark]*

If you gave the full quark configuration of the proton and neutron in your equation, you'll still get the mark.

2.2   If the electron and positron have negligible kinetic energy, the momentum of the particles must also be negligible / approximately zero *[1 mark]*. Since the total momentum before the annihilation is (approximately) zero, and momentum must be conserved, the total momentum after must also be zero, so the gamma ray photons must move off with equal velocities in opposite directions *[1 mark]*.

2.3   Rate of antineutrino interaction detection = 3 per hour

1 hour = $60 \times 60 = 3600$ s

So, number of antineutrino interactions in 1 s = $3 \div 3600$

                          $= 8.33... \times 10^{-4}$

area of tank face = $1.91 \times 1.37 = 2.6167$ m^2

                    $= 2.6167 \times 10^4$ cm^2

total antineutrinos incident on tank per second = number incident per second per cm^2 × area of face

total antineutrinos = $5 \times 10^{13} \times 2.6167 \times 10^4$

                     $= 1.30835 \times 10^{18}$ antineutrinos

So the ratio of detected antineutrino interactions to total incident antineutrinos per second $= \frac{8.33... \times 10^{-4}}{1.30835 \times 10^{18}}$

                      $= 6.369... \times 10^{-22}$

                      $= \textbf{6} \times \textbf{10}^{-22}$ **(to 1 s.f.)**

(You could also write this as $8.33... \times 10^{-4} : 1.30835 \times 10^{18}$, which simplifies to $\textbf{1 : 2} \times \textbf{10}^{21}$ **(to 1 s.f.)**)

[2 marks for correct value, otherwise 1 mark for correct calculation of total number of antineutrinos on the tank per second]

The ratio of antineutrino interactions to incident antineutrinos is incredibly small, so the likelihood of neutrinos undergoing particle interactions is very small *[1 mark]*.

3.1   Calculate the potential difference across the variable resistor:
$V_{variable} = V_{supply} - V_{fixed} = 12 - 4.5 = 7.5$ V
Calculate the resistance of the variable resistor:
ratio of the resistances = ratio of potential differences
(since the current through both resistors is the same)
$$\frac{R_{variable}}{R_{fixed}} = \frac{V_{variable}}{V_{fixed}}$$
$$R_{variable} = \frac{V_{variable}}{V_{fixed}} \times R_{fixed} = \frac{7.5}{4.5} \times 9.0 = \mathbf{15\ \Omega}$$
[2 marks for correct answer, otherwise 1 mark for correct use of Ohm's law]

You could also have directly calculated the current through the circuit and used $R = V \div I$.

3.2   Calculate the potential difference across the variable resistor:
$V_{variable} = V_{supply} - V_{fixed} = 12 - 5.4 = 6.6$ V
Calculate the resistance of the variable resistor:
ratio of the resistances = ratio of potential differences
$$\frac{R_{variable}}{R_{fixed}} = \frac{V_{variable}}{V_{fixed}}$$
$$R_{variable} = \frac{V_{variable}}{V_{fixed}} \times R_{fixed} = \frac{6.6}{5.4} \times 9.0 = 11\ \Omega$$
The resistance of the variable resistor is directly proportional to the height of the sliding contact above the bottom of the coil, L.
Since resistance has decreased by a factor of $\frac{11}{15}$, so will L.
$$L = \frac{11}{15} \times 0.3 = 0.22 \text{ m}$$
The decrease in length equals the change in the spring's length:
$\Delta L = 0.3 - 0.22 = 0.08$ m
Use Hooke's law: $F = k\Delta L$
The force causing the spring's compression is the weight of the mass, mg. $mg = k\Delta L$, so:
$$k = \frac{mg}{\Delta L} = \frac{1.5 \times 9.81}{0.08} = 183.9... \text{ Nm}^{-1} = \mathbf{180\ Nm^{-1}\ (to\ 2\ s.f.)}$$
[4 marks for correct answer, otherwise 1 mark for calculating the new resistance of the variable resistor, 1 mark correctly calculating the new position of the sliding contact and 1 mark for calculating the change in the spring's length]

Pages 157-159: Mixed Questions — 3

1   A *[1 mark]*
2   D *[1 mark]*
Rearrange $F = BQv$ for v:
$$v = \frac{F}{BQ} = \frac{4.8 \times 10^{-15}}{0.015 \times 1.60 \times 10^{-19}} = 2.0 \times 10^6 \text{ ms}^{-1}$$
3   D *[1 mark]*
$$C = \frac{Q}{V} \text{ so } V = \frac{Q}{C} = \frac{0.0352}{2200 \times 10^{-6}} = 16 \text{ V}$$
$$E = \frac{V}{d} = \frac{16}{0.50 \times 10^{-3}} = 32\ 000 \text{ Vm}^{-1}$$
4   B *[1 mark]*
$Q = mc\Delta\theta$, so $\Delta\theta = 1506 \div (0.0145 \times 3157) = 32.8...$
So after heating, $T = 275.0 + 32.8... = 307.8...$ K
Average KE $= \frac{3}{2}kT = \frac{3}{2} \times 1.38 \times 10^{-23} \times 307.8...$
$$= 6.37... \times 10^{-21} \text{ J} = 6.4 \times 10^{-21} \text{ J (to 2 s.f.)}$$
5.1   E.g.

[1 mark for gravitational field lines that are evenly spaced and vertical with arrows pointing in the correct direction and an equipotential line drawn perpendicular to them]

5.2   The net energy supplied to the tea is
$Q = 140 - 22 = 118$ kJ $= 118\ 000$ J
Rearrange $Q = mc\Delta\theta$ for m:
$$m = \frac{Q}{c\Delta\theta} = \frac{118 \times 10^3}{4200 \times (100.0 - 6.0)} = 0.2988... \text{ kg}$$
$$= 298.8... \text{ g}$$
Subtract this from the initial amount to find the mass of tea consumed:
$510 - 298.8... = 211.1...$ g $= \mathbf{210}$ g (to 2 s.f.)
[2 marks for correct answer, otherwise 1 mark for correctly calculating the mass of the remaining tea]

5.3   The volume of the capsule will increase if the surrounding pressure is low, and decrease if it is high in order to equalise the internal and external pressure *[1 mark]*. Since pressure decreases with height, the capsule expands as its altitude increases. This causes the bottom of the expanding capsule to move downwards, and so the mechanism moves the dial to display an increase in altitude *[1 mark]*.

6.1   E.g. the torch would only emit light while it was being shaken, as energy could not be stored for later use *[1 mark]*. / The flux cut by the coil would vary as the magnet moved through and away from the coil, so the brightness of the torch would increase and decrease *[1 mark]*.

6.2   Due to Lenz's law, the induced emf opposes the change that caused it *[1 mark]*. So the current that flows in the coil (due to the induced emf) has a magnetic field which applies an upwards force on the magnet, reducing the overall downwards resultant force on the magnet and so reducing its acceleration and final speed *[1 mark]*.

6.3   Time to halve = 1.5 mins = $1.5 \times 60 = 90$ s
Time to halve = $0.69RC$
So, RC = time to halve $\div 0.69 = 90 \div 0.69 = 130.434...$ s
LED won't light up after the p.d. drops to below 0.25 V. When discharging, the voltage across the capacitor and so LED is equal to $V = V_0 e^{\frac{-t}{RC}}$. Rearrange for t:
$$\ln\left(\frac{V}{V_0}\right) = \frac{-t}{RC}$$
$$t = -RC\ln\left(\frac{V}{V_0}\right) = -130.434... \times \ln\left(\frac{0.25}{2.2}\right)$$
$$= 283.663... \text{ s} = \mathbf{280}\text{ s (to 2 s.f.)}$$
[2 marks for correct answer, otherwise 1 mark for calculating the time constant RC]

Pages 160-161: Mixed Questions — 4

1.1   E.g. the centripetal force acting on the satellite is equal to the gravitational attraction between the satellite and the Earth,
so $\frac{m_1 v^2}{r} = \frac{Gm_1 m_2}{r^2}$ where m_1 is the mass of the satellite,
v is the satellite's linear velocity, r is the radius of the satellite's orbit, G is the gravitational constant and m_2 is the mass of the Earth *[1 mark]*. Cancelling and rearranging for v gives
$$v = \sqrt{\frac{Gm_2}{r}}.$$
v is inversely proportional to $\sqrt{r}$, so as r has increased the linear speed of the satellite must decrease *[1 mark]*.

1.2   26 hours = $26 \times 60 \times 60 = 93\ 600$ s
First calculate the angular velocity of the satellite:
$$\omega = \frac{\theta}{t} = \frac{2\pi}{93\ 600} = 6.71... \times 10^{-5} \text{ rads}^{-1}$$
Rearrange $V = -\frac{GM}{r}$ for r:
$$r = -\frac{GM}{V} = -\frac{6.67 \times 10^{-11} \times 5.97 \times 10^{24}}{-8.94 \times 10^6} = 4.45... \times 10^7 \text{ m}$$
$$F = m\omega^2 r = 142 \times (6.71... \times 10^{-5})^2 \times 4.45... \times 10^7$$
$$= 28.5... = \mathbf{29}\text{ N (to 2 s.f.)}$$
[3 marks for correct answer, otherwise 1 mark for calculating the angular velocity of the satellite and 1 mark for calculating the radius of the satellite's orbit]

You could also have found the linear speed, v, and used $F = mv^2 \div r$ to find the force.

1.3   Plutonium-238 has 238 nucleons, so one 1 mol = 238 g.

So number of

plutonium atoms in 50.0 mg $= \dfrac{50.0 \times 10^{-3}}{238} \times 6.02 \times 10^{23}$

$= 1.264... \times 10^{20}$

5.593 MeV $= 5.593 \times 10^{6} \times 1.60 \times 10^{-19} = 8.9488 \times 10^{-13}$ J

So the number of decays needed to produce 250 kJ is:

$250\,000 \div (8.9488 \times 10^{-13}) = 2.793... \times 10^{17}$

Rearrange $N = N_0 e^{-\lambda t}$ for t:

$$\frac{N}{N_0} = e^{-\lambda t} \Rightarrow \ln\left(\frac{N}{N_0}\right) = -\lambda t \Rightarrow -\frac{1}{\lambda}\ln\left(\frac{N}{N_0}\right) = t$$

Substitute the numbers in to calculate t:

$$t = -\frac{1}{2.51 \times 10^{-10}} \ln\left(\frac{(1.264... \times 10^{20}) - (2.793... \times 10^{17})}{1.264... \times 10^{20}}\right)$$

$= 8.8103... \times 10^{6}$ s $= \mathbf{8.8 \times 10^{6}}$ **s (to 2 s.f.)**

[3 marks for correct answer, otherwise 1 mark for correctly calculating the number of atoms in the sample and 1 mark for correctly calculating the number of decays that must occur]

2.1   First calculate the period of the carriage's swing, by modelling it as a simple pendulum with a bob at its centre of mass:

$T = 2\pi \times \sqrt{\dfrac{l}{g}} = 2\pi \times \sqrt{\dfrac{22}{9.81}} = 9.409...$ s

Find the angular frequency ω:

$\omega = 2\pi f = \dfrac{2\pi}{T} = \dfrac{2\pi}{9.409...} = 0.6677...$ rad s^{-1}

Maximum displacement from rest position is equal to the amplitude, so $A = 13$ m

Maximum speed, $v_{max} = \omega A = 0.6677... \times 13$

$= 8.6809...$ ms$^{-1} = \mathbf{8.7\ ms^{-1}}$ **(to 2 s.f.)**

[3 marks for correct answer, otherwise 1 mark for correctly calculating the period of the carriage's swing and 1 mark for correctly calculating the angular frequency]

2.2   How to grade your answer:

Level 0:   There is no relevant information. *[No marks]*

Level 1:   A connection is made between the rotation of the chamber and the centripetal force acting on the rider. Answer is incomplete and lacks clarity. *[1 to 2 marks]*

Level 2:   A brief explanation of how the ride works is given, including a connection made between the frequency of rotation of the chamber and the frictional force acting on the rider. The answer is generally clear but lacks key details. *[3 to 4 marks]*

Level 3:   A clear and detailed explanation of how the ride works is given, including the connection between the frequency of rotation of the chamber and the frictional force acting on the rider. The answer is clear and complete. *[5 to 6 marks]*

Indicative content:

As the ride starts rotating, the rider undergoes centripetal acceleration.

For there to be centripetal acceleration, there must be a centripetal force acting on the rider that is directed towards the centre of the chamber.

This is the normal force exerted by the wall of the chamber on the rider.

As the frequency of rotation of the chamber increases, the centripetal acceleration increases.

This means the normal force acting on the rider also increases.

The maximum possible frictional force acting upwards on the rider is proportional to the normal force, so this also increases with the frequency of rotation of the chamber.

Eventually the frequency of rotation is high enough that the maximum frictional force acting upwards on the rider will be able to equal their weight and prevent them from sliding.

So when the floor of the chamber moves downwards, the friction equals their weight and there is no net force acting upwards or downwards on the rider so they remain 'stuck' to the wall.

Physics Data and Formulae

Here's a list of all the data and formulae you'll be given in the exams. You'll need it when answering questions in this book.

Fundamental Constants and Values

Quantity, symbol	Value
speed of light in vacuo, c	3.00×10^8 ms^{-1}
permeability of free space, μ_0	$4\pi \times 10^{-7}$ Hm^{-1}
permittivity of free space, ε_0	8.85×10^{-12} Fm^{-1}
magnitude of charge of electron, e	1.60×10^{-19} C
the Planck constant, h	6.63×10^{-34} Js
gravitational constant, G	6.67×10^{-11} Nm^{2}kg^{-2}
the Avogadro constant, N_A	6.02×10^{23} mol^{-1}
molar gas constant, R	8.31 JK^{-1}mol^{-1}
the Boltzmann constant, k	1.38×10^{-23} JK^{-1}
the Stefan constant, σ	5.67×10^{-8} Wm^{-2}K^{-4}
the Wien constant, α	2.90×10^{-3} mK
electron rest mass, m_e	9.11×10^{-31} kg
	5.5×10^{-4} u
electron charge/mass ratio, $\frac{e}{m_e}$	1.76×10^{11} Ckg^{-1}
proton rest mass, m_p	$1.67(3) \times 10^{-27}$ kg
	1.00728 u
proton charge/mass ratio, $\frac{e}{m_p}$	9.58×10^7 Ckg^{-1}
neutron rest mass, m_n	$1.67(5) \times 10^{-27}$ kg
	1.00867 u
gravitational field strength, g	9.81 Nkg^{-1}
acceleration due to gravity, g	9.81 ms^{-2}
atomic mass unit, u	1.661×10^{-27} kg
	931.5 MeV

Astronomical Data

Mass of the Sun = 1.99×10^{30} kg
Mean radius of the Sun = 6.96×10^8 m
Mass of the Earth = 5.97×10^{24} kg
Mean radius of Earth = 6.37×10^6 m

The Quadratic Equation and Geometric Equations

quadratic equation: $x = \dfrac{-b \pm \sqrt{b^2 - 4ac}}{2a}$
arc length = $r\theta$
circumference of circle = $2\pi r$
area of circle = πr^2
curved surface area of cylinder = $2\pi rh$
surface area of sphere = $4\pi r^2$
volume of sphere = $\dfrac{4}{3}\pi r^3$

Year 1
Section One — Particles

Photon symbol = γ Photon rest energy = 0 MeV

Leptons

Name	Symbol	Rest energy / MeV
electron	e$^\pm$	0.510999
muon	$\mu^\pm$	105.659
electron neutrino	ν_e	0
muon neutrino	ν_μ	0

		Lepton Number
Particles	e$^-$, ν_e, μ^-, ν_μ	+1
Antiparticles	e$^+$, $\overline{\nu}_e$, μ^+, $\overline{\nu}_\mu$	−1

Mesons

Name	Symbol	Rest energy / MeV
π meson	$\pi^\pm$	139.576
	π^0	134.972
K meson	K$^\pm$	493.821
	K^0	497.762

Baryons

Name	Symbol	Rest energy / MeV
proton	p	938.257
neutron	n	939.551

Quarks

Type	Charge	Baryon Number	Strangeness
u	$+\frac{2}{3}e$	$+\frac{1}{3}$	0
d	$-\frac{1}{3}e$	$+\frac{1}{3}$	0
s	$-\frac{1}{3}e$	$+\frac{1}{3}$	−1

Section Two — Electromagnetic Radiation and Quantum Phenomena

photon energy	$E = hf = \dfrac{hc}{\lambda}$
energy levels	$hf = E_1 - E_2$
photoelectric effect	$hf = \phi + E_{k(max)}$
de Broglie wavelength	$\lambda = \dfrac{h}{p} = \dfrac{h}{mv}$

Section Three — Waves

wave speed and period	$c = f\lambda \quad f = \dfrac{1}{T}$
first harmonic	$f = \dfrac{1}{2l}\sqrt{\dfrac{T}{\mu}}$
fringe spacing	$w = \dfrac{\lambda D}{s}$
diffraction grating	$d\sin\theta = n\lambda$
refractive index of a substance s,	$n = \dfrac{c}{c_s}$

For two substances with refractive indices of n_1 and n_2:

law of refraction	$n_1 \sin\theta_1 = n_2 \sin\theta_2$
critical angle (for $n_1 > n_2$)	$\sin\theta_c = \dfrac{n_2}{n_1}$

Section Four — Mechanics

moments	moment $= Fd$
velocity	$v = \dfrac{\Delta s}{\Delta t}$
acceleration	$a = \dfrac{\Delta v}{\Delta t}$
equations of motion	$v = u + at \qquad s = \left(\dfrac{u+v}{2}\right)t$
	$v^2 = u^2 + 2as \qquad s = ut + \dfrac{at^2}{2}$
force and impulse	$F = ma \qquad F = \dfrac{\Delta(mv)}{\Delta t}$
	$F\Delta t = \Delta(mv)$
work and energy	$W = Fs\cos\theta$
	$E_k = \frac{1}{2}mv^2 \qquad \Delta E_p = mg\Delta h$
power	$P = \dfrac{\Delta W}{\Delta t} \qquad P = Fv$
	efficiency $= \dfrac{\text{useful output power}}{\text{input power}}$

Section Five — Materials

density	$\rho = \dfrac{m}{V}$
Hooke's law	$F = k\Delta L$
energy stored	$E = \frac{1}{2}F\Delta L$
tensile stress $= \dfrac{F}{A}$	tensile strain $= \dfrac{\Delta L}{L}$
Young modulus $= \dfrac{\text{tensile stress}}{\text{tensile strain}}$	

Section Six — Electricity

current and potential difference	$I = \dfrac{\Delta Q}{\Delta t} \qquad V = \dfrac{W}{Q}$
resistance and resistivity	$R = \dfrac{V}{I} \qquad \rho = \dfrac{RA}{L}$
resistors in series	$R_T = R_1 + R_2 + R_3 + \ldots$
resistors in parallel	$\dfrac{1}{R_T} = \dfrac{1}{R_1} + \dfrac{1}{R_2} + \dfrac{1}{R_3} + \ldots$
power	$P = VI = I^2R = \dfrac{V^2}{R}$
emf	$\varepsilon = \dfrac{E}{Q} \qquad \varepsilon = I(R + r)$

Year 2

Section Seven — Further Mechanics

Circular Motion

magnitude of angular speed	$\omega = \dfrac{v}{r} = 2\pi f$
centripetal acceleration	$a = \dfrac{v^2}{r} = \omega^2 r$
centripetal force	$F = \dfrac{mv^2}{r} = m\omega^2 r$

Simple Harmonic Motion

acceleration and displacement	$a = -\omega^2 x \quad x = A\cos(\omega t)$
speed	$v = \pm\,\omega\sqrt{(A^2 - x^2)}$
maximum speed and acceleration	$v_{max} = \omega A \quad a_{max} = \omega^2 A$
for a mass-spring system	$T = 2\pi\sqrt{\dfrac{m}{k}}$
for a simple pendulum	$T = 2\pi\sqrt{\dfrac{l}{g}}$

Section Eight — Thermal Physics

energy to change temperature	$Q = mc\Delta\theta$
energy to change state	$Q = ml$
gas law	$pV = nRT \quad pV = NkT$

Kinetic theory

model of kinetic theory	$pV = \dfrac{1}{3}Nm(c_{rms})^2$
kinetic energy of a gas molecule	$\dfrac{1}{2}m(c_{rms})^2 = \dfrac{3}{2}kT = \dfrac{3RT}{2N_A}$

Section Nine — Gravitational and Electric Fields

Gravitational Fields

force between two masses	$F = \dfrac{Gm_1 m_2}{r^2}$
gravitational field strength	$g = \dfrac{F}{m}$
magnitude of gravitational field strength in a radial field	$g = \dfrac{GM}{r^2}$
gravitational potential	$V = -\dfrac{GM}{r} \qquad g = -\dfrac{\Delta V}{\Delta r}$
work done in a gravitational field	$\Delta W = m\Delta V$

Electric Fields

force between two point charges	$F = \dfrac{1}{4\pi\varepsilon_0}\dfrac{Q_1 Q_2}{r^2}$
force on a charge	$F = EQ$
electric potential	$V = \dfrac{1}{4\pi\varepsilon_0}\dfrac{Q}{r}$
electric field strength	$E = \dfrac{\Delta V}{\Delta r}$
electric field strength for a uniform field	$E = \dfrac{V}{d}$
electric field strength for a radial field	$E = \dfrac{1}{4\pi\varepsilon_0}\dfrac{Q}{r^2}$
work done in an electric field	$\Delta W = Q\Delta V$

Section Ten — Capacitors

capacitance	$C = \dfrac{Q}{V}$ $\qquad C = \dfrac{A\varepsilon_0\varepsilon_r}{d}$
energy stored	$E = \dfrac{1}{2}QV = \dfrac{1}{2}CV^2 = \dfrac{1}{2}\dfrac{Q^2}{C}$
capacitor charging	$Q = Q_0\left(1 - e^{-\frac{t}{RC}}\right)$
decay of charge	$Q = Q_0 e^{-\frac{t}{RC}}$
time constant $= RC$	

Section Eleven — Magnetic Fields

force on a current in a magnetic field	$F = BIl$
force on a moving charge in a magnetic field	$F = BQv$
magnetic flux	$\Phi = BA$
magnetic flux linkage	$N\Phi = BAN\cos\theta$
transformer equations	$\dfrac{N_s}{N_p} = \dfrac{V_s}{V_p}$
	efficiency $= \dfrac{I_s V_s}{I_p V_p}$
alternating current	$I_{\text{rms}} = \dfrac{I_0}{\sqrt{2}}$ $\qquad V_{\text{rms}} = \dfrac{V_0}{\sqrt{2}}$

Induced emf

magnitude of induced emf	$\varepsilon = N\dfrac{\Delta\Phi}{\Delta t}$
induced emf in a rotating coil	$\varepsilon = BAN\omega\sin\omega t$

Section Twelve — Nuclear Physics

inverse square law for γ radiation	$I = \dfrac{k}{x^2}$
nuclear radius	$R = R_0 A^{\frac{1}{3}}$
energy-mass equation	$E = mc^2$
radioactive decay	$\dfrac{\Delta N}{\Delta t} = -\lambda N$ $\qquad N = N_0 e^{-\lambda t}$
activity	$A = \lambda N$
half-life	$T_{\frac{1}{2}} = \dfrac{\ln 2}{\lambda}$

Section Thirteen: Option A — Astrophysics

1 astronomical unit $= 1.50 \times 10^{11}$ m, 1 light year $= 9.46 \times 10^{15}$ m

1 parsec $= 2.06 \times 10^5$ AU $= 3.26$ ly $= 3.08 \times 10^{16}$ m

$$M = \frac{\text{angle subtended by image at eye}}{\text{angle subtended by object at unaided eye}}$$

telescope in normal adjustment	$M = \dfrac{f_o}{f_e}$
Rayleigh criterion	$\theta \approx \dfrac{\lambda}{D}$
magnitude equation	$m - M = 5\log\left(\dfrac{d}{10}\right)$
Wien's law	$\lambda_{\max} T = 2.9 \times 10^{-3}$ m K
Stefan's law	$P = \sigma A T^4$
Schwarzschild radius	$R_s \approx \dfrac{2GM}{c^2}$
Doppler shift	$\dfrac{\Delta f}{f} = -\dfrac{\Delta\lambda}{\lambda} = \dfrac{v}{c}$ for $v \ll c$
red shift	$z = -\dfrac{v}{c}$
Hubble's law	$v = Hd$

Hubble constant, $H = 65$ km s^{-1}Mpc^{-1}

Section Thirteen: Option B — Medical Physics

lens equations	$P = \dfrac{1}{f}$ $\quad m = \dfrac{v}{u}$ $\quad \dfrac{1}{f} = \dfrac{1}{u} + \dfrac{1}{v}$
threshold of hearing	$I_0 = 1.0 \times 10^{-12}$ W m^{-2}
intensity level	intensity level $= 10\log\left(\dfrac{I}{I_0}\right)$
absorption	$I = I_0 e^{-\mu x}$ $\qquad \mu_m = \dfrac{\mu}{\rho}$
ultrasound imaging	$Z = pc$ $\qquad \dfrac{I_r}{I_i} = \left(\dfrac{z_2 - z_1}{z_2 + z_1}\right)^2$
half-lives	$\dfrac{1}{T_E} = \dfrac{1}{T_B} + \dfrac{1}{T_P}$

Section Thirteen: Option C — Engineering Physics

moment of inertia	$I = \Sigma mr^2$
angular kinetic energy	$E_K = \frac{1}{2}I\omega^2$
angular motion equations	$\omega_2 = \omega_1 + \alpha t$ $\qquad \omega_2^2 = \omega_1^2 + 2\alpha\theta$
	$\theta = \omega_1 t + \dfrac{\alpha t^2}{2}$ $\qquad \theta = \dfrac{(\omega_1 + \omega_2)t}{2}$
torque	$T = I\alpha$ $\qquad T = Fr$
angular momentum	angular momentum $= I\omega$
angular impulse	$T\Delta t = \Delta(I\omega)$
work done and power	$W = T\theta$ $\qquad P = T\omega$

Thermodynamics and heat engines

thermodynamics	$Q = \Delta U + W$ $\qquad W = p\Delta V$
adiabatic change	$pV^\gamma = $ constant
isothermal change	$pV = $ constant
heat engine efficiency	$= \dfrac{W}{Q_H} = \dfrac{Q_H - Q_C}{Q_H}$
maximum theoretical efficiency	$= \dfrac{T_H - T_C}{T_H}$

work done per cycle = area of loop

input power = calorific value × fuel flow rate

indicated power = (area of p-V loop)

$\qquad\qquad$ × (number of cycles per second)

$\qquad\qquad$ × (number of cylinders)

output or brake power $P = T\omega$

friction power = indicated power − brake power

refrigerator	$COP_{\text{ref}} = \dfrac{Q_C}{W} = \dfrac{Q_C}{Q_H - Q_C}$
heat pump	$COP_{\text{hp}} = \dfrac{Q_H}{W} = \dfrac{Q_H}{Q_H - Q_C}$

Section Thirteen: Option D — Turning Points in Physics

electron motion in fields	$F = \dfrac{eV}{d}$ $\qquad r = \dfrac{mv}{Be}$
	$\frac{1}{2}mv^2 = eV$ $\qquad F = Bev$
Milikan's experiment	$\dfrac{QV}{d} = mg$ $\qquad F = 6\pi\eta r v$
Maxwell's formula	
	$c = \dfrac{1}{\sqrt{\mu_0\varepsilon_0}}$ $\qquad \lambda = \dfrac{h}{p} = \dfrac{h}{\sqrt{2meV}}$
special relativity	$t = \dfrac{t_0}{\sqrt{1 - \dfrac{v^2}{c^2}}}$ $\qquad E = mc^2 = \dfrac{m_0 c^2}{\sqrt{1 - \dfrac{v^2}{c^2}}}$
	$l = l_0\sqrt{1 - \dfrac{v^2}{c^2}}$